APOCRYPHA

OF THE EARLY CHURCH

APOCRYPHA
OF THE EARLY CHURCH

G. Paul Robinson

TATE PUBLISHING
AND ENTERPRISES, LLC

Published by Tate Publishing & Enterprises, LLC
127 E. Trade Center Terrace | Mustang, Oklahoma 73064 USA
1.888.361.9473 | www.tatepublishing.com

Tate Publishing is committed to excellence in the publishing industry. The company reflects the philosophy established by the founders, based on Psalm 68:11,
"The Lord gave the word and great was the company of those who published it."

Published in the United States of America

ISBN: 978-1-62854-243-1
1. Religion / Christian Ministry / General
2. Religion / Biblical Studies / Bible Study Guides
16.04.06

Dedicated to the men and women, theologians, clergy, and "*lay persons*", who have conscientiously studied the ancient Christian, non-Christian and Hebrew writings for the revealed truth. Many Christian theologians and scholars have taken the bold step to suggest that these sacred writings may have included at least a portion of the Apocrypha (*ie. hidden books*) as well as the canonized writings of the Holy Bible.

TABLE OF CONTENTS

INTRODUCTION

Almost all Christians (*and those of other faiths*) know something about the Holy Bible[1]. It is the most widely-circulated document in history. It's books have been studied by Christians worldwide for at least 1,633 years after the books were canonized and bound together as Holy scripture. Individual books were studied much earlier, dating back to a decade or so after Christ's death and resurrection.

In addition to the books of the Holy Bible, approximately 200+ manuscripts were written during those first few centuries after Christ's death. These were the "*hidden books*" or apocryphal books which did not carry over into the canonized Holy scripture in 367 A.D. A number of apocryphal manuscripts have been discovered which were written within the first century or so after Christ's birth and resurrection. This book will focus on 30 of the earliest and most prominent manuscripts in terms of early community involvement and theology. The remaining manuscripts will be listed by name and approximate date in the *Appendix*.

Due to the magnitude of these works, many will include only excerpts (*i.e. the most Christo-centric passages*) although some manuscripts will be included in their entirety. Some of these important works in the formation of the early Church were written by early historians, apologists or theologians. Another grouping involved stories about Jesus, Mary, the Apostles and others. Almost all of these Christian stories or apocryphal manuscripts were called "*pseudepigrapha*", that is, they were attributed to false or unknown authors. Many contained heretical teachings of the first centuries.

One may genuinely ask at this point, "*What relevance do these apocryphal books have to Christianity?*" After all, the ancients rejected

---

[1] The Holy Bible refers to the sacred scriptures of Judaism and Christianity, usually compiled in a single volume. The Hebrew Bible contains 39 books. The Christian Bible adds to the Hebrew Bible some 27 more books of the New Testament, giving a total of 66 books. *Please note that the Catholic and Eastern Orthodox bibles (73 books) include the deuterocanonical books of Tobit, Judith, parts of Esther, 1 and 2 Maccabees, Wisdom, Sirach, Baruch, and parts of Daniel.*

many of these documents for various reasons (*below*).

It is fair to say that the non-canonized Apocrypha have not undergone the same bibiical, historical or textual scrutiny that the Holy scriptures have undergone; therefore, most would conclude that these manuscripts are isolated instances or occurrences which may or may not be based upon historical fact and/or were not eye-witnessed by the disciples or Apostles of Jesus the Christ as was the case of the much more authoritative New Testament. Four "*Criteria for Canonicity*" were generally used by the early Church to justify the selection of the canonized books which were included in the New Testament:

- Apostolic Origin — attributed to and based on the preaching/teaching of the first-generation apostles (or their close companions).
- Universal Acceptance — acknowledged by all major Christian communities in the ancient world (end of the fourth century).
- Liturgical Use — read publicly when early Christian communities gathered for the Lord's Supper (their weekly worship services).
- Consistent Message — containing a theological outlook similar to other writings.

As one studies these apocryphal books, the relevance of these books to Christianity becomes more appropriate. Although some are written from an heretical point of view (*ie. Gnostic, etc.*) and most do not reveal the authorship, many of these manuscripts provide us with additional community and theological information to similar, contemporary works in the Holy Bible. Many modern movies and books have seized upon the scenarios in these apocryphal, ancient writings *(ie. Da Vinci code, etc.)* to present an "*historical fiction*" sequence of events which at times, unfortunately, presents non-Biblical views of Christianity. Oftentimes, these depictions are in contrast or disagreement with the New Testament. The auyhot is reminded of St. Paul's eloquent words to the Colossians (2:8):

> "See to it that no one takes you captive through hollow and deceptive philosophy, which depends on human tradition and the elemental spiritual forces of this world rather than on Christ."

Having said that, these are nonetheless valuable manuscripts. The scope of this book includes the apocryphal books of the early Church (*ie. New Testament period*) although it should be noted that the Catholic and Orthodox Churches elevate some of the *Old Testament* Apocrypha (*ie. Tobit, Judith, parts of Esther, 1 and 2 Maccabees, Wisdom, Sirach, Baruch, and other parts of Daniel*) to *"deuterocanonical"* status; that is, they include these books in their Holy Bible for informational rather than theological doctrine use. The Anglicans also refer to these books for informational purposes.

The first chapter of *Apocrypha of the Early Church* gives a brief insight into the deliberations and councils responsible for the canonization of the New Testament. It also includes the primary heresies of the early Church. The second and third chapters, respectively, contain the *all-important* treatises of the earliest non-Christian historians and Christian apologists and the writings of the earliest *Apostolic Fathers* who were contemporaries and associates of St. Paul, St. Peter, St. John and others. It also includes *Church Fathers* who came later and formulated the foundational doctrines.

The fourth chapter contains the most *Christo-centric* passages of the earliest apocryphal writings which were not canonical and, therefore, didn't survive the selection process of the Holy scriptures as we know it today. Again, many of these have [... sections omitted.]. due to their length and/or relevance to the Gospel message. Some of the shorter manuscripts are included in their entirety; however, some of these works have sections missing. Care has been taken to retain the main thought or theology of each manuscript.

The Appendix includes additional apocryphal manuscripts by name and date only because they are not considered primary or main works of the early Church. An additional reference guide is furnished for further insight into these intriguing manuscripts.

Acknowledgements

Introduction

En.wikipedia.org references a diverse, global compilation of biblical scholarship. Wikipedia® is a registered trademark of the Wikimedia Foundation, Inc., a non-profit organization. Used by permission . All rights reserved.

Gotquestions.org is a compilation of conservative, Evangelical biblical scholarship. © Copyright 2002-2010 Got Questions Ministries - Used by permission . All rights reserved.

Biblegateway.com, the world's largest Christian website, is a Christian, mission-centered enterprise, focusing on making Scripture freely available on the Web in multiple languages and translations. Used by permission . All rights reserved.

EarlyChristianWritings.com is the most complete collection of Christian texts before the Council of Nicaea in 325 A.D.. The "Early Christian Writings: New Testament, Apocrypha, Gnostics, Church Fathers" site is copyright © Peter Kirby. Used by permission . All rights reserved.

APOCRYPHA OF THE EARLY CHURCH © Copyright 2015, represents years of research and compilation and could be viewed as a complementary work of the first two publications. The New Testament, as indicated by comprehensive Bible studies of the first work and, particularly, the earliest 29 books of the Apocrypha as indicated in this work, represent the most reliable scholarship and documentation on the historical Jesus.

HE *STILLED* THE STORM © Copyright 2014, represents the in-depth research and compilation of selected, controversial Church and Bible-related topics which were researched as a result of Bible studies across America and the Caribbean. This book is obviously not intended to provide all of the answers to mankind's quest for eternal truth in the scriptures and the Church. It is intended to provide a factual, provocative account of Bible and Church-related issues which have molded our world society and moral values.

Introduction

THE CHRIST *REVEALED* teaching series © Copyright 2013, 2015. is the author's first published work. The foundational, *Christo-centric* Bible studies include three from the Old Testament and four studies from the New Testament. Each of the series is conveniently divided into 3 courses and contain areas for personal notation for future reference. The work also contains a popular Lenten Series:

- **Cornerstone Series**
  - The Gospel of John
  - The Acts of the Apostles
  - The Epistle to the Romans
- **Synoptic Gospels Series**
  - The Gospel of Matthew
  - The Gospel of Mark
  - The Gospel of Luke
- **Missionary Series**
  - Galatians and the "Prison" Epistles
  - The Epistles to the Corinthians
  - Thessalonians and the "Pastoral" Epistles
- **Major Apostles Series**
  - The Epistle to the Hebrews
  - The Letters of James, Peter and John
  - The Revelation of John
- **Genesis Series**
  - The Book Of Genesis
  - The Book of Exodus
  - The Book of Deuteronomy
- **Major Prophets Series**
  - The Books of Isaiah and Ezekiel
  - The Books of Jeremiah and Daniel
  - The Book of Psalms
- **Wisdom Series**
  - The Book of Job
  - The Book of Proverbs
  - The Book of Ecclesiastes
- **Lenten Series:**
  - Christ and His chosen Apostles
  - Why Judaism will not accept Chrisrianity
  - Understanding Islam
  - Eastern Religions
  - Summary: Major Religions of the World

The Record of the Historical Jesus

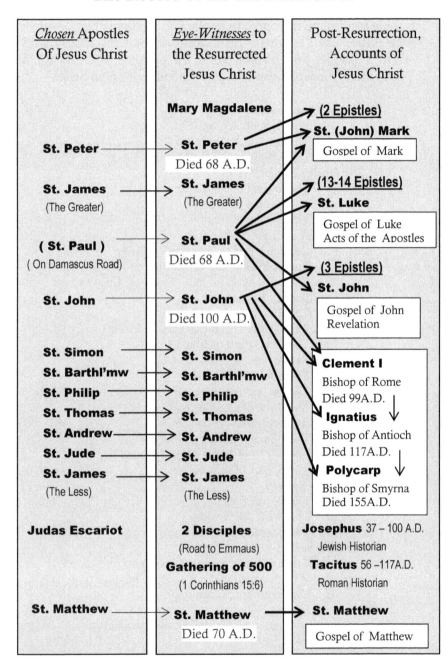

Chosen Apostles Of Jesus Christ	*Eye-Witnesses* to the Resurrected Jesus Christ	Post-Resurrection, Accounts of Jesus Christ
	Mary Magdalene	**(2 Epistles)** **St. (John) Mark** Gospel of Mark
St. Peter	**St. Peter** Died 68 A.D.	
St. James (The Greater)	**St. James** (The Greater)	**(13-14 Epistles)** **St. Luke** Gospel of Luke Acts of the Apostles
(St. Paul) (On Damascus Road)	**St. Paul** Died 68 A.D.	**(3 Epistles)** **St. John**
St. John	**St. John** Died 100 A.D.	Gospel of John Revelation
St. Simon	**St. Simon**	**Clement I** Bishop of Rome Died 99A.D.
St. Barthl'mw	**St. Barthl'mw**	
St. Philip	**St. Philip**	**Ignatius** Bishop of Antioch Died 117A.D.
St. Thomas	**St. Thomas**	
St. Andrew	**St. Andrew**	**Polycarp** Bishop of Smyrna Died 155A.D.
St. Jude	**St. Jude**	
St. James (The Less)	**St. James** (The Less)	
Judas Escariot	**2 Disciples** (Road to Emmaus) **Gathering of 500** (1 Corinthians 15:6)	**Josephus** 37 – 100 A.D. Jewish Historian **Tacitus** 56 –117A.D. Roman Historian
St. Matthew	**St. Matthew** Died 70 A.D.	**St. Matthew** Gospel of Matthew

I. THE NEW TESTAMENT CANON

Perhaps most of Christendom believe that the 27 books of the New Testament is not only inspired by God but limited and controlled by God insofar as the total number of books are concerned. We are mindful of the last words that St. John wrote in his revelation:

> I warn everyone who hears the words of the prophecy of this scroll: If anyone adds anything to them, God will add to that person the plagues described in this scroll. And if anyone takes words away from this scroll of prophecy, God will take away from that person any share in the tree of life and in the Holy City, which are described in this scroll.(Revelation 22:18-19 NIV)

Perhaps this is a warning assigned to the Book of Revelation as it states. Many extrapolate the meaning to include the entire New Testament.

There are approximately 200+ manuscripts and fragments of manuscripts which were not canonized (*i.e.Apocrypha*) by the early Church. A number of manuscripts were permanently lost and the only record that we have is through comments made in the writings of the early Church Fathers.

The book also attempts to trace the early Church heresies, the varied opinions of the early Church Fathers *(including those who were determined heretical)*, and finally suggest reasons why the apocryphal works may have not been positively considered for canonized scripture. Sometimes this is almost self-evident and sometimes it is very difficult. It is apparent from the number of councils and synods that the subject of canonization was not taken lightly. It is ultimately up to the reader to decide the fate of these aprocryphal writings.

The Early Councils

Pre-ecumenical councils, those earlier than 325 A.D., were mostly local or provincial. Some, held in the second half of the 3rd century involved more than one province. The *sui generis* Council of Jerusalem was a meeting, described in Acts 15 and possibly in Galatians 2, of the apostles and elders of the local Church in Jerusalem.[2]

1. Council of Jerusalem (c. 50),
2. Council of Rome (155),
3. Second Council of Rome (193),
4. Council of Ephesus (193),
5. Council of Carthage (251),
6. Council of Iconium (258),
7. Council of Antioch (264),
8. Councils of Arabia (246–247),
9. Council of Elvira (306),
10. Council of Carthage (311)
11. Synod of Neo-Caesarea (c. 314)
12. Council of Ancyra (314)
13. Council of Arles (314).

The first seven ecumenical councils, from the First Council of Nicaea (325 A.D.) to the Second Council of Nicaea (787 A.D.), represented an attempt to reach an orthodox consensus and to establish a unified Christendom as the state Church of the Roman Empire[3].

1. First Council of Nicaea (325)
2. First Council of Constantinople (381)
3. Council of Ephesus (431)
4. Council of Chalcedon (451)
5. Second Council of Constantinople (553)
6. Third Council of Constantinople (680)
7. Second Council of Nicaea (787)

---

[2] http://en.wikipedia.org/wiki/Ancient_Church_councils_(pre-ecumenical)
[3] http://en.wikipedia.org/wiki/First_seven_Ecumenical_Councils

The New Testament Canon Deliberations

	Ignatius 110 A.D. (Ig)	Polycarp 110 A.D. (Po)	Marcion 140 A.D. (M)	Valentinus 145 A.D. (Va)	Justin Martyr 155 A.D. (JM)	Irenaeus 180 A.D. (Ir)	Clement 190 A.D. (C)	Tertullian 205 A.D. (I)	Muratorian Canon 250 A.D. (MC)	Origen 220 A.D. (O)	Eusebius 310 A.D. (E)	Codex Sinaiticus 350 A.D. (CS)	Athanasius 367 A.D. (A)	Didymus the Blind 350 A.D. (D)	Peshitta 400 A.D. (P)	Vulgate 400 A.D. (V)
Gospel according to Matthew	✓	✓	×	✓	✓	✓	✓	✓	✓	✓	✓	✓	✓	✓	✓	✓
Gospel according to Mark		✓		✓	✓	✓	✓	✓	✓	✓	✓	✓	✓	✓	✓	✓
Gospel according to Luke	✓	✓	✓ᶜ	✓	✓	✓	✓	✓	✓	✓	✓	✓	✓	✓	✓	✓
Gospel according to John			×	✓	✓	✓	✓	✓	✓	✓	✓	✓	✓	✓	✓	✓
Acts	✓	✓	×			✓	✓	✓	✓	✓	✓	✓	✓	✓	✓	✓
Romans	✓	✓	✓ᶜ	✓		✓	✓	✓	✓	✓	✓	✓	✓	✓	✓	✓
I Corinthians	✓	✓	✓ᶜ	✓		✓	✓	✓	✓	✓	✓	✓	✓	✓	✓	✓
II Corinthians		✓	✓ᶜ	✓		✓	✓	✓	✓	✓	✓	✓	✓	✓	✓	✓
Galatians		✓	✓ᶜ	✓		✓	✓	✓	✓	✓	✓	✓	✓	✓	✓	✓
Ephesians	✓	✓	✓ᶜ	✓		✓	✓	✓	✓	✓	✓	✓	✓	✓	✓	✓
Philippians	·	✓	✓ᶜ	✓		✓	✓	✓	✓	✓	✓	✓	✓	✓	✓	✓
Colossians	✓	·	✓ᶜ	✓		✓	✓	✓	✓	✓	✓	✓	✓	✓	✓	✓
I Thessalonians	✓	✓	✓ᶜ			✓	✓	✓	✓	✓	✓	✓	✓	✓	✓	✓
II Thessalonians		✓	✓ᶜ			✓	✓	✓	✓	✓	✓	✓	✓	✓	✓	✓
I Timothy		✓	×			✓	✓	✓	✓	✓	✓	✓	✓	✓	✓	✓
II Timothy		✓	×			✓	✓	✓	✓	✓	✓	✓	✓	✓	✓	✓
Titus			×			✓	✓	✓	✓	✓	✓	✓	✓	✓	✓	✓
Philemon			✓ᶜ					✓	✓	✓	✓	✓	✓		✓	✓
Hebrews		✓				√	✓	✓		✓	√?	✓	✓	✓	✓	✓
James						√				?	?	✓	✓	✓	✓	✓
I Peter		✓		✓	✓	✓	✓		✓	✓	✓	✓	✓	✓	✓	✓
II Peter										?	?	✓	✓	✓		✓
I John		✓		✓	✓	✓	✓	✓	✓	✓	✓	✓	✓	✓	√	✓
II John					√			✓		?	?	✓	✓	×	·	✓
III John		✓								?	?	✓	✓	×	·	✓
Jude							✓	✓	✓	✓	?	✓	✓	√	·	✓
Revelation of John				✓	✓	✓	✓	✓	✓	✓	✓	✓	✓	✓		✓

Symbol	Opinion of Authority
✓	accepted; true; scriptural; or quoted from very approvingly
√	possible approving quotation or allusion
✓ᶜ	acceptable, but only with changes
?	dubious; disputed; or useful for inspiration
∴	spurious (in the classification of Eusebius)
×	false; heretical; heterodox; quoted from very disapprovingly
·	not mentioned or quoted from; opinion unknown

The Finalized
New Testament Canon

Christian writing[4]	Date A..D.	Author (if known)
1. James	45-50	St.James
2. 1 Thessalonians	52-54	St. Paul
3. 2 Thessalonians	53-55	St. Paul
4. 1 Corinthians	53-59	St. Paul
5. 2 Corinthians	54-60	St. Paul
6. Romans	58-60	St. Paul
7. Jude	60-70	St. Paul
8. Gospel of Mark	63-65	St. (John)Mark
9. Gospel of Luke	64-65	St. Luke
10. Ephesians	64-65	St. Paul
11. Philippians	64-65	St. Paul
12. Colossians	64-65	St. Paul
13. Philemon	64-65	St. Paul
14. Acts of the Apostles	64-65	St. Luke
15. Book of Hebrews	67-68	(St. Paul?)
16. Gospel of Matthew	65-66	St.Matthew
17. 1 Peter	65-68	St. Peter
18. 2 Peter	66-68	St. Peter
19. 1 Timothy	66-67	St. Paul
20. Galatians	67-68	St. Paul
21. 2 Timothy	67-68	St. Paul
22. Titus	67-68	St. Paul
23. Gospel of John	90-100	St. John
24. 1 John	90-100	St. John
25. 2 John	90-100	St. John
26. 3 John	90-100	St. John
27. Revelation of John	90-100	St. John

[4] In his Easter letter of 367, Athanasius, Bishop of Alexandria, gave a list of the books that would become the twenty-seven-book NT canon.

Early Apocryphal (Canon) Deliberations

	Ignatius 110 A.D. (Ig)	Polycarp 110 A.D. (Po)	Marcion 140 A.D. (M)	Valentinus 145 A.D. (Va)	Justin Martyr 155 A.D. (JM)	Irenaeus 180 A.D. (Ir)	Clement 190 A.D. (C)	Tertullian 205 A.D. (T)	Muratorian Canon 250 A.D. (MC)	Origen 220 A.D. (O)	Eusebius 310 A.D. (E)	Codex Sinaiticus 350 A.D. (CS)	Athanasius 367 A.D. (A)	Didymus the Blind 350 A.D. (D)	Peshitta 400 A.D. (P)	Vulgate 400 A.D. (V)
	Ig	Po	M	Va	JM	Ir	C	T	MC	O	E	CS	A	D	P	V
Gospel of Thomas										×	×					
Gospel of Truth				✓		×										
Gospel of the Twelve										×						
Gospel of Peter										?	✕					
Gospel of Basilides								×		×						
Gospel of the Egyptians							✓			×						
Gospel of the Hebrews							✓			?	✕				✓	
Gospel of Matthias								.		×	×					
New Traditions of Matthias							✓									
Preaching of Peter				✓			✓			×						
Acts of Andrew											×					
Acts of Paul							✓	×	.	?	×					
Acts of John											×					
Epistle to the Laodiceans									?							✓
I Clement						✓	✓			?				✓		
Epistle of Barnabas							✓			?	✕	✓	.	✓		
Didache							✓			?	✕		?	✓		
Shepherd of Hermas					✓	✓	?	?		?	✕?	✓	?	✓		
Apocalypse of Peter							✓		✓		✕					

Symbol	Opinion of Authority
✓	accepted; true; scriptural; or quoted from very approvingly
✓	possible approving quotation or allusion
✗	acceptable, but only with changes
?	dubious; disputed; or useful for inspiration
✕	spurious (in the classification of Eusebius)
×	false; heretical; heterodox; quoted from very disapprovingly
.	not mentioned or quoted from; opinion unknown

Heretical Teaching

Many of the faithful in the early Church were adjudged Saints by their peers and early Church Fathers. Many had heretical views to the early Church doctrines and were excommunicated. Ironically, some within the hierarchy of the early Church Fathers who were very instrumental in the early formulation of the New Testament and, would have eventually attained sainthood, fell from grace in the early Church through one or more extreme positions and were ultimately labeled heretic.

Formal heresy is "*the willful and persistent adherence to an error in matters of faith*" on the part of a baptised member of the catholic (*i.e. universal*) Church. As such it is a grave sin and involves *ipso facto* excommunication. Here "*matters of faith*" means dogmas which have been proposed by the "infallible" Magisterium of the Church and, in addition to this intellectual error, "*pertinacity in the will*" in maintaining it in opposition to Church teaching.[5]

Primary Heresies in the Early Church

Gnosticism heresy	**1st century** – Taught that Christ only appeared to be a man.
Montanism heresy	**2nd century** – Taught of Christ's imminent return
Sabellianism heresy	**3rd century** – Taught that Jesus Christ and God the Father were not distinct persons
Arianism heresy	**4th century** – Taught that Christ was a creature made by God
Pelagianism heresy	**5th century** – Denied doctrine of original sin, stated that man is morally neutral and can achieve heaven
Apollinarius heresy	**5th century** - Taught that Jesus was a combination of the divine Logos spirit, a sensitive human soul and a human body.

---

[5] http://en.wikipedia.org/wiki/List_of_Christian_heresies

6

The New Testament Canon

Major Heresy / Author	Belief	Dispensation
Gnosticism, Gnostic systems can be discerned some centuries before the Christian Era Gnosticism may have been earlier than the 1st century, thus predating Jesus Christ It spread through the Mediterranean and Middle East before and during the 2nd and 3rd centuries, becoming a dualistic heresy to Judaism, Christianity and Hellenic philosophy in areas controlled by the Roman Empire and Arian Goths.	Gnosis is 'knowledge'. We become closer to God as we gain knowledge. Humans are divine souls trapped a material world created by an imperfect god, the demiurge. Gnosticism is a rejection and vilification of the human body and of the material world or cosmos. Gnosticism teaches duality in Material (Matter) versus Spiritual or Body (evil) versus Soul (good). And that the material world will be destroyed by the spiritual God in order to free mankind from the reign of the false God or Demiurge.	Condemned by Emperor Theodosius I decree in 382, Condemned by synod of Zaragoza in 380., Dealt as heresy by Irenaeus, Hippolytus, and Philaster, and Epiphanius of Salamis
Adoptionism, Theodotus of Byzantium, a leather merchant, in Rome c.190	Belief that Jesus was born as a mere (non-divine) man, was supremely virtuous and that he was adopted later as "Son of God" by the descent of Spirit .	Theodotus was excommunicated by Pope Victor and Paul was condemned by the Synod of Antioch in 268
Apollinarism, Apollinaris of Laodicea(died 390)	Belief that Jesus had a humanbody and lower soul (the seat of the emotions) but a divine mind. Apollinaris further taught that the souls of men were propagated by other souls, as well as their bodies.	Declared to be a heresy in 381 by the First Council of Constantinople
Arianism, The doctrine is associated with Arius (ca. A.D. 250—336) who lived and taught in Alexandria, Egypt.	Denial of the true divinity of Jesus Christ taking various specific forms, but all agreed that Jesus Christ was created by the Father, that he had a beginning in time, and that the title "Son of God" was a courtesy one.	Arius was first pronounced a heretic at theFirst Council of Nicea, he was later exonerated as a result of imperial pressure and finally declared a heretic after his death. The heresy was finally resolved in 381 by the First Council of Constantinople

The New Testament Canon

Major Heresy / Author	Belief	Dispensation
Docetism, Tendencies existed in the 1st century, but it was most notably embraced by Gnostics in subsequent centuries.	Belief that Jesus' physical body was an illusion, as was his crucifixion; that is, Jesus only seemed to have a physical body and to physically die, but in reality he could not die.	Docetism was rejected by the ecumenical councils and mainstream Christianity, and largely died out during the first millennium A.D..
Macedonians, Allegedly founded in 4th century by Bishop Macedonius I of Constantinople, Eustathius of Sebaste was their principal theologian.	While accepting the divinity of Jesus Christ as affirmed at Nicea in 325, they denied that of the Holy Spirit which they saw as a creation of the Son, and a servant of Father/Son	Opposed by the Cappadocian Fathers and condemned at the First Council of Constantinople.
Sabellianism, First formally stated by Noetus of Smyrna c.190, refined by Sabellius c.210 who applied the names merely to different roles of God in the history and economy of salvation.	Belief that the Father, Son, and Holy Spirit are three characterizations of one God, rather than three distinct "persons" in one God.	Noetus was condemned by the presbyters of Smyrna. Tertullian wrote *Adversus Praxeam* against this tendency and Sabellius was condemned by Pope Callistus.
Manichaeism (Gnostic) , Founded in 210–276 A.D. by Mani	A major dualistic religion stating that good and evil are equally powerful, and that material things are evil.	Condemned by Emperor Theodosius I decree in 382
Valentianism, **(Gnostic)** sect was founded by Ex-Catholic Bishop Valentinus	A Gnostic and dualistic sect. n theology, dualism can refer to the relationship between God and creation. The Christian dualism of God and creation exists in some traditions of Christianity, like Paulicianism, ,Catharism, and Gnosticism.	Considered heresy by Irenaeus andEpiphanius of Salamis
Antinomianism, (Gnostic) (e.g. Ophites and Nicolaitans) taught that since matter was opposed to the spirit, the body was unimportant.	Any view which holds that Christians are freed by grace from obligations of any moral law. St Paul had to refute a charge of this type . (Romans 3:8)[17]	Decree on Justification, chapter XV Council of Trent

The New Testament Canon

Major Heresy / Author	Belief	Dispensation
Donatism, Named for their second leader Donatus Magnus	Donatists were rigorists, holding that the Church must be a Church of saints, not sinners, and that sacraments administered by *traditores* were invalid. They also regarded martyrdom as the supreme Christian virtue and regarded those that actively sought martyrdom as saints.	Condemned by Pope Melchiades
Marcionism, Originates in the teachings of Marcion of Sinope at Rome around the year 144.	An Early Christian dualist belief system. Marcion affirmed Jesus Christ as the savior sent by God and Paul as his chief apostle, but he rejected the Hebrew Bible and the Hebrew God. Marcionists believed that the wrathful Hebrew God was a separate and lower entity than the all-forgiving God of Testament.	Many early apologists, such as Tertullian on his *Adversus Marcionem* (year 207) condemned Marcionism
Montanism, Named for its founder founder Montanus, ontanism originated at Hierapolis. It spread rapidly to other regions in the Roman Empire during the period before Christianity was generally tolerated or legal.	The belief that the prophecies of the Montanists superseded and fulfilled the doctrines proclaimed by the Apostles.The encouragement of ecstatic prophesying. The view that Christians who fell from grace could not be redeemed. Remarriage was fobidden.	The Churches of Asia Minorexcommunicated Mont anism Around 177, Apollinarius, Bishop of Hierapolis, presided over asynod which condemned the New Prophecy. The leaders of the Churches of Lyon and Vienne in Gaul responded to the New Prophecy in 177
Pelagianism, named after Pelagius (ad. 354 – ad. 420/440	Belief that original sin did not taint human nature and that mortal will is still capable of choosing good and revil without Divine aid.	Attacked in the Council of Diospolis and condemned in 418 at Council of Carthage , Council of Ephesus in 431. refuted by Augustine of Hippo.

(This page is intentionally blank.)

II. EARLIEST HISTORIANS & APOLOGISTS

The earliest prominent historians to the time of Christ were Judaeus Philo of Alexandria, a Greek historian who was a contemporary of Jesus the Christ, Flavius Josephus, a Jewish historian who lived a generation beyond the ministry of Christ, and PubliusTacitus, a Roman historian who lived almost two generations beyond the time of Christ. These accurate historians were important in that they were non-Christians commenting on Christianity. They were not biased towards Christianity as so often is reported by the non-Christian world regarding documents.

Philo's concept of the Logos as God's creative principle influenced early Christology. He was a Hellenized (*Greek*) Jew and also influenced the synthesis of both traditions. Josephus' works provide valuable insight into first century Judaism and the background of Early Christianity. He reported Jesus' "*wonderful works*", His ministry of truth, His messiahship and His resurrection.

Tacitus reports on Christ's crucifixion during the reign of Tiberius at the hands of one of our procurators, Pontius Pilatus. He also states that Christ was born of a virgin.

Justin Martyr was a foremost apologist of the Christian faith after the turn of the first century. His momentous work, *On the Resurrection*, gives "*full credit to God, the Father of the universe, who is the perfect intelligence, the truth. And the Word, being His Son, came to us, having put on flesh, revealing both Himself and the Father, giving to us in Himself resurrection from the dead, and eternal life afterwards.*" His insights on the Resurrection are both detailed and thought-provoking.

Tertullian, the architect of the Trinitarian concept of the Godhead, wrote his famous Apology on Christianity around the turn of the second century. He defended Chritianity to the rulers of the Roman empire and detailed the crucifixion and circumstances around the resurrection, He also detailed Christ's appearances after His resurrectuon.

11

Philo of Alexandria
(20 BC – 50 A.D.)

A Greek Historian

Philo of Alexandria, a Hellenized Jew also called Judaeus Philo, is a figure that spans two cultures, the Greek and the Hebrew. When Hebrew mythical thought met Greek philosophical thought in the first century B.C.E. it was only natural that someone would try to develop speculative and philosophical justification for Judaism in terms of Greek philosophy.

Thus Philo produced a synthesis of both traditions developing concepts for future Hellenistic interpretation of messianic Hebrew thought, especially by Clement of Alexandria, Christian Apologists like Athenagoras, Theophilus, Justin Martyr, Tertullian, and by Origen. He may have influenced Paul, his contemporary, and perhaps the authors of the Gospel of John and the Epistle to the Hebrews. In the process, he laid the foundations for the development of Christianity in the West and in the East, as we know it today. Philo's primary importance is in the development of the philosophical and theological foundations of Christianity.[6]

In Christology, the concept that the Christ is the Logos (*Greek: Λόγος for "word", "discourse" or "reason"*) has been important in establishing the doctrine of the divinity and morality of Jesus Christ and his position as God the Son in the Trinity as set forth in the Chalcedonian Creed.

The pivotal and the most developed doctrine in Philo's writings on which hinges his entire philosophical system, is his doctrine of the Logos. By developing this doctrine he fused Greek philosophical concepts with Hebrew religious thought and provided the foundation for Christianity, first in the development of the Christian Pauline myth and speculations of John, later in the Hellenistic Christian Logos and Gnostic doctrines of the second century.

All other doctrines of Philo hinge on his interpretation of divine existence and action. The term *Logos* was widely used in the Greco-

---

[6] http://www.iep.utm.edu/philo/

12

Roman culture and in Judaism. Through most schools of Greek philosophy, this term was used to designate a rational, intelligent and thus vivifying principle of the universe. This principle was deduced from an understanding of the universe as a living reality and by comparing it to a living creature. Ancient people did not have the dynamic concept of *"function,"* therefore, every phenomenon had to have an underlying factor, agent, or principle. In the Septuagint version of the Old Testament the term logos (*Hebrew* davar) was used frequently to describe God's utterances (*Gen. 1:3, 6,9; 3:9,11; Ps. 32:9*), God's action (*Zech. 5:1-4; Ps. 106:20; Ps. 147:15*), and messages of prophets by means of which God communicated his will to his people (*Jer. 1:4-19, 2:1-7; Ezek. 1:3; Amos 3:1*). Logos is used here only as a figure of speech designating God's activity or action. In the so-called Jewish wisdom literature we find the concept of Wisdom (*hokhmah* and *sophia*) which could be to some degree interpreted as a separate personification or individualization *(hypostatization)*.

In the Hebrew culture it was a part of the metaphorical and poetic language describing divine wisdom as God's attribute and it clearly refers to a human characteristic in the context of human earthly existence. The Greek, metaphysical concept of the Logos is in sharp contrast to the concept of a personal God described in anthropomorphic terms typical of Hebrew thought. Philo made a synthesis of the two systems and attempted to explain Hebrew thought in terms of Greek philosophy by introducing the Stoic concept of the Logos into Judaism. In the process the Logos became transformed from a metaphysical entity into an extension of a divine and transcendental anthropomorphic being and mediator between God and men. Philo offered various descriptions of the Logos.

The concept derives from the opening of the Gospel of John, which is often simply translated into English as: "In the beginning was the Word, and the Word was with God, and the Word was God." In the translations, "*Word*" is used for *Logos* (λόγος), but in theological discourse, this is often left untranslated. At the same time, this Word offers light to everyone coming into the world (John 1:9), a theme soon developed, with help of Philo, Middle Platonic, and/or Stoic thought, by Justin, Origen, and others.

Flavius Josephus
(37 – 100 A.D.)

A Jewish Historian

Titus Flavius Josephus[7], also called **Joseph ben Matityahu** (Biblical Hebrew: מתתיהו בן יוסף, *Yosef ben Matityahu*), was a scholar who witnessed the sack of Jerusalem, a first-century Romano-Jewish historian and hagiographer who was born in Jerusalem, then part of Roman Judea, to a father of priestly descent and a mother who claimed royal ancestry.

He initially fought against the Romans during the First Jewish–Roman War as the head of Jewish forces in Galilee, until surrendering into Roman forces led by Vespasian after the six-week siege of Jotapata. Josephus claims the Jewish Messianic prophecies that initiated the First Roman-Jewish War made reference to Vespasian becoming Emperor of Rome. In response Vespasian decided to keep Josephus as a hostage and interpreter. After Vespasian did become Emperor, he granted Josephus his freedom, at which time Josephus assumed the emperor's family name of Flavius.

Flavius Josephus fully defected to the Roman side and was granted Roman citizenship. He became an advisor and friend of Vespasian's son Titus, serving as his translator when Titus led the Siege of Jerusalem, which resulted when the Jewish revolt did not surrender in the city's destruction and the looting and destruction of Herod's Temple (*Second Temple*). Josephus recorded Jewish history, with special emphasis on the first century A.D. and the First Jewish–Roman War, including the Siege of Masada, but the imperial patronage of his work has sometimes caused it to be characterized as pro-Roman propaganda.

Josephus belonged to a distinguished priestly family, whose paternal ancestors he himself traces back five generations; his mother's family claimed descent from the Machabeans. He received a good education, and association with distinguished scholars developed his intellectual gifts, more especially his memory and

---

[7] http://en.wikipedia.org/wiki/Josephus

power of judgment. He also made himself fully acquainted with and tried the leading politico-religious Jewish parties of his age, the Essenes, Pharisees, and Sadducees.

The first work of Josephus was the "*Jewish War*" (*Peri tou Ioudaikou polemou*) in seven books. This is mainly based on his memoranda made during the war of independence (66-73), on the memoirs of Vespasian, and on letters of King Agrippa. While his story of warlike events is reliable, the account of his own doings is strongly tinctured with foolish self-adulation. Josephus's second work, the "Jewish Antiquities" (*Ioudaike Archaiologia*), contains in twenty books the whole history of the Jews from the Creation to the outbreak of the revolt in A.D. 66. Books I-XI are based on the text of the Septuagint, though at times he also repeats traditional explanations current among the Jews in later times. He also quotes numerous passages from Greek authors whose writings are now lost. On the other hand he made allowance for the tastes of his Gentile contemporaries by arbitrary omissions as well as by the free embellishment of certain scenes. Books XII-XX, in which he speaks of the times preceding the coming of Christ and the foundation of Christianity, are our only sources for many historical events. In these the value of the statements is enhanced by the insertion of dates which are otherwise wanting, and by the citation of authentic documents which confirm and supplement the Biblical narrative. The story of Herod the Great is contained in books XV-XVII.[8]

Excerpts from Antiquities of the Jews, Book 18, Chapter 3.

Sedition of the Jews against Pontius Pilate concerning Christ, and what befell Paulina and the Jews at Rome.

But now Pilate, the procurator of Judea, removed the army from Cesarea to Jerusalem, to take their winter quarters there, in order to abolish the Jewish laws. So he introduced Caesar's effigies, which were upon the ensigns, and brought them into the city; whereas our law forbids us the very making of images; on which account the former procurators were wont to make their entry into the city with

---

[8] http://www.earlychristianwritings.com/info/josephus-cathen.html

such ensigns as had not those ornaments. Pilate was the first who brought those images to Jerusalem, and set them up there; which was done without the knowledge of the people, because it was done in the night time; but as soon as they knew it, they came in multitudes to Cesarea, and interceded with Pilate many days that he would remove the images; and when he would not grant their requests, because it would tend to the injury of Caesar, while yet they persevered in their request, on the sixth day he ordered his soldiers to have their weapons privately, while he came and sat upon his judgment-seat, which seat was so prepared in the open place of the city, that it concealed the army that lay ready to oppress them; and when the Jews petitioned him again, he gave a signal to the soldiers to encompass them routed, and threatened that their punishment should be no less than immediate death, unless they would leave off disturbing him, and go their ways home. But they threw themselves upon the ground, and laid their necks bare, and said they would take their death very willingly, rather than the wisdom of their laws should be transgressed; upon which Pilate was deeply affected with their firm resolution to keep their laws inviolable, and presently commanded the images to be carried back from Jerusalem to Cesarea.

But Pilate undertook to bring a current of water to Jerusalem, and did it with the sacred money, and derived the origin of the stream from the distance of two hundred furlongs. However, the Jews were not pleased with what had been done about this water; and many ten thousands of the people got together, and made a clamor against him, and insisted that he should leave off that design. Some of them also used reproaches, and abused the man, as crowds of such people usually do.

So he habited a great number of his soldiers in their habit, who carried daggers under their garments, and sent them to a place where they might surround them. So he bid the Jews himself go away; but they boldly casting reproaches upon him, he gave the soldiers that signal which had been beforehand agreed on; who laid upon them much greater blows than Pilate had commanded them, and equally punished those that were tumultuous, and those that were not; nor did they spare them in the least: and since the people were unarmed, and were caught by men prepared for what they were about, there were a great number of them slain by this means, and others of them ran away wounded. And thus an end was put to this sedition.

Now there was about this time Jesus, a wise man, if it be lawful to call him a man; for he was a doer of wonderful works, a teacher of such men as receive the truth with pleasure. He drew over to him both many of the Jews and many of the Gentiles. **He was [*the*] Christ.** And when Pilate, at the suggestion of the principal men amongst us, had condemned him to the cross, those that loved him at the first did not forsake him. **For he appeared to them alive again the third day as the divine prophets had foretold** these and other wonderful things and the tribe of Christians, so named from him, are not extinct at this day.

Cornelius Tacitus
(56 – 117 A.D.)

A Roman Historian

Publius (or **Gaius**) **Cornelius Tacitus**[9] was a senator and a historian of the Roman Empire. The surviving portions of his two major works—the *Annals* and the *Histories*—examine the reigns of the Roman Emperors Tiberius, Claudius, Nero, and those who reigned in the Year of the Four Emperors (*A.D. 69*). These two works span the history of the Roman Empire from the death of Augustus in A.D. 14 to the years of the First Jewish–Roman War in A.D. 70. (*Annals XV*)

There are substantial lacunae in the surviving texts, including a gap in the *Annals* that is four books long.Other writings by him discuss oratory (in dialogue format, see *Dialogus de oratoribus*), Germania (in *De origine et situ Germanorum*), and the life of his father-in-law, Agricola, the Roman general responsible for much of the Roman conquest of Britain, mainly focusing on his campaign in Britannia (*De vita et moribus Iulii Agricolae*).Tacitus is considered to be one of the greatest Roman historians. He lived in what has been called the Silver Age of Latin literature. He is known for the brevity and compactness of his Latin prose, as well as for his penetrating insights into the psychology of power politics.

The *Annals* and the *Histories*, published separately, were meant to form a single edition of thirty books. Although Tacitus wrote the *Histories* before the *Annals*, the events in the *Annals* precede the *Histories*; together they form a continuous narrative from the death of Augustus (14) to the death of Domitian (96). Though most has been lost, what remains is an invaluable record of the era. The first half of the Annals survived in a single copy of a manuscript from Corvey Abbey, and the second half from a single copy of a manuscript from Monte Cassino, and so it is remarkable that they survived at all.The *Annals* is Tacitus' final work, covering the period from the death of Augustus Caesar in 14 A.D.. He wrote at least sixteen books, but books 7–10 and parts of books 5, 6, 11 and 16 are

---

[9] http://en.wikipedia.org/wiki/Tacitus

missing. Book 6 ends with the death of Tiberius and books 7–12 presumably covered the reigns of Caligula and Claudius. The remaining books cover the reign of Nero, perhaps until his death in June 68 or until the end of that year, to connect with the *Histories*. The second half of book 16 is missing (ending with the events of 66). We do not know whether Tacitus completed the work; he died before he could complete his planned histories of Nerva and Trajan, and no record survives of the work on Augustus Caesar and the beginnings of the Empire with which he had planned to finish his work. The *Annals* is one of the earliest secular historical records to mention Christ.

Excerpts from "Annals, Book 15, Chapter 44"[10]

Such indeed were the precautions of human wisdom. The next thing was to seek means of propitiating the gods, and recourse was had to the Sibylline books, by the direction of which prayers were offered to Vulcanus, Ceres, and Proserpina. Juno, too, was entreated by the matrons, first, in the Capitol, then on the nearest part of the coast, whence water was procured to sprinkle the fane and image of the goddess. **Christus, from whom the name had its origin, suffered the extreme penalty during the reign of Tiberius at the hands of one of our procurators, Pontius Pilatus,** and a most mischievous superstition, thus checked for the moment, again broke out not only in Judæa, the first source of the evil, but even in Rome, where all things hideous and shameful from every part of the world find their centre and become popular. Accordingly, an arrest was first made of all who pleaded guilty; then, upon their information, an immense multitude was convicted, not so much of the crime of firing the city, as of hatred against mankind. Mockery of every sort was added to their deaths. Covered with the skins of beasts, they were torn by dogs and perished, or were nailed to crosses, or were doomed to the flames and burnt, to serve as a nightly illumination, when daylight had expired[11]

---

[10] http://www.perseus.tufts.edu/hopper/text?doc=Tac.+Ann.+1.1
[11] Tacitus, *Annals* 15.44, translated by Church and Brodribb.

19

Justin Martyr
(100 - 165 A.D.)

An Early Apologist

Justin Martyr[12], also known as Saint Justin (*c. 100 – 165 A.D.*), was an early Christian apologist, and is regarded as the foremost interpreter of the theory of the Logos in the 2nd century. He was martyred, alongside some of his students, and is considered a saint by the Roman Catholic Church, the Anglican Church, and the Eastern Orthodox Church.

Most of his works are lost, but two apologies and a dialogue did survive. The *First Apology*, his most well known text, passionately defends the morality of the Christian life, and provides various ethical and philosophical arguments to convince the Roman emperor, Antoninus, to abandon the persecution of the fledgling sect. Further, he also makes the theologically-innovative suggestion that the "seeds of Christianity" (manifestations of the Logos acting in history) actually predated Christ's incarnation. The earliest mention of Justin is found in the *Oratio ad Graecos* by Tatian who, after calling him "the most admirable Justin," quotes a saying of his and says that the Cynic Crescens laid snares for him. Irenaeus speaks of Justin's martyrdom and of Tatian as his disciple. Irenaeus quotes Justin twice and shows his influence in other places. Eusebius of Caesarea deals with him at some length, and names the following works:

- The First Apology
- Second Apology of Justin Martyr
- Discourse to the Greeks
- On the Sovereignty of God
- The Psalmist
- On the Soul
- Dialogue with Trypho.
- On the Resurrection

---

[12] http://en.wikipedia.org/wiki/Justin_Martyr

20

Excerpts from "The Resurrection"

Chapter 1 – The self-evidencing Power of the Truth.

The word of truth is free, and carries its own authority, disdaining to fall under any skilful argument, or to endure the logical scrutiny of its hearers. But it would be believed for its own nobility, and for the confidence due to Him who sends it. Now the word of truth is sent from God; wherefore the freedom claimed by the truth is not arrogant. For being sent with authority, it were not fit that it should be required to produce proof of what is said; since neither is there any proof beyond itself, which is God.

For every proof is more powerful and trustworthy than that which it proves; since what is disbelieved, until proof is produced, gets credit when such proof is produced, and is recognised as being what it was stated to be. But nothing is either more powerful or more trustworthy than the truth; so that he who requires proof of this is like one who wishes it demonstrated why the things that appear to the senses do appear. For the test of those things which are received through the reason, is sense; but of sense itself there is no test beyond itself. As then we bring those things which reason hunts after, to sense, and by it judge what kind of things they are, whether the things spoken be true or false, and then sit in judgment no longer, giving full credit to its decision; so also we refer all that is said regarding men and the world to the truth, and by it judge whether it be worthless or no.

But the utterances of truth we judge by no separate test, giving full credit to itself. And God, the Father of the universe, who is the perfect intelligence, is the truth. And the Word, being His Son, came to us, having put on flesh, revealing both Himself and the Father, giving to us in Himself resurrection from the dead, and eternal life afterwards. And this is Jesus Christ, our Saviour and Lord. He, therefore, is Himself both the faith and the proof of Himself and of all things. Wherefore those who follow Him, and know Him, having faith in Him as their proof, shall rest in Him. But since the adversary does not cease to resist many, and uses many and divers arts to ensnare them, that he may seduce the faithful from their faith, and that he may prevent the faithless from believing, it seems to me necessary that we also, being armed with the invulnerable doctrines of the faith, do battle against him in behalf of the weak.

Chapter 2 – Objections to the Resurrection of the Flesh.

They who maintain the wrong opinion say that there is no resurrection of the flesh; giving as their reason that it is impossible that what is corrupted and dissolved should be restored to the same as it had been. And besides the impossibility, they say that the salvation of the flesh is disadvantageous; and they abuse the flesh, adducing its infirmities, and declare that it only is the cause of our sins, so that if the flesh, say they, rise again, our infirmities also rise with it. And such sophistical reasons as the following they elaborate: If the flesh rise again, it must rise either entire and possessed of all its parts, or imperfect.

But its rising imperfect argues a want of power on God's part, if some parts could be saved, and others not; but if all the parts are saved, then the body will manifestly have all its members. But is it not absurd to say that these members will exist after the resurrection from the dead, since the Saviour said, "*They neither marry, nor are given in marriage, but shall be as the angels in heaven?*" And the angels, say they, have neither flesh, nor do they eat, nor have sexual intercourse; therefore there shall be no resurrection of the flesh. By these and such like arguments, they attempt to distract men from the faith. And there are some who maintain that even Jesus Himself appeared only as spiritual, and not in flesh, but presented merely the appearance of flesh: these persons seek to rob the flesh of the promise. First, then, let us solve those things which seem to them to be insoluble; then we will introduce in an orderly manner the demonstration concerning the flesh, proving that it partakes of salvation.

[… sections omitted.]

For if the flesh were deprived of food, drink, and clothing, it would be destroyed; but being deprived of lawless desire, it suffers no harm. And at the same time He foretold that, in the future world, sexual intercourse should be done away with; as He says, *"The children of this world marry, and are given in marriage; but the children of the world to come neither marry nor are given in marriage, but shall be like the angels in heaven."* Let not, then, those that are unbelieving marvel, if in the world to come He do away with those acts of our fleshly members which even in this present life are abolished.

[… sections omitted.].

Chapter 3 – The Resurrection of Christ proves that the Body rises.

If He had no need of the flesh, why did He heal it? And what is most forcible of all, He raised the dead. Why? Was it not to show what the resurrection should be? How then did He raise the dead? Their souls or their bodies? Manifestly both. If the resurrection were only spiritual, it was requisite that He, in raising the dead, should show the body lying apart by itself, and the soul living apart by itself. But now He did not do so, but raised the body, confirming in it the promise of life. Why did He rise in the flesh in which He suffered, unless to show the resurrection of the flesh? And wishing to confirm this, when His disciples did not know whether to believe He had truly risen in the body, and were looking upon Him and doubting,

He said to them, *"Ye have not yet faith, see that it is I"* and He let them handle Him, and showed them the prints of the nails in His hands. And when they were by every kind of proof persuaded that it was Himself, and in the body, they asked Him to eat with them, that they might thus still more accurately ascertain that He had in verity risen bodily; and He did eat honey-comb and fish. And when He had thus shown them that there is truly a resurrection of the flesh, wishing to show them this also, that it is not impossible for flesh to ascend into heaven (*as He had said that our dwelling-place is in heaven*), *"He was taken up into heaven while they beheld,"* as He was in the flesh. If, therefore, after all that has been said, any one demand demonstration of the resurrection, he is in no respect different from the Sadducees, since the resurrection of the flesh is the power of

God, and, being above all reasoning, is established by faith, and seen in works.

[... sections omitted.].

Chapter 10 – The Body saved and will, therefore, rise.

The resurrection is a resurrection of the flesh which died. For the spirit dies not; the soul is in the body, and without a soul it cannot live. The body, when the soul forsakes it, is not. For the body is the house of the soul; and the soul the house of the spirit. These three, in all those who cherish a sincere hope and unquestioning faith in God, will be saved. Considering, therefore, even such arguments as are suited to this world, and finding that, even according to them, it is not impossible that the flesh be regenerated; and seeing that, besides all these proofs, the Saviour in the whole Gospel shows that there is salvation for the flesh, why do we any longer endure those unbelieving and dangerous arguments, and fail to see that we are retrograding when we listen to such an argument as this: that the soul is immortal, but the body mortal, and incapable of being revived? For this we used to hear from Pythagoras and Plato, even before we learned the truth. If then the Saviour said this, and proclaimed salvation to the soul alone, what new thing, beyond what we heard from Pythagoras and Plato and all their band, did He bring us? But now He has come proclaiming the glad tidings of a new and strange hope to men.

For indeed it was a strange and new thing for God to promise that He would not keep incorruption in incorruption, but would make corruption incorruption. But because the prince of wickedness could in no other way corrupt the truth, he sent forth his apostles (*evil men who introduced pestilent doctrines*), choosing them from among those who crucified our Saviour; and these men bore the name of the Saviour, but did the works of him that sent them, through whom the name itself has been spoken against. But if the flesh do not rise, why is it also guarded, and why do we not rather suffer it to indulge its desires? Why do we not imitate physicians, who, it is said, when they get a patient that is despaired of and incurable, allow him to indulge his desires? For they know that he is dying; and this indeed those who hate the flesh surely do, casting it out of its inheritance, so far as they can; for on this account they also despise it, because it is shortly to become a corpse. But if our physician Christ, God, having rescued us from our desires, regulates our flesh with His own wise and temperate rule, it is evident that He guards it from sins because it possesses a hope of salvation, as physicians do not suffer men whom they hope to save to indulge in what pleasures they please.

Excerpts from "The First Apology"

[Note: This excerpt XLV in Justin Martyr's writings is extremely important because it mirrors the lost ending to the Gospel of Mark 16:9-16 which were found in later manuscripts but not in the earliest manuscripts.]

Chapter 1 – Address.

To the Emperor Titus Ælius Adrianus Antoninus Pius Augustus Caesar, and to his son Verissimus the Philosopher, and to Lucius the Philosopher, the natural son of Caesar, and the adopted son of Pius, a lover of learning, and to the sacred Senate, with the whole People of the Romans, I, Justin, the son of Priscus and grandson of Bacchius, natives of Flavia Neapolis in Palestine, present this address and petition in behalf of those of all nations who are unjustly hated and wantonly abused, myself being one of them.

[… sections omitted.].

Chapter 13 - Christians serve God rationally.

What sober-minded man, then, will not acknowledge that we are not atheists, worshipping as we do the Maker of this universe, and declaring, as we have been taught, that He has no need of streams of blood and libations and incense; whom we praise to the utmost of our power by the exercise of prayer and thanksgiving for all things wherewith we are supplied, as we have been taught that the only honour that is worthy of Him is not to consume by fire what He has brought into being for our sustenance, but to use it for ourselves and those who need, and with gratitude to Him to offer thanks by invocations and hymns for our creation, and for all the means of health, and for the various qualities of the different kinds of things, and for the changes of the seasons; and to present before Him petitions for our existing again in incorruption through faith in Him.

Our teacher of these things is Jesus Christ, who also was born for this purpose, and was crucified under Pontius Pilate, procurator of Judaea, in the times of Tiberius Caesar; and that we reasonably worship Him, having learned that He is the Son of the true God Himself, and holding Him in the second place, and the prophetic Spirit in the third, we will prove. For they proclaim our madness to consist in this, that we give to a crucified man a place second to the unchangeable and eternal God, the Creator of all; for they do not discern the mystery that is herein, to which, as we make it plain to you, we pray you to give heed.

[... sections omitted.].

Chapter 19 – The Resurrection possible.

And to any thoughtful person would anything appear more incredible, than, if we were not in the body, and some one were to say that it was possible that from a small drop of human seed bones and sinews and flesh be formed into a shape such as we see? For let this now be said hypothetically: if you yourselves were not such as you now are, and born of such parents [and causes], and one were to show you human seed and a picture of a man, and were to say with confidence that from such a substance such a being could be produced, would you believe before you saw the actual production? No one will dare to deny [*that such a statement would surpass belief*]. In the same way, then, you are now incredulous because you have never seen a dead man rise again.

But as at first you would not have believed it possible that such persons could be produced from the small drop, and yet now you see them thus produced, so also judge ye that it is not impossible that the bodies of men, after they have been dissolved, and like seeds resolved into earth, should in God's appointed time rise again and put on incorruption. For what power worthy of God those imagine who say, that each thing returns to that from which it was produced, and that beyond this not even God Himself can do anything, we are unable to conceive; but this we see clearly, that they would not have believed it possible that they could have become such and produced from such materials, as they now see both themselves and the whole world to be. And that it is better to believe even what is impossible to our own nature and to men, than to be unbelieving like the rest of the world, we have learned; for we know that our Master Jesus Christ said, that *"what is impossible with men is possible with God,"* and, *"Fear not them that kill you, and after that can do no more; but fear Him who after death is able to cast both soul and body into hell."* And hell is a place where those are to be punished who have lived wickedly, and who do not believe that those things which God has taught us by Christ will come to pass.

[... sections omitted.].

Chapter 32 – Christ predicted by Moses.

Moses then, who was the first of the prophets, spoke in these very words: "The sceptre shall not depart from Judah, nor a lawgiver from between his feet, until He come for whom it is reserved; and He shall be the desire of the nations, binding His foal to the vine, washing His robe in the blood of the grape." It is yours to make accurate inquiry, and ascertain up to whose time the Jews had a lawgiver and king of their own. Up to the time of Jesus Christ, who taught us, and interpreted the prophecies which were not yet understood, [they had a lawgiver] as was foretold by the holy and divine Spirit of prophecy through Moses, *"that a ruler would not fail the Jews until He should come for whom the kingdom was reserved"* (*for Judah was the forefather of the Jews, from whom also they have their name of Jews)*; and after He (*i.e., Christ*) appeared, you began to rule the Jews, and gained possession of all their territory.

And the prophecy, *"He shall be the expectation of the nations,"* signified that there would be some of all nations who should look for Him to come again. And this indeed you can see for yourselves, and be convinced of by fact. For of all races of men there are some who look for Him who was crucified in Judaea, and after whose crucifixion the land was straightway surrendered to you as spoil of war. And the prophecy, "*binding His foal to the vine, and washing His robe in the blood of the grape,*" was a significant symbol of the things that were to happen to Christ, and of what He was to do. For the foal of an ass stood bound to a vine at the entrance of a village, and He ordered His acquaintances to bring it to Him then; and when it was brought, He mounted and sat upon it, and entered Jerusalem, where was the vast temple of the Jews which was afterwards destroyed by you. And after this He was crucified, that the rest of the prophecy might be fulfilled.

For this "*washing His robe in the blood of the grape*" was predictive of the passion He was to endure, cleansing by His blood those who believe on Him. For what is called by the Divine Spirit through the prophet "*His robe,*" are those men who believe in Him in whom abideth the seed of God, the Word. And what is spoken of as "*the blood of the grape,*" signifies that He who should appear would have blood, though not of the seed of man, but of the power of God. And the first power after God the Father and Lord of all is the Word, who is also the Son; and of Him we will, in what follows, relate how He took flesh and became man. For as man did not make the blood of the vine, but God, so it was hereby intimated that the blood should not be of human seed, but of divine power, as we have said above. And Isaiah, another prophet, foretelling the same things in other words, spoke thus: "*A star shall rise out of Jacob, and a flower shall spring from the root of Jesse; and His arm shall the nations trust.*" And a star of light has arisen, and a flower has sprung from the root of Jesse--this Christ. For by the power of God He was conceived by a virgin of the seed of Jacob, who was the father of Judah, who, as we have shown, was the father of the Jews; and Jesse was His forefather according to the oracle, and He was the son of Jacob and Judah according to lineal descent.

Chapter 33 – Manner of Christ's birth predicted.

And hear again how Isaiah in express words foretold that He should be born of a virgin; for he spoke thus: "*Behold, a virgin shall conceive, and bring forth a son, and they shall say for His name, 'God with us.'*" For things which were incredible and seemed impossible with men, these God predicted by the Spirit of prophecy as about to come to pass, in order that, when they came to pass, there might be no unbelief, but faith, because of their prediction. But lest some, not understanding the prophecy now cited, should charge us with the very things we have been laying to the charge of the poets who say that Jupiter went in to women through lust, let us try to explain the words. This, then, "*Behold, a virgin shall conceive,*" signifies that a virgin should conceive without intercourse.

For if she had had intercourse with any one whatever, she was no longer a virgin; but the power of God having come upon the virgin, overshadowed her, and caused her while yet a virgin to conceive. And the angel of God who was sent to the same virgin at that time brought her good news, saying, "*Behold, thou shalt conceive of the Holy Ghost, and shalt bear a Son, and He shall be called the Son of the Highest, and thou shalt call His name Jesus; for He shall save His people from their sins,*"--as they who have recorded all that concerns our Saviour Jesus Christ have taught, whom we believed, since by Isaiah also, whom we have now adduced, the Spirit of prophecy declared that He should be born as we intimated before. It is wrong, therefore, to understand the Spirit and the power of God as anything else than the Word, who is also the first-born of God, as the foresaid prophet Moses declared; and it was this which, when it came upon the virgin and overshadowed her, caused her to conceive, not by intercourse, but by power. **And the name Jesus in the Hebrew language means Swthr (Saviour) in the Greek tongue.** Wherefore, too, the angel said to the virgin, "*Thou shalt call His name Jesus, for He shall save His people from their sins.*" And that the prophets are inspired by no other than the Divine Word, even you, as I fancy, will grant.

Chapter 34 – Place of Christ's birth foretold.

And hear what part of earth He was to be born in, as another prophet, Micah, foretold. He spoke thus: "*And thou, Bethlehem, the land of Judah, art not the least among the princes of Judah; for out of thee shall come forth a Governor, who shall feed My people.*" Now there is a village in the land of the Jews, thirty-five stadia from Jerusalem, in which Jesus Christ was born, as you can ascertain also from the registers of the taxing made under Cyrenius, your first procurator in Judaea.

[... sections omitted.].

Chapter 35 –Other fulfilled prophecies.

And how Christ after He was born was to escape the notice of other men until He grew to man's estate, also came to pass, hear what was foretold regarding this. There are the following predictions:--"*Unto us a child is born, and unto us a young man is given, and the government shall be upon His shoulders;*" which is significant of the power of the cross, for to it, when He was crucified, He applied His shoulders, as shall be more clearly made out in the ensuing discourse. And again the same prophet Isaiah, being inspired by the prophetic Spirit, said, "*I have spread out my hands to a disobedient and gainsaying people, to those who walk in a way that is not good. They now ask of me judgment, and dare to draw near to God.*"

And again in other words, through another prophet, He says, "*They pierced My hands and My feet, and for My vesture they cast lots.*" And indeed David, the king and prophet, who uttered these things, suffered none of them; but Jesus Christ stretched forth His hands, being crucified by the Jews speaking against Him, and denying that He was the Christ. And as the prophet spoke, they tormented Him, and set Him on the judgment-seat, and said, Judge us. And the expression, "*They pierced my hands and my feet,*" was used in reference to the nails of the cross which were fixed in His hands and feet. And after He was crucified they cast lots upon His vesture, and they that crucified Him parted it among them. And that these things did happen, you can ascertain from the Acts of Pontius Pilate. And we will cite the prophetic utterances of another prophet, Zephaniah, to the effect that He was foretold expressly as to sit upon the foal of an ass and to enter Jerusalem. The words are these: "*Rejoice greatly, O daughter of Zion; shout, O daughter of Jerusalem: behold, thy King cometh unto thee; lowly, and riding upon an ass, and upon a colt the foal of an ass.*"

[... sections omitted.].

Chapter 41 – The Crucifixion predicted. .

And again, in another prophecy, the Spirit of prophecy, through the same David, intimated that Christ, after He had been crucified, should reign, and spoke as follows: "*Sing to the Lord, all the earth, and day by day declare His salvation. For great is the Lord, and greatly to be praised, to be feared above all the gods. For all the gods of the nations are idols of devils; but God made the heavens. Glory and praise are before His face, strength and glorying are in the habitation of His holiness. Give Glory to the Lord, the Father everlasting. Receive grace, and enter His presence, and worship in His holy courts. Let all the earth fear before His face; let it be established, and not shaken. Let them rejoice among the nations. The Lord hath reigned from the tree.*"

[… sections omitted.].

Chapter 45 – Christ's session in Heaven foretold.

And that God the Father of all would bring Christ to heaven after He had raised Him from the dead, and would keep Him there until He has subdued His enemies the devils, and until the number of those who are foreknown by Him as good and virtuous is complete, on whose account He has still delayed the consummation--hear what was said by the prophet David. These are his words: "*The Lord said unto My Lord, Sit Thou at My right hand, until I make Thine enemies Thy footstool. The Lord shall send to Thee the rod of power out of Jerusalem; and rule Thou in the midst of Thine enemies. With Thee is the government in the day of Thy power, in the beauties of Thy saints: from the womb of morning have I begotten Thee.*" That which he says, "*He shall send to Thee the rod of power out of Jerusalem,*" is predictive of the mighty, word, which His apostles, going forth from Jerusalem, preached everywhere; and though death is decreed against those who teach or at all confess the name of Christ, we everywhere both embrace and teach it. And if you also read these words in a hostile spirit, ye can do no more, as I said before, than kill us; which indeed does no harm to us, but to you and all who unjustly hate us, and do not repent, brings eternal punishment by tire.

[... sections omitted.].

Chapter 48 – Christ's work and death foretold.

And that it was predicted that our Christ should heal all diseases and raise the dead, hear what was said. There are these words: "*At His coming the lame shall leap as an hart, and the tongue of the stammerer shall be clear speaking: the blind shall see, and the lepers shall be cleansed; and the dead shall rise, and walk about.*" And that He did those things, you can learn from the Acts of Pontius Pilate. And how it was predicted by the Spirit of prophecy that He and those who hoped in Him should be slain, hear what was said by Isaiah. These are the words: "*Behold now the righteous perisheth, and no man layeth it to heart; and just men are taken away, and no man considereth. From the presence of wickedness is the righteous man taken, and his burial shall be in peace: he is taken from our midst.*"

[... sections omitted.].

Chapter 49 – His rejection by the Jews foretold.

And again, how it was said by the same Isaiah, that the Gentile nations who were not looking for Him should worship Him, but the Jews who always expected Him should not recognize Him when He came. And the words are spoken as from the person of Christ; and they are these "*I was manifest to them that asked not for Me; I was found of them that sought Me not: I said, Behold Me, to a nation that called not on My name. I spread out My hands to a disobedient and gainsaying people, to those who walked in a way that is not good, but follow after their own sins; a people that provoketh Me to anger to My face.*"

For the Jews having the prophecies, and being always in expectation of the Christ to come, did not recognise Him; and not only so, but even treated Him shamefully. But the Gentiles, who had never heard anything about Christ, until the apostles set out from Jerusalem and preached concerning Him, and gave them the prophecies, were filled with joy and faith, and cast away their idols, and dedicated themselves to the Unbegotten God through Christ. And that it was foreknown that these infamous things should be uttered against those who confessed Christ, and that those who slandered Him, and said that it was well to preserve the ancient customs, should be miserable, hear what was briefly said by Isaiah; it is this: "*Woe unto them that call sweet bitter, and bitter sweet.*"

[... sections omitted.].

Chapter 50 – His humiliation predicted.

But that, having become man for our sakes, He endured to suffer and to be dishonoured, and that He shall come again with glory, hear the prophecies which relate to this; they are these: *"Because they delivered His soul unto death, and He was numbered with the transgressors, He has borne the sin of many, and shall make intercession for the transgressors. For, behold, My Servant shall deal prudently, and shall be exalted, and shall be greatly extolled. As many were astonished at Thee, so marred shall Thy form be before men, and so hidden from them Thy glory; so shall many nations wonder, and the kings shall shut their mouths at Him. For they to whom it was not told concerning Him, and they who have not heard, shall understand. O Lord, who hath believed our report? and to whom is the arm of the Lord revealed? We have declared before Him as a child, as a root in a dry ground. He had no form, nor glory; and we saw Him, and there was no form nor comeliness: but His form was dishonoured and marred more than the sons of men. A man under the stroke, and knowing how to bear infirmity, because His face was turned away: He was despised, and of no reputation. It is He who bears our sins, and is afflicted for us; yet we did esteem Him smitten, stricken, and afflicted. But He was wounded for our transgressions, He was bruised for our iniquities, the chastisement of peace was upon Him, by His stripes we are healed. All we, like sheep, have gone astray; every man has wandered in his own way. And He delivered Him for our sins; and He opened not His mouth for all His affliction. He was brought as a sheep to the slaughter, and as a lamb before his shearer is dumb, so He openeth not His mouth. In His humiliation, His judgment was taken away."*

Accordingly, after He was crucified, even all His acquaintances forsook Him, having denied Him; and afterwards, when He had risen from the dead and appeared to them, and had taught them to read the prophecies in which all these things were foretold as coming to pass, and when they had seen Him ascending into heaven, and had believed, and had received power sent thence by Him upon them, and went to every race of men, they taught these things, and were called apostles.

[... sections omitted.].

Chapter 57 – Weekly worship of the Christians.

And we afterwards continually remind each other of these things. And the wealthy among us help the needy; and we always keep together; and for all things wherewith we are supplied, we bless the Maker of all through His Son Jesus Christ, and through the Holy Ghost. And on the day called Sunday, all who live in cities or in the country gather together to one place, and the memoirs of the apostles or the writings of the prophets are read, as long as time permits; then, when the reader has ceased, the president verbally instructs, and exhorts to the imitation of these good things. Then we all rise together and pray, and, as we before said, when our prayer is ended, bread and wine and water are brought, and the president in like manner offers prayers and thanksgivings, according to his ability, and the people assent, saying Amen; and there is a distribution to each, and a participation of that over which thanks have been given, and to those who are absent a portion is sent by the deacons.

And they who are well to do, and willing, give what each thinks fit; and what is collected is deposited with the president, who succours the orphans and widows and those who, through sickness or any other cause, are in want, and those who are in bonds and the strangers sojourning among us, and in a word takes care of all who are in need. But Sunday is the day on which we all hold our common assembly, because it is the first day on which God, having wrought a change in the darkness and matter, made the world; and Jesus Christ our Saviour on the same day rose from the dead. For He was crucified on the day before that of Saturn (Saturday); and on the day after that of Saturn, which is the day of the Sun, having appeared to His apostles and disciples, He taught them these things, which we have submitted to you also for your consideration.

Tertullian
(160 – 225 A.D.)

An Early Apologist

Quintus Septimius Florens Tertullianus, anglicised as **Tertullian,** was a prolific early Christian author from Carthage in the Roman province of Africa. He is the first Christian author to produce an extensive corpus of Latin Christian literature. He also was a notable early Christian apologist and a polemicist against heresy. Though conservative, he did originate and advance new theology to the early Church. He is perhaps most famous for being the oldest extant Latin writer to use the term **Trinity** (*Latin: trinitas*), and giving the oldest extant formal exposition of a Trinitarian theology.

Other Latin formulations that first appear in his work are "three Persons, one Substance" as the Latin "*tres Personae, una Substantia*" (itself from the Koine Greek "*treis Hypostases, Homoousios*"). However, unlike many Church fathers, he was never canonized by the Catholic Church, as several of his later teachings directly contradicted the actions and teachings of the apostles.

Jerome says that Tertullian lived to a great age, but there is no reliable source attesting to his survival beyond the estimated year 225 A.D.. In spite of his schism from the Church, he continued to write against heresy, especially Gnosticism. Thus, by the doctrinal works he published, Tertullian became the teacher of Cyprian and the predecessor of Augustine, who, in turn, became the chief founder of Latin theology.[13]

Excerpts from "The Apology"

Chapter 1

Rulers of the Roman Empire, if, seated for the administration of justice on your lofty tribunal, under the gaze of every eye, and

---

[13] http://en.wikipedia.org/wiki/Tertullian

occupying there all but the highest position in the state, you may not openly inquire into and sift before the world the real truth in regard to the charges made against the Christians; if in this case alone you are afraid or ashamed to exercise your authority in making public inquiry with the carefulness which becomes justice; if, finally, the extreme severities inflicted on our people in recently private judgments, stand in the way of our being permitted to defend ourselves before you, you cannot surely forbid the Truth to reach your ears by the secret pathway of a noiseless book. She has no appeals to make to you in regard of her condition, for that does not excite her wonder. She knows that she is but a sojourner on the earth, and that among strangers she naturally finds foes; and more than this, that her origin, her dwelling-place, her hope, her recompense, her honours, are above. One thing, meanwhile, she anxiously desires of earthly rulers--not to be condemned unknown.

[... sections omitted.].

Chapter 5

To say a word about the origin of laws of the kind to which we now refer, there was an old decree that no god should be consecrated by the emperor till first approved by the senate. Marcus AEmilius had experience of this in reference to his god Alburnus. And this, too, makes for our case, that among you divinity is allotted at the judgment of human beings. Unless gods give satisfaction to men, there will be no deification for them the god will have to propitiate the man. Tiberius accordingly, in whose days the Christian name made its entry into the world, having himself received intelligence from Palestine of events which had clearly shown the truth of Christ's divinity, brought the matter before the senate, with his own decision in favour of Christ.

[... sections omitted.].

Chapter 21

Then, too, the common people have now some knowledge of

Christ, and think of Him as but a man, one indeed such as the Jews condemned, so that some may naturally enough have taken up the idea that we are worshippers of a mere human being. But we are neither ashamed of Christ --for we rejoice to be counted His disciples, and in His name to suffer--nor do we differ from the Jews concerning God.

We must make, therefore, a remark or two as to Christ's divinity. In former times the Jews enjoyed much of God's favour, when the fathers of their race were noted for their righteousness and faith. So it was that as a people they flourished greatly, and their kingdom attained to a lofty eminence; and so highly blessed were they, that for their instruction God spake to them in special revelations, pointing out to them beforehand how they should merit His favor and avoid His displeasure. But how deeply they have sinned, puffed up to their fall with a false trust in their noble ancestors, turning from God's way into a way of sheer impiety, though they themselves should refuse to admit it, their present national ruin would afford sufficient proof.

The sacred writers withal, in giving previous warning of these things, all with equal clearness ever declared that, in the last days of the world, God would, out of every nation, and people, and country, choose for Himself more faithful worshippers, upon whom He would bestow His grace, and that indeed in ampler measure, in keeping with the enlarged capacities of a nobler dispensation. Accordingly, He appeared among us, whose coming to renovate and illuminate man's nature was pre-announced by God--I mean Christ, that Son of God. And so the supreme Head and Master of this grace and discipline, the Enlightener and Trainer of the human race, God's own Son, was announced among us, born, but not so born as to make Him ashamed of the name of Son or of His paternal origin. It was not His lot to have as His father, by incest with a sister, or by violation of a daughter or another's wife, a god in the shape of serpent, or ox, or bird, or lover, for his vile ends transmuting himself into the gold of Danaus. They are your divinities upon whom these base deeds of Jupiter were done.

But the Son of God has no mother in any sense which involves impurity; she, whom men suppose to be His mother in the ordinary way, had never entered into the marriage bond. But, first, I shall discuss His essential nature, and so the nature of His birth will be understood. We have already asserted that God made the world, and all which it contains, by His Word, and Reason, and Power. It is abundantly plain that your philosophers, too, regard the Logos; that is, the Word and Reason as the Creator of the universe.

[... sections omitted.].

But, lo, on the third day there a was a sudden shock of earthquake, and the stone which sealed the sepulchre was rolled away, and the guard fled off in terror without a single disciple near, the grave was found empty of all but the clothes of the buried One. **But nevertheless, the leaders of the Jews, whom it nearly concerned both to spread abroad a lie, and keep back a people tributary and submissive to them from the faith, gave it out that the body of Christ had been stolen by His followers.**

For the Lord, you see, did not go forth into the public gaze, lest the wicked should be delivered from their error; that faith also, destined to a great reward, might hold its ground in difficulty. But He spent forty days with some of His disciples down in Galilee, a region of Judea, instructing them in the doctrines they were to teach to others.

Thereafter, having given them commission to preach the gospel through the world, He was encompassed with a cloud and taken up to heaven, a fact more certain far than the assertions of your Proculi concerning Romulus. All these things Pilate did to Christ; and now in fact a Christian in his own convictions, he sent word of Him to the reigning Caesar, who was at the time Tiberius. Yes, and the Caesars too would have believed on Christ, if either the Caesars had not been necessary for the world, or if Christians could have been Caesars. His disciples also, spreading over the world, did as their Divine Master bade them; and after suffering greatly themselves from the persecutions of the Jews, and with no unwilling heart, as having faith undoubting in the truth, at last by Nero's cruel sword sowed the seed of Christian blood at Rome. Yes, and we shall prove that even your own gods are effective witnesses for Christ.

III.   APOSTOLIC &
EARLY CHURCH FATHERS

In addition to the early historians and apologists of the formative Church in the last section, the three Apostolic fathers and subsequent Church Fathers provided a record and foundational theology of the early Church. Since these historical works are not in the New Testament canon, they, too, are considered Apocrypha although their importance to the early Church cannot be over emphasized. Although these fathers lived relatively early in the Church (*ie. 1-2 centuries*), St. Augustine's works, which dated as late as the end of the fourth century, have also been included since most scholars regard him as the theological architect of many of the primary theological doctrines in the western Roman Catholic Church.

There were three Apostolic Fathers: Clement I of Rome, Ignatius of Antioch, and Polycarp of Smyrna. These men were extremely important to the life of the early Christian Church from a number of perspectives. ***Their works provide an undeniable roadmap to the historical Jesus Christ***. First and foremost, their close relationship with the Apostles and disciples provided a direct, non-broken line to first-hand accounts of the Christ and His ministry. For instance, St. Clement I (*not to be confused with Clement II of Alexandria*) was a contemporary of St. John, St. Peter and the other Apostles. He was also mentioned in St. Paul's epistle.   Therefore, he was also acquainted with St. Luke. He was ordained Bishop of Rome by St. Peter.   His letters to the Corinthians provide us an historical account of the earliest Christian Church.

Ignatius of Antioch was a contemporary of St. Clement, was a disciple of St. John and St. Paul and, presumably, knew the other Apostles. He knew Polycarp as his Christian mentor. His works included such fundamental Christian concepts as ecclesiology, the sacraments, the role of bishops, and Biblical Sabbath.

Polycarp of Smyrna was a contemporary of Ignatius of Antioch and his disciple. Perhaps more importatntly, he was a disciple of St. John the Apostle and St. John ordained him Bishop of Smyrna.

39

(Pope) Clement I of Rome
(- 99 A.D.)

St. Clement of Rome[14]. Clement calls on the Christians of Corinth to maintain harmony and order. According to Tertullian, Clement was consecrated by Saint Peter. Tradition identifies him as the fourth Pope and Bishop of Rome and his epistle asserts Rome's apostolic authority over its audience, the Church in Corinth. He is mentioned by name in St. Paul's epistle to the Philippians 4.3. He was the first Apostolic Father of the Church.

Clément's only existing, genuine text is a letter to the Christian congregation in Corinth, often called the First Epistle of Clement or 1 Clement. It is the earliest Christian epistle outside of the New Testament. His epistle, 1 Clement *(c 96)*, was copied and widely read in the Early Church.

The history of 1 Clement clearly and continuously shows Clement as the author of this letter. It is considered the earliest authentic Christian document outside of the New Testament. In the epistle Clement uses the terms bishop and presbyter interchangeably for the higher order of ministers above deacons. The letters of Ignatius of Antioch indicate the several congregations were headed by individual bishops but that Rome's congregation was not. In some congregations, particularly in Egypt, the distinction between bishops and presbyters seems to have become established only later. But by the middle of that century all the leading Christian centers had bishops.

Excerpts from Clement's First Epistle to the Corinthians

The Church of God which sojourneth in Rome to the Church of God which sojourneth in Corinth, to them which are called and sanctified by the will of God through our Lord Jesus Christ. Grace to you and peace from Almighty God through Jesus Christ be multiplied. By reason of the sudden and repeated calamities and reverses which are befalling us, brethren, we consider that we have

---

[14] http://en.wikipedia.org/wiki/Pope_Clement_I

been somewhat tardy in giving heed to the matters of dispute that have arisen among you, dearly beloved, and to the detestable and unholy sedition, so alien and strange to the elect of God, which a few headstrong and self-willed persons have kindled to such a pitch of madness that your name, once revered and renowned and lovely in the sight of all men, hath been greatly reviled.

[... sections omitted.].

But, to pass from the examples of ancient days, let us come to those champions who lived nearest to our time. Let us set before us the noble examples which belong to our generation. By reason of jealousy and envy the greatest and most righteous pillars of the Church were persecuted, and contended even unto death. Let us set before our eyes the good Apostles. There was Peter who by reason of unrighteous jealousy endured not one but many labors, and thus having borne his testimony went to his appointed place of glory. By reason of jealousy and strife Paul by his example pointed out the prize of patient endurance. After that he had been seven times in bonds, had been driven into exile, had been stoned, had preached in the East and in the West, he won the noble renown which was the reward of his faith, having taught righteousness unto the whole world and having reached the farthest bounds of the West; and when he had borne his testimony before the rulers, so he departed from the world and went unto the holy place, having been found a notable pattern of patient endurance.

[... sections omitted.].

Let us fix our eyes on the blood of Christ and understand how precious it is unto His Father, because being shed for our salvation it won for the whole world the grace of repentance. Let us review all the generations in turn, and learn how from generation to generation the Master hath given a place for repentance unto them that desire to turn to Him. Noah preached repentance, and they that obeyed were saved. Jonah preached destruction unto the men of Nineveh; but they, repenting of their sins, obtained pardon of God by their supplications and received salvation, albeit they were aliens from God. The ministers of the grace of God through the

Holy Spirit spake concerning repentance. Yea and the Master of the universe Himself spake concerning repentance with an oath: for, as I live saith the Lord, I desire not the death of the sinner, so much as his repentance, and He added also a merciful judgment: Repent ye, O house of Israel, of your iniquity; say unto the sons of My people, Though your sins reach from the earth even unto the heaven, and though they be redder than scarlet and blacker than sackcloth, and ye turn unto Me with your whole heart and say Father, I will give ear unto you as unto a holy people. And in another place He saith on this wise, Wash, be ye clean. Put away your iniquities from your souls out of My sight. Cease from your iniquities; learn to do good; seek out judgment; defend him that is wronged: give judgment for the orphan, and execute righteousness for the widow; and come and let us reason together, saith He; and though your sins be as crimson, I will make them white as snow; and though they be as scarlet, I will make them white as wool. And if ye be willing and will hearken unto Me, ye shall eat the good things of the earth; but if ye be not willing, neither hearken unto Me, a sword shall devour you; for the mouth of the Lord hath spoken these things. Seeing then that He desireth all His beloved to be partakers of repentance, He confirmed it by an act of His almighty will.

[... sections omitted.].

For Christ is with them that are lowly of mind, not with them that exalt themselves over the flock. The scepter of the majesty of God, even our Lord Jesus Christ, came not in the pomp of arrogance or of pride, though He might have done so, but in lowliness of mind, according as the Holy Spirit spake concerning Him. For He saith Lord, who believed our report? and to whom was the arm of the Lord revealed? We announced Him in His presence. As a child was He, as a root in a thirsty ground. There is no form in Him, neither glory. And we beheld Him, and He had no form nor comeliness, but His form was mean, lacking more than the form of men. He was a man of stripes and of toil, and knowing how to bear infirmity: for His face is turned away. He was dishonored and held of no account. He beareth our sins and suffereth pain for our sakes: and we accounted Him to be in toil and in stripes and in affliction. And He was wounded for our sins and hath been afflicted for our iniquities. The chastisement of our peace is upon Him. With His bruises we were healed.

We all went astray like sheep, each man went astray in his own path: and the Lord delivered Him over for our sins. And He openeth not His mouth, because He is afflicted. As a sheep He was led to slaughter; and as a lamb before his shearer is dumb, so openeth He not His mouth. In His humiliation His judgment was taken away. His generation who shall declare? For His life is taken away from the earth. For the iniquities of my people He is come to death. And I will give the wicked for His burial, and the rich for His death; for He wrought no iniquity, neither was guile found in His mouth. And the Lord desireth to cleanse Him from His stripes. If ye offer for sin, your soul shall see along lived seed. And the Lord desireth to take away from the toil of His soul, to show Him light and to mould Him with understanding, to justify a Just One that is a good servant unto many. And He shall bear their sins. Therefore He shall inherit many, and shall divide the spoils of the strong; because His soul was delivered unto death, and He was reckoned unto the transgressors; and He bare the sins of many, and for their sins was He delivered up.

[… sections omitted.].

Look ye, brethren, lest His benefits, which are many, turn unto judgment to all of us, if we walk not worthily of Him, and do those things which are good and well pleasing in His sight with concord. For He saith in a certain place, The Spirit of the Lord is a lamp searching the closets of the belly. Let us see how near He is, and how that nothing escapeth Him of our thoughts or our devices which we make. It is right therefore that we should not be deserters from His will. Let us rather give offense to foolish and senseless men who exalt themselves and boast in the arrogance of their words, than to God. Let us fear the Lord Jesus [Christ], whose blood was given for us. Let us reverence our rulers; let us honor our elders; let us instruct our young men in the lesson of the fear of God. Let us guide our women toward that which is good: let them show forth their lovely disposition of purity; let them prove their sincere affection of gentleness; let them make manifest the moderation of their tongue through their silence; let them show their love, not in factious preferences but without partiality towards all them that fear God, in holiness. Let our children be partakers of the instruction which is in Christ: let them learn how lowliness of mind prevaileth with God, what power chaste love hath with God, how the fear of Him is good and great and saveth all them that walk therein in a pure mind with holiness. For He is the searcher out of the intents and desires; whose breath is in us, and when He listeth, He shall take it away.

[... sections omitted.].

The Apostles received the Gospel for us from the Lord Jesus Christ; Jesus Christ was sent forth from God. So then Christ is from God, and the Apostles are from Christ. Both therefore came of the will of God in the appointed order. Having therefore received a charge, and having been fully assured through the resurrection of our Lord Jesus Christ and confirmed in the word of God with full assurance of the Holy Ghost, they went forth with the glad tidings that the kingdom of God should come. So preaching everywhere in country and town, they appointed their firstfruits, when they had proved them by the Spirit, to be bishops and deacons unto them that should believe. And this they did in no new fashion; for indeed it had been written concerning bishops and deacons from very ancient times; for thus saith the scripture in a certain place, I will appoint their bishops in righteousness and their deacons in faith. And what marvel, if they which were entrusted in Christ with such a work by God appointed the aforesaid persons?

[... sections omitted.].

Let us therefore cleave to the guiltless and righteous: and these are the elect of God. Wherefore are there strifes and wraths and factions and divisions and war among you? Have we not one God and one Christ and one Spirit of grace that was shed upon us? And is there not one calling in Christ? Wherefore do we tear and rend asunder the members of Christ, and stir up factions against our own body, and reach such a pitch of folly, as to forget that we are members one of another? Remember the words of Jesus our Lord: for He said, Woe unto that man; it were good for him if he had not been born, rather than that at he should offend one of Mine elect. It were better for him that a millstone were hanged about him, and be cast into the sea, than that he should pervert one of Mine elect. Your division hath perverted many; it hath brought many to despair, many to doubting, and all of us to sorrow. And your sedition still continueth.

Take up the epistle of the blessed Paul the Apostle. What wrote he first unto you in the beginning of the Gospel? Of a truth he charged you in the Spirit concerning himself and Cephas and Apollos, because that even then ye had made parties. Yet that making of parties brought less sin upon you; for ye were partisans of Apostles that were highly reputed, and of a man approved in their sight. But now mark ye, who they are that have perverted you and diminished the glory of your renowned love for the brotherhood. It is shameful, dearly beloved, yes, utterly shameful and unworthy of your conduct in Christ, that it should be reported that the very steadfast and ancient Church of the Corinthians, for the sake of one or two persons, maketh sedition against its presbyters. And this report hath reached not only us, but them also which differ from us, so that ye even heap blasphemies on the Name of the Lord by reason of your folly, and moreover create peril for yourselves.

Let us therefore root this out quickly, and let us fall down before the Master and entreat Him with tears, that He may show Himself propitious and be reconciled unto us, and may restore us to the seemly and pure conduct which belongeth to our love of the brethren. For this is a gate of righteousness opened unto life, as it is written; Open me the gates of righteousness, that I may enter in thereby and preach the Lord. This is the gate of the Lord; the righteous shall enter in thereby. Seeing then that many gates are opened, this is that gate which is in righteousness, even that which is in Christ, whereby all are blessed that have entered in and direct their path in holiness and righteousness, performing all things without confusion. Let a man be faithful, let him be able to expound a deep saying, let him be wise in the discernment of words, let him be strenuous in deeds, let him be pure; for so much the more ought he to be lowly in mind, in proportion as he seemeth to be the greater; and he ought to seek the common advantage of all, and not his own.

Let him that hath love in Christ fulfill the commandments of Christ. Who can declare the bond of the love of God? Who is sufficient to tell the majesty of its beauty? The height, where unto love exalteth, is unspeakable. Love joineth us unto God; love covereth a multitude of sins; love endureth all things, is long-suffering in all things. There is nothing coarse, nothing arrogant in love. Love hath no divisions, love maketh no seditions, love doeth all things in concord. In love were all the elect of God made perfect; without love nothing is well pleasing to God: in love the Master took us unto Himself; for the love which He had toward us, Jesus Christ our Lord hath given His blood for us by the will of God, and His flesh for our flesh and His life for our lives.

Ye see, dearly beloved, how great and marvelous a thing is love, and there is no declaring its perfection. Who is sufficient to be found therein, save those to whom God shall vouchsafe it? Let us therefore entreat and ask of His mercy, that we may be found blameless in love, standing apart from the factiousness of men. All the generations from Adam unto this day have passed away: but they that by God's grace were perfected in love dwell in the abode of the pious; and they shall be made manifest in the visitation of the Kingdom of God. For it is written; Enter into the closet for a very little while until Mine anger and Mine wrath shall pass away, and I will remember a good day and will raise you from your tombs. Blessed were we, dearly beloved, if we should be doing the commandments of God in concord of love, to the end that our sins may through love be forgiven us. For it is written; Blessed are they whose iniquities are forgiven, and whose sins are covered. Blessed is the man to whom the Lord shall impute no sin, neither is guile in his mouth. This declaration of blessedness was pronounced upon them that have been elected by God through Jesus Christ our Lord, to whom be the glory for ever and ever. Amen.

For all our transgressions which we have committed through any of the wiles of the adversary, let us entreat that we may obtain forgiveness. Yea and they also, who set themselves up as leaders of faction and division, ought to look to the common ground of hope.

For such as walk in fear and love desire that they themselves should fall into suffering rather than their neighbors; and they pronounce condemnation against themselves rather than against the harmony which hath been handed down to us nobly and righteously.

Finally may the All seeing God and Master of spirits and Lord of all flesh, who chose the Lord Jesus Christ, and us through Him for a peculiar people, grant unto every soul that is called after His excellent and holy Name faith, fear, peace, patience, long-suffering, temperance, chastity and soberness, that they may be well pleasing unto His Name through our High priest and Guardian Jesus Christ, through whom unto Him be glory and majesty, might and honor, both now and for ever and ever. Amen.

Now send ye back speedily unto us our messengers Claudius Ephebus and Valerius Bito, together with Fortunatus also, in peace and with joy, to the end that they may the more quickly report the peace and concord which is prayed for and earnestly desired by us, that we also may the more speedily rejoice over your good order. The grace of our Lord Jesus Christ be with you and with all men in all places who have been called by God and through Him, through whom be glory and honor, power and greatness and eternal dominion, unto Him, from the ages past and forever and ever. Amen.

Ignatius of Antioch
(35 – 107 A.D.)

Ignatius of Antioch[15] (*also known as Theophorus*) was the third Bishop or Patriarch of Antioch. It is believed that St. Ignatius, along with his friend Polycarp, with great probability were disciples of the apostles St. John and St. Paul. En route to his martyrdom in Rome, Ignatius wrote a series of letters which have been preserved. Important topics addressed in these letters include ecclesiology, the sacraments, the role of bishops, and Biblical Sabbath. He is the second after Clement to mention Paul's epistles. He was sentenced to die in the Coliseum which is to say, he was eaten by lions.

Excerpts from "Ignatius to Polycarp"

Ignatius, who is also Theophorus, unto Polycarp who is bishop of the Church of the Smyrnaeans or rather who hath for his bishop God the Father and Jesus Christ, abundant greeting. Welcoming thy godly mind which is grounded as it were on an immovable rock, I give exceeding glory that it hath been vouchsafed me to see thy blameless face,whereof I would fain have joy in God. I exhort thee in the grace wherewith thou art clothed to press forward in thy course and to exhort all men that they may be saved. Vindicate thine officein all diligence of flesh and of spirit. Have a care for union, than which there is nothing better. Bear all men, as the Lord also beareth thee. Suffer all men in love, as also thou doest.

Give thyself to unceasing prayers. Ask for larger wisdom than thou hast. Be watchful, and kept hy spirit from slumbering. Speak to each man severally after the manner of God. Bear the maladies of all, as a perfect athlete. Where there is more toil, there is much gain.

[... sections omitted.].

Despise not slaves, whether men or women. Yet let not these

---

[15] http://en.wikipedia.org/wiki/Ignatius_of_Antioch

again be puffed up, but let them serve the more faithfully to the glory of God, that they may obtain a better freedom from God. Let them not desire to be set free at the public cost, lest they be found slaves of lust. Flee evil arts, or rather hold thou discourse about these. Tell my sisters to love the Lord and tobe content with their husbands in flesh and in spirit.in like manner also charge my brothers in the name of Jesus Christ to love their wives, as the Lord loved the Church. If any one is able to abide in chastity to the honour of the flesh of the Lord, let him so abide without boasting. If he boast, he is lost; and if it be known beyond the bishop, he is polluted.

It becometh men and women too, when they marry, to unite themselves with the consent of the bishop, that the marriage may be after the Lord and not after concupiscence. Let all things be done to the honour of God. Give ye heed to the bishop, that God also may give heed to you. I am devoted to those who are subject to the bishop, the presbyters, the deacons. May it be granted me to have my portion with them in the presence of God. Toil together one with another, struggle together, run together, suffer together, lie down together, rise up together, as God's stewards and assessors and ministers. Please the Captain in whose army ye serve, from whom also ye will receive your pay. Let none of you be found a deserter. Let your baptism abide with you as you shield; your faith as your helmet; your love as your spear; your patience as your body armour. Let your works be your deposits, that ye may receive your assets due to you. Be ye therefore long-suffering one with another in gentleness, as God is with you. May I have joy of you always. Seeing that the Church which is in Antioch of Syria hath peace, as it hath been reported to me, through your prayers, I myself also have been the more comforted since God hath banished my care; if so be I may through suffering attain unto God, that I may be found a disciple through your intercession.

It becometh thee, most blessed Polycarp, to call together a godly council and to elect some one among you who is very dear to you and zealous also, who shall be fit to bear the name of God's courier to appoint him, I say, that he may go to Syria and glorify your zealous love unto the glory of God. A Christian hath no authority over himself, but giveth his time to God. This is God's work, and yours also, when ye shall complete it for I trust in the Divine grace, that ye are ready for an act of well-doing which is meet for God. Knowing the fervour of your sincerity, I have exhorted you in a short letter.

Since I have not been able to write to all theChurches, by reason of my sailing suddenly from Troasto Neapolis, as the Divine will enjoineth, thou shaltwrite to the Churches in front, as one possessing themind of God, to the intent that they also may do thissame thing -- let those who are able send messengers,and the rest letters by the persons who are sent bythee, that ye may be glorified by an ever memorabledeed -- for this is worthy of thee.

I salute all by name, and especially the wife of Epitropus with her whole household and her children's.I salute Attalus my beloved. I salute him that shall be appointed to go to Syria. Grace shall be with himalways, and with Polycarp who sendeth him. I bid you farewell always in our God Jesus Christ, in whom abide ye in the unity and supervisionof God. I salute Alce, a name very dear to me. Fare yewell in the Lord.

Ignatius to Smyrnaeans. Ignatius, who is also Theophorus, to the Church of God the Father and of Jesus Christ the beloved, to her who hath by mercy obtained every gift, filled with faith and love, not lacking in any gift, most Godlike, and the mother of saints, to her which is in Smyrna in Asia, much joy in the blameless spirit and word of God. I glorify God even Jesus Christ, who hath thus made you wise; for I perceived that ye were perfected in immovable faith, as though ye were nailed to the cross of our Lord Jesus Christ in flesh and in spirit, and firmly fixed in love in the blood of Christ, being fully persuaded with regard to our Lord, that he was truly of the race of David according to the flesh, the Son of God according to the will and power of God; truly born of a virgin; baptized by John, that all righteousness might be fulfilled by him; truly nailed for us unto the cross in the flesh in the time of Pontius Pilate and Herod the tetrarch; from the fruit of which cross are we, even from his divinely blessed passion, that he might raise up a sign unto the ages, by means of the resurrection, even unto the saints and them that believe in him, whether they be among the Jews or the Gentiles, in one body of his Church. All these things did he suffer for our sake, to the end that we might be saved. And he truly suffered, even as he truly raised himself up; not as certain unbelievers say, that he suffered in semblance, they themselves only existing in semblance; and even according to their opinions shall it happen unto them, since they are bodiless and of the nature of devils. For I also know and believe, that he exists in the flesh even after the resurrection. And when he came unto them who were with Peter he said unto them, Take, handle me, and see that I am not a spirit without a body; and straightway they touched him and believed, being convinced by his flesh and his spirit. On this account also they despised death, and were found superior to death. But after his resurrection, he ate and drank with them, as being in the flesh, though spiritually he was united to the Father.

These things do I exhort you, beloved, knowing that such is your faith. But I put you on your guard against beasts in human shape, whom not only doth it behove you not to receive, but, if it is possible, not even to meet. But only pray for them, if by any means they may repent; and this is difficult, but it is in the power of Jesus Christ, our true life. For if these things were done by our Lord only in appearance, then in appearance only am I bound. And why have I given myself up unto death, to fire, to sword, to wild beasts? but nearness to the sword is nearness to God; to be among the wild beasts is to be in the arms of God; only let it be in the name of Jesus Christ. I endure all things that I may suffer together with him, since he who became perfect man strengtheneth me. Whom some in ignorance deny, but have rather been denied of him, being advocates of death rather than of the truth. Whom the prophets have not convinced, nor the law of Moses, nor until now the gospel, nor the sufferings which each of us severally have endured; for of a truth they think that our sufferings also are in appearance. For how doth a man benefit me, if he praise me but blasphemeth my Lord, not confessing that he lived in the flesh? But he who confesseth not this, hath denied him completely, being dead while he liveth. But it hath not seemed good unto me to write their names, which are those of unbelievers; but may it not even happen unto me to remember them, until they repent of their errors with regard to the passion, which is our resurrection.

Let no man be deceived. Even the heavenly things, and the glory of the angels, and the principalities, both visible and invisible, if they believe not on the blood of Christ, for them also is there condemnation. Let him who receiveth it, receive it in reality. Let not high place puff up any man. For the whole matter is faith and love, to which there is nothing preferable.

Consider those who hold heretical opinions with regard to the grace of Jesus Christ which hath come unto us, how opposite they are to the mind of God. They have no care for love, nor concerning the widow, nor concerning the orphan, nor concerning the afflicted, nor concerning him who is bound or loosed, nor concerning him who is hungry or thirsty. They refrain from the eucharist and from prayer, because they do not confess that the eucharist is the flesh of our Saviour Jesus Christ, which suffered for our sins, and which the Father of his goodness raised up. They, therefore, who speak against the gift of God, die disputing. But it were better for them to love, that they might also rise again. It is, therefore, proper to abstain from such, and not to speak concerning them, either in private or in public; but to attend to the prophets, and especially to the gospel, in which the passion hath been revealed unto us, and the resurrection hath been perfected. But avoid divisions, as being the beginning of evils. Do ye all follow the bishop, as Jesus Christ doth the Father; and follow the presbyters as the apostles; and have respect unto the deacons as unto the commandment of God. Let no one, apart from the bishop, do any of the things that appertain unto the Church.

Let that eucharist alone be considered valid which is celebrated in the presence of the bishop, or of him to whom he shall have entrusted it. Wherever the bishop appear, there let the multitude be; even as wherever Christ Jesus is, there is the Catholic Church. It is not lawful either to baptize, or to hold a love-feast without the consent of the bishop; but whatsoever he shall approve of, that also is well pleasing unto God, to the end that whatever is done may be safe and sure. It is reasonable for the future to be vigilant, and while we have yet time, to repent unto God. It is well to honour God and the bishop; he who honoureth the bishop, is honoured of God; he who doeth anything without the knowledge of the bishop, serveth the devil. Let all things, therefore, abound unto you in grace, for ye are worthy. Ye have refreshed me in all things, and Jesus Christ hath refreshed you. Ye have loved me both when absent and present. May God requite you, through whom, by enduring all things, ye shall attain unto him. Ye have done well in that ye have received as servants of Christ, who is God, Philo and Rheus Agathopus, who have followed me for the sake of God; who also return thanks unto the Lord in your behalf, because ye have refreshed them in every way. Nothing shall be lost unto you. My spirit is given for yours, and my bonds, which ye have not despised, nor have been ashamed of them; nor shall the perfect faith, even Jesus Christ, be ashamed of you.

Your prayer hath come unto the Church which is at Antioch in Syria, whence I salute all, being bound with the most god like bonds, not being worthy to be from thence, being the last of them. But according to his will, I was thought worthy, not from any merit of which I am conscious, but of the grace of God, which I pray may be given unto me in perfection, that, by means of your prayer, I may attain unto God. In order, therefore, that your work may be perfect, both on earth and in heaven, it is fitting, for the honour of God, that your Church should elect a divine ambassador, who, when he has come unto Syria, may congratulate them that they are at peace, and have received their proper greatness, and that their own governing body has been restored to them. It hath, therefore, appeared unto me to be a worthy thing to send some one of yours with the epistle, that he may glorify together with them the prosperity which hath happened unto them in accordance with God, and because that by your prayer it hath already attained unto the harbour. Since ye are perfect, think also such things as be perfect; for if ye are willing to do well, God is ready to grant you the opportunity.

The love of the brethren who are in Troas saluteth you, whence also I write unto you by means of Burrhus, whom ye, together with the Ephesians your brethren, sent along with me, who hath in all respects refreshed me; and would that all imitated him, who is a pattern of the service of God. Grace shall requite him in all things; I salute also your bishop, who is worthy of God, and your godlike presbyters, the deacons, who are my fellow-servants, and all of you, both individually and in common, in the name of Jesus Christ, in his flesh and his blood, in his passion and resurrection, both fleshly and spiritual, in the unity both of God and of yourselves. Grace be unto you, mercy, peace, and patience for ever. I salute the families of my brethren, together with their wives and children, and the virgins who are called widows. Fare ye well in the power of the spirit. Philo, who is with me, saluteth you. I salute the house of Tavias, which I pray may be fixed in faith and love, both fleshly and spiritual. I salute Alce, the name desired by me, and Daphnus the incomparable, and Eutecnus, and all by name. Farewell in the grace of God.

Excerpts from "Martyrdom of Ignatius"

Desire Of Ignatius For Martyrdom. When Trajan, not long since, succeeded to the empire of the Romans, Ignatius, the disciple of John the apostle, a man in all respects of an apostolic character, governed the Church of the Antiochians with great care, having with difficulty escaped the former storms of the many persecutions under Domitian, inasmuch as, like a good pilot, by the helm of prayer and fasting, by the earnestness of his teaching, and by his [constant spiritual labour, he resisted the flood that rolled against him, fearing [only] lest he should lose any of those who were deficient in courage, or apt to suffer from their simplicity. Wherefore he rejoiced over the tranquil state of the Church, when the persecution ceased for a little time, but was grieved as to himself, that he had not yet attained to a true love to Christ, nor reached the perfect rank of a disciple. For he inwardly reflected, that the confession which is made by martyrdom, would bring him into a yet more intimate relation to the Lord. Wherefore, continuing a few years longer with the Church, and, like a divine lamp, enlightening every one's understanding by his expositions of the [Holy] Scriptures, he [at length] attained the object of his desire.

Ignatius Is Condemned By Trajan. For Trajan, in the ninth year of his reign, being lifted up [with pride], after the victory he had gained over the Scythians and Dacians, and many other nations, and thinking that the religious body of the Christians were yet wanting to complete the subjugation of all things to himself, and [thereupon] threatening them with persecution unless they should agree to worship daemons, as did all other nations, thus compelled all who were living godly lives either to sacrifice [*to idols*] or die. Wherefore the noble soldier of Christ [*Ignatius*], being in fear for the Church of the Antiochians, was, in accordance with his own desire, brought before Trajan, who was at that time staying at Antioch, but was in haste [*to set forth*] against Armenia and the Parthians. And when he was set before the emperor Trajan, [*that prince*] said unto him, "*Who art thou, eked wretch, who settest thyself to transgress our commands, and persuadest others to do the same, so that they should miserably perish?*" Ignatius replied, "*No one ought to call Theophorus wicked; for all evil spirits have departed from the servants of God. But if, because I am an enemy to these [spirits], you call me wicked in respect to them, I quite agree with you; for inasmuch as I have Christ the King of heaven [within me], I destroy all the devices of these [evil spirits].*"

Trajan answered, "*And who is Theophorus?*" Ignatius replied, "*He who has Christ within his breast.*" Trajan said, "*Do we not then seem to you to have the gods in our mind, whose assistance we enjoy in fighting against our enemies?*" Ignatius answered, "*Thou art in error when thou callest the daemons of the nations gods. For there is but one God, who made heaven, and earth, and the sea, and all that are in them; and one Jesus Christ, the only-begotten Son of God, whose kingdom may I enjoy.*" Trajan said, "*Do you mean Him who was crucified under Pontius Pilate?*" Ignatius replied, "*I mean Him who crucified my sin, with him who was the inventor of it, and who has condemned [and cast down] all the deceit and malice of the devil under the feet of those who carry Him in their heart.*" Trajan said, "*Dost thou then carry within thee Him that was crucified?*" Ignatius replied, "*Truly so; for it is written, 'I will dwell in them, and walk in them.'*" Then Trajan pronounced sentence as follows "*We command that Ignatius, who affirms that he carries about within him Him that was crucified, be bound by soldiers, and carried to the great [city] Rome, there to be devoured by the beasts, for the gratification of the people.*"

When the holy martyr heard this sentence, he cried out with joy, "*I thank thee, O Lord, that Thou hast vouchsafed to honour me with a perfect love towards Thee, and hast made me to be bound with iron chains, like Thy Apostle Paul.*" Having spoken thus, he then, with delight, clasped the chains about him; and when he had first prayed for the Church, and commended it with tears to the Lord, he was hurried away by the savage cruelty of the soldiers, like a distinguished ram the leader of a goodly flock, that he might be carried to Rome, there to furnish food to the bloodthirsty beasts.

Ignatius Sails To Smyrna. Wherefore, with great alacrity and joy, through his desire to suffer, he came down from Antioch to Seleucia, from which place he set sail. And after a great deal of suffering he came to Smyrna, where he disembarked with great joy, and hastened to see the holy Polycarp, [*formerly*] his fellow-disciple, and [*now*] bishop of Smyrna. For they had both, in old times, been disciples of St. John the Apostle. Being then brought to him, and having communicated to him some spiritual gifts, and glorying in his bonds, he entreated of him to labour along with him for the fulfilment of his desire; earnestly indeed asking this of the whole Church (*for the cities and Churches of Asia had welcomed the holy man through their bishops, and presbyters, and deacons, all hastening to meet him, if by any means they might receive from him some spiritual gift*), but above all, the holy Polycarp, that, by means of the wild beasts, he soon disappearing from this world, might be manifested before the face of Christ.

Ignatius Writes To The Churches. And these things he thus spake, and thus testified, extending his love to Christ so far as one who was about to secure heaven through his good confession, and the earnestness of those who joined their prayers to his in regard to his [*approaching*] conflict; and to give a recompense to the Churches, who came to meet him through their rulers, sending letters of thanksgiving to them, which dropped spiritual grace, along with prayer and exhortation. Wherefore, seeing all men so kindly affected towards him, and fearing lest the love of the brotherhood should hinder his zeal towards the Lord, while a fair door of suffering martyrdom was opened to him, he wrote to the Church of the Romans the Epistle which is here subjoined. (*See the Epistle as formerly given.*)

Ignatius Is Brought To Rome. Having therefore, by means of this Epistle, settled, as he wished, those of the brethren at Rome who were unwilling [*for his martyrdom*]; and setting sail from Smyrna (for Christophorus was pressed by the soldiers to hasten to the public spectacles in the mighty [*city*] Rome, that, being given up to the wild beasts in the sight of the Roman people, he might attain to the crown for which he strove), he [*next*] landed at Troas. Then, going on from that place to Neapolis, he went [*on foot*] by Philippi through Macedonia, and on to that part of Epirus which is near Epidamnus; and finding a ship in one of the seaports, he sailed over the Adriatic Sea, and entering from it on the Tyrrhene, he passed by the various islands and cities, until, when Puteoli came in sight, he was eager there to disembark, having a desire to tread in the footsteps of the Apostle Paul.

[... sections omitted.].

Ignatius Is Devoured By The Beasts At Rome. They pushed forth therefore from the place which is called Portus; and (*the fame of all relating to the holy martyr being already spread abroad*) we met the brethren full of fear and joy; rejoicing indeed because they were thought worthy to meet with Theophorus, but struck with fear because so eminent a man was being led to death. Now he enjoined some to keep silence who, in their fervent zeal, were saying that they would appease the people, so that they should not demand the destruction of this just one. He being immediately aware of this through the Spirit, and having saluted them all, and begged of them to show a true affection towards him, and having dwelt [on this point] at greater length than in his Epistle, and having persuaded them not to envy him hastening to the Lord, he then, after he had, with all the brethren kneeling *[beside him]*, entreated the Son of God in behalf of the Churches, that a stop might be put to the persecution, and that mutual love might continue among the brethren, was led with all haste into the amphitheatre.

Then, being immediately thrown in, according to the command of Caesar given some time ago, the public spectacles being just about to close (*for it was then a solemn day, as they deemed it, being that which is called the thirteenth in the Roman tongue, on which the people were wont to assemble in more than ordinary numbers*), he was thus cast to the wild beasts close, beside the temple, that so by them the desire of the holy martyr Ignatius should be fulfilled, according to that which is written.

[... sections omitted.].

Ignatius Appears In A Vision. After his death Now these things took place on the thirteenth day before the Kalends of January, that is, on the twentieth of December, Sun and Senecio being then the consuls of the Romans for the second time. Having ourselves been eye-witnesses of these things, and having spent the whole night in tears within the house, and having entreated the Lord, with bended knees and much prayer, that He would give us weak men full assurance respecting the things which were done, it came to pass, on our filling into a brief slumber, that some of us saw the blessed Ignatius suddenly standing by us and embracing us, while others beheld him again praying for us, and others still saw him dropping with sweat, as if he had just come from his great labour, and standing by the Lord.

When, therefore, we had with great joy witnessed these things, and had compared our several visions together, we sang praise to God, the giver of all good things, and expressed our sense of the happiness of the holy [*martyr*]; and now we have made known to you both the day and the time [*when these things happened*], that, assembling ourselves together according to the time of his martyrdom, we may have fellowship with the champion and noble martyr of Christ, who trode under foot the devil, and perfected the course which, out of love to Christ, he had desired, in Christ Jesus our Lord; by whom, and with whom, be glory and power to the Father, with the Holy Spirit, for evermore! Amen.

Polycarp of Smyrna
(69 – 155 A.D.)

St. Polycarp of Smyrna[16] was a Christian bishop of Smyrna (*now İzmir in Turkey*). It is recorded that "*He had been a disciple of John.*" According to the *Martyrdom of Polycarp* he died a martyr, bound and burned at the stake, then stabbed when the fire failed to touch him. Polycarp is regarded as a saint in the Roman Catholic, Eastern Orthodox, Oriental Orthodox, Anglican,. and Lutheran Churches.

It is recorded by Irenaeus, who heard him speak in his youth, and by Tertullian, that he had been a disciple of John the Apostle. Saint Jerome wrote that Polycarp was a disciple of John and that John had ordained him bishop of Smyrna. The early tradition that expanded upon the *Martyrdom* to link Polycarp in competition and contrast with John the Apostle who, though many people had tried to kill him, was not martyred but died of old age after being exiled to the island of Patmos, is embodied in the Coptic language fragmentary papyri (*the "Harris fragments"*) dating to the 3rd to 6th centuries

Both Polycarp and Irenaeus viewed the "John" as the apostle who wrote the Gospel, letters and Revelation. Other traditional advocates follow Eusebius in insisting that the apostolic connection of Polycarp was with John the Evangelist, and that this John, the author of the Gospel of John, was the same as the Apostle John. Polycarp, 155, tried and failed to persuade Anicetus, Bishop of Rome, to have the West celebrate Passover on 14 Nisan, as in the East. He rejected the suggestion that the East use the Western date. In *c* 155, the Smyrnans demanded Polycarp's execution as a Christian, and he died a martyr.

Excerpts from "Polycarp to the Philippians"

Polycarp prologue. Polycarp and the presbyters that are with him unto the Church of Godwhich sojourneth at Philippi; mercy

---

[16] http://en.wikipedia.org/wiki/Polycarp

unto you and peace from GodAlmighty and Jesus Christ our Savior be multiplied. I rejoiced with you greatly in our Lord Jesus Christ, for that ye received the followers of the true Love and escorted them on their way, as befitted you--those men encircled in saintly bonds which are the diadems of them that be truly chosen of God and our Lord; and that the steadfast root of your faith which was famed from primitive times abideth until now and beareth fruit unto our Lord Jesus Christ, who endured to face even death for our sins, whom God raised, having loosed the pangs of Hades; on whom, though ye saw Him not, ye believe with joy unutterable and full of glory; unto which joy many desire to enter in; forasmuch as ye know that it is by grace ye are saved, not of works, but by the will of God through Jesus Christ.

Wherefore gird up your loins and serve God in fear and truth, forsaking the vain and empty talking and the error of the many, for that ye have believed on Him that raised our Lord Jesus Christ from the dead and gave unto him glory and a throne on His right hand;unto whom all things were made subject that are in heaven and that are on the earth; to whom every creature that hath breath doeth service; who cometh as judge of quick and dead; whose blood God will require of them that are disobedient unto Him. Now He that raised Him from the dead will raise us also; if we do His will and walk in His commandments and love the things which He loved, abstaining from all unrighteousness, covetousness, love of money, evil speaking, false witness; not rendering evil for evil or railing for railing or blow for blow or cursing for cursing but remembering the words which the Lord spake, as He taught; Judge not that ye be not judged. Forgive, and it shall be forgiven to you. Have mercy that ye may receive mercy. With what measure ye mete, it shall be measured to you again; and again Blessed are the poor and they that are persecuted for righteousness' sake, for theirs is the kingdom of God.

These things, brethren, I write unto you concerning righteousness, not because I laid this charge upon myself, but because ye invited me . For neither am I, nor is any other like unto me, able to follow the wisdom of the blessed and glorious Paul, who when he came among you taught face to face with the men of that day the word which concerneth truth carefully and surely; who also, when he was absent,wrote a letter unto you, into the which if ye look diligently, ye shall be able to be builded up unto the faith given to you, which is the mother of us all, while hope followeth after and love goeth before--love toward God and Christ and toward our neighbor. For if any man be occupied with these, he hath fulfilled the commandment of righteousness; for he that hath love is far from all sin.

But the love of money is the beginning of all troubles. Knowing therefore that we brought nothing into the world neither can we carry anything out, let us arm ourselves with the armor of righteousness, and let us teach ourselves first to walk in the commandment of the Lord; and then our wives also, to walk in the faith that hath been given unto them and in love and purity, cherishing their own husbands in all truth and loving all men equally in all chastity, and to train their children in the training of the fear of God. Our widows must be sober-minded as touching the faith of the Lord,making intercession without ceasing for all men, abstaining from all calumny, evil speaking, false witness, love of money, and every evil thing, knowing that they are God's altar, and that all sacrifices are carefully inspected, and nothing escapeth Him either of their thoughts or intents or any of the secret things of the heart.

Knowing then that God is not mocked, we ought to walk worthily of His commandment and His glory. In like manner deacons should be blameless in the presence of His righteousness, as deacons of God and Christ and not of men; not calumniators, not double-tongued, not lovers of money, temperate inall things, compassionate, diligent, walking according to the truthof the Lord who became a minister *(deacon)* of all. For if we be well pleasing unto Him in this present world, we shall receive the future world also, according as He promised us to raise us from thedead, and that if we conduct ourselves worthily of Him we shall also reign with Him, if indeed we have faith. In like manner also the younger men must be blameless in all things, caring for purity before everything and curbing themselves from every evil. For it is a good thing to refrain from lusts in the world, for every lust warreth against the Spirit, and **neither whoremongers nor effeminate persons nor defilers of themselves with men shall inherit the**

kingdom of God, neither they that do untoward things.

Wherefore it is right to abstain from all these things, submittingyourselves to the presbyters and deacons as to God and Christ. The virgins must walk in a blameless and pure conscience. And the presbyters also must be compassionate, merciful towards all men, turning back the sheep that are gone astray, visiting all the infirm, not neglecting a widow or an orphan or a poor man but providing always for that which is honorable in the sight of God and of men, abstaining from all anger, respect of persons, unrighteous judgment, being far from all love of money, not quick to believe anything against any man, not hasty in judgment, knowing that we all are debtors of sin.

If then we entreat the Lord that He would forgive us, we also ought to forgive for we are before the eyes of our Lord and God, and we must all stand at the judgment-seat of Christ, and each man must give an account of himself. Let us therefore so serve Him with fear and all reverence, as Hehimself gave commandment and the Apostles who preached the Gospel tous and the prophets who proclaimed beforehand the coming of our Lord;being zealous as touching that which is good, abstaining from offenses and from the false brethren and from them that bear the name of the Lord in hypocrisy, who lead foolish men astray.

For every one who shall not confess that Jesus Christ is come in the flesh, is antichrist and whosoever shall not confess the testimony of the Cross, is of the devil; and whosoever shall pervertthe oracles of the Lord to his own lusts and say that there is neither resurrection nor judgment, that man is the firstborn of Satan. Wherefore let us forsake the vain doing of the many and their false teachings, and turn unto the word which was delivered unto us from the beginning, being sober unto prayer and constant in fastings, entreating the all-seeing God with supplications that *He* bring us not into temptation, according as the Lord said, The Spirit is indeed willing, but the flesh is weak. Let us therefore without ceasing hold fast by our hope and by the earnest of our righteousness, which is Jesus Christ who took up our sins in His own body upon the tree, who did no sin, neither was guile found in His mouth, but for our sakes He endured all things, that we might live in Him. Let us therefore become imitators of His endurance;

and if we should suffer for His name's sake, let us glorify Him. For He gave this example to us in His own person, and we believed this.

I exhort you all therefore to be obedient unto the word of righteousness and to practice all endurance, which also ye saw withyour own eyes in the blessed Ignatius and Zosimus and Rufus, yea and in others also who came from among yourselves, as well as in Paul himself and the rest of the Apostles; being persuaded that all these ran not in vain but in faith andrighteousness, and that they are in their due place in the presence of the Lord, with whom also they suffered. For they loved not the present world, but Him that died for our sakes and was raised byGod for us.

[... sections omitted.].

For I am persuaded that ye are well trained in the sacred writings, and nothing is hidden from you. But to myself this is not granted. Only, as it is said in these scriptures, Be ye angry and sin not, and Let not the sun set on your wrath. Blessed is he that remembereth this; and I trust that this is in you. Now may the God and Father of our Lord Jesus Christ, and the eternal High-priest Himself the Son of God Jesus Christ, build you up infaith and truth, and in all gentleness and in all avoidance of wrath and in forbearance and long suffering and in patient endurance and inpurity; and may He grant unto you a lot and portion among His saints, and to us with you, and to all that are under heaven, who shall believe on our Lord and God Jesus Christ and on His Father tha raised him from the dead.

Pray for all the saints. Pray also for kings and powers and princes and for them that persecute and hate you and for the enemies of the cross, that your fruit may be manifest among all men, that ye may be perfect in Him. Ye wrote to me, both ye yourselves and Ignatius, asking that if anyone should go to Syria he might carry thither the letters from you. And this I will do, if I get a fit opportunity, either I myself, orhe whom I shall send to be ambassador on your behalf also. For they comprise faith and endurance and everykind of edification, which pertaineth unto our Lord. Moreover concerning Ignatius himself and those that were with him, if ye haveany sure tidings, certify us I write these things to you by Crescens, whom I commended to you recently and now commend unto you for he hath walked blamelessly with us; and I believe also with you in like manner. But ye shall have his sister commended, when she shall come to you. Fare ye well in the Lord Jesus Christ in grace, ye and all yours. Amen.

[... sections omitted.].

Excerpts from "Martyrdom of Polycarp"

Internal evidence goes far to establish the credit which Eusebius lends to this specimen of the martyrologies, certainly not the earliest if we accept that of Ignatius as genuine. As an encyclical of one of" *the seven Churches*" to another of the same Seven, and as bearing witness to their aggregation with others into the unity of "*the Holy and Catholic Church,*" it is a very interesting witness, not only to an article of the creed, but to the original meaning and acceptation of the same. More than this, it is evidence of the strength of Christ perfected in human weakness; and thus it affords us an assurance of grace equal to our day in every time of need. When I see in it, however, an example of what a noble army of martyrs, women and children included, suffered in those days "*for the testimony of Jesus,*" and in order to hand down the knowledge of the Gospel to these boastful ages of our own, I confess myself edified by what I read, chiefly because I am humbled and abashed in comparing what a Christian used to be, with what a Christian is, in our times, even at his best estate.

That this Epistle has been interpolated can hardly be doubted, when we compare it with the unvarnished specimen, in Eusebius. As for the "*fragrant smell*" that came from the fire, many kinds of wood emit the like in burning; and, apart from Oriental warmth of colouring, there seems nothing incredible in the narrative if we except "*the dove*" (*xvi.*), which, however, is probably a corrupt reading, as suggested by our translators. The blade was thrust into the martyr's left side; and this, opening the heart, caused the outpouring of a flood, and not a mere trickling.

But, though Greek thus amended is a plausible conjecture, there seems to have been nothing of the kind in the copy quoted by Eusebius. On the other hand, note the truly catholic and scriptural testimony "We love the martyrs, but the Son of God we worship it is impossible for us to worship any other." Bishop Jacobson assigns more than fifty pages to this martyrology, with a Latin version and abundant notes. To these I must refer the student, who may wish to see this attractive history in all the light of critical scholarship and, often, of admirable comment.

The following is the original *Introductory Notice.* The following letter purports to have been written by the Church at Smyrna to the Church at Philomelium, and through that Church to the whole Christian world, in order to give a succinct account of the circumstances attending the martyrdom of Polycarp. It is the earliest of all the Martyria, and has generally been accounted both the most interesting and authentic. Not a few, however, deem it interpolated in several passages, and some refer it to a much later date than the middle of the second century, to which it has been commonly ascribed. We cannot tell how much it may owe to the writers (*xxii.*) who successively transcribed it. Great part of it has been engrossed by Eusebius in his Ecclesiastical History *(iv.)*; and it is instructive to observe, that some of the most startling miraculous phenomena recorded in the text as it now stands, have no place in the narrative as given by that early historian of the Church. Much discussion has arisen respecting several particulars contained in this Martyrium; but into these disputes we do not enter, having it for our aim simply to present the reader with as faithful a translation as possible of this very interesting monument of Christian antiquity.

The Church of God which sojourns at Smyrna, to the Church of God sojourning in Philomelium, and to all the congregations of the Holy and Catholic Church in every place Mercy, peace, and love from God the Father, and our Lord Jesus Christ, be multiplied.

Subject Of Which We Write. We have written to you, brethren, as to what relates to the martyrs, and especially to the blessed Polycarp, who put an end to the persecution, having, as it were, set a seal upon it by his martyrdom. For almost all the events that happened previously [*to this one*], took place that the Lord might show us from above a martyrdom becoming the Gospel. For he waited to be delivered up, even as the Lord had done, that we also might become his followers, while we look not merely at what concerns ourselves but have regard also to our neighbours. For it is the part of a true and well-founded love, not only to wish one's self to be saved, but also all the brethren.

The Wonderful Constancy Of The Martyrs. All the martyrdoms, then, were blessed and noble which took place according to the will of God. For it becomes us who profess greater piety than others, to ascribe the authority over all things to God. And truly, who can fail to admire their nobleness of mind, and their patience, with that love towards their Lord which they displayed? Who, when they were so torn with scourges, that the frame of their bodies, even to the very inward veins and arteries, was laid open, still patiently endured, while even those that stood by pitied and bewailed them. But they reached such a pitch of magnanimity, that not one of them let a sigh or a groan escape them; thus proving to us all that those holy martyrs of Christ, at the very time when they suffered such torments, were absent from the body, or rather, that the Lord then stood by them, and communed with them. And, looking to the grace of Christ, they despised all the torments of this world, redeeming themselves from eternal punishment by [the suffering of] a single hour. For this reason the fire of their savage executioners appeared cool to them. For they kept before their view escape from that fire which is eternal and never shall be quenched, and looked forward with the eyes of their heart to those good things which are laid up for such as endure; things "which ear hath not heard, nor eye seen, neither have entered into the heart of man," but were revealed by the Lord to them, inasmuch as they were no longer men, but had already become angels. And, in like manner, those who were condemned to the wild beasts endured dreadful tortures, being stretched out upon beds full of spikes, and subjected to various other kinds of torments, in order that, if it were possible, the tyrant might, by their lingering tortures, lead them to a denial [*of Christ*]. The Constancy Of Germanicus;

The Death Of Polycarp Is Demanded. For the devil did indeed invent many things against them; but thanks be to God, he could not prevail over all. For the most noble Germanicus strengthened the timidity of others by his own patience, and fought heroically with the wild beasts. For, when the proconsul sought to persuade him, and urged him to take pity upon his age, he attracted the wild beast towards himself, and provoked it, being desirous to escape all the more quickly from an unrighteous and impious world. But upon this the whole multitude, marvelling at the nobility of mind displayed by the devout and godly race of Christians, cried out, "*Away with the Atheists; let Polycarp be sought out!*" Quintus The Apostate Now one named Quintus, a Phrygian, who was but lately come from Phrygia, when he saw the wild beasts, became afraid. This was the man who forced himself and some others to come forward voluntarily [*for trial*]. Him the proconsul, after many entreaties, persuaded to swear and to offer sacrifice. Wherefore, brethren, we do not commend those who give themselves up [to suffering], seeing the Gospel does not teach so to do.

The Departure And Vision Of Polycarp. But the most admirable Polycarp, when he first heard [that he was sought for], was in no measure disturbed, but resolved to continue in the city. However, in deference to the wish of many, he was persuaded to leave it. He departed, therefore, to a country house not far distant from the city. There he stayed with a few [*friends*], engaged in nothing else night and day than praying for all men, and for the Churches throughout the world, according to his usual custom. And while he was praying, a vision presented itself to him three days before he was taken; and, behold, the pillow under his head seemed to him on fire. Upon this, turning to those that were with him, he said to them prophetically," *I must be burnt alive.*"

Polycarp Is Betrayed By A Servant. And when those who sought for him were at hand, he departed to another dwelling, whither his pursuers immediately came after him. And when they found him not, they seized upon two youths [that were there], one of whom, being subjected to torture, confessed. It was thus impossible that he should continue hid, since those that betrayed him were of his own household. The Irenarch then (*whose office is the same as that of the Cleronomus*), by name Herod, hastened to bring him into the stadium. [*This all happened*] that he might fulfil his special lot, being made a partaker of Christ, and that they who betrayed him might undergo the punishment of Judas himself.

[... sections omitted.].

Polycarp Refuses To Revile Christ. Now, as Polycarp was entering into the stadium, there came to him a voice from heaven, saying, *"Be strong, and show thyself a man, O Polycarp!"* No one saw who it was that spoke to him; but those of our brethren who were present heard the voice. And as he was brought forward, the tumult became great when they heard that Polycarp was taken. And when he came near, the proconsul asked him whether he was Polycarp. On his confessing that he was, [the proconsul] sought to persuade him to deny [*Christ*], saying, *"Have respect to thy old age,"* and other similar things, according to their custom, [*such as*], *"Swear by the fortune of Caesar; repent, and say, Away with the Atheists."* But Polycarp, gazing with a stern countenance on all the multitude of the wicked heathen then in the stadium, and waving his hand towards them, while with groans he looked up to heaven, said, *"Away with the Atheists."*

Then, the proconsul urging him, and saying, *"Swear, and I will set thee at liberty, reproach Christ;"* Polycarp declared, *"Eighty and six years have I served Him, and He never did me any injury how then can I blaspheme my King and my Saviour?"*

Polycarp Confesses Himself A Christian. And when the proconsul yet again pressed him, and said, *"Swear by the fortune of Caesar,"* he answered, *"Since thou art vainly urgent that, as thou sayest, I should swear by the fortune of Caesar, and pretendest not to know who and what I am, hear me declare with boldness, I am a Christian. And if you wish to learn what the doctrines of Christianity are, appoint me a day, and thou shalt hear them."* The proconsul replied, *"Persuade the people."* But Polycarp said, *"To thee I have thought it right to offer an account [of my faith]; for we are taught to give all due honour (which entails no injury upon ourselves) to the powers and authorities which are ordained of God. But as for these, I do not deem them worthy of receiving any account from me."*

No Threats Have Any Effect On Polycarp. The proconsul then said to him, *"I have wild beasts at hand ; to these will I cast thee, except thou repent."* But he answered, *"Call them then, for we are not accustomed to repent of what is good in order to adopt that which is evil; and it is well for me to be changed from what is evil to what is righteous."*

But again the proconsul said to him, "*I will cause thee to be consumed by fire, seeing thou despisest the wild beasts, if thou wilt not repent.*" But Polycarp said, "*Thou threatenest me with fire which burneth for an hour, and after a little is extinguished, but art ignorant of the fire of the coming judgment and of eternal punishment, reserved for the ungodly. But why tarriest thou? Bring forth what thou wilt.*"

Polycarp Is Sentenced To Be Burned. While he spoke these and many other like things, he was filled with confidence and joy, and his countenance was full of grace, so that not merely did it not fall as if troubled by the things said to him, but, on the contrary, the proconsul was astonished, and sent his herald to proclaim in the midst of the stadium thrice, "*Polycarp has confessed that he is a Christian.*" This proclamation having been made by the herald, the whole multitude both of the heathen and Jews, who dwelt at Smyrna, cried out with uncontrollable fury, and in a loud voice, "*This is the teacher of Asia, the father of the Christians, and the overthrower of our gods, he who has been teaching many not to sacrifice, or to worship the gods.*" Speaking thus, they cried out, and besought Philip the Asiarch to let loose a lion upon Polycarp. But Philip answered that it was not lawful for him to do so, seeing the shows of wild beasts were already finished. Then it seemed good to them to cry out with one consent, that Polycarp should be burnt alive. For thus it behooved the vision which was revealed to him in regard to his pillow to be fulfilled, when, seeing it on fire as he was praying, he turned about and said prophetically to the faithful that were with him," *I must be burnt alive.*"

The Funeral Pile Is Erected. This, then, was carried into effect with greater speed than it was spoken, the multitudes immediately gathering together wood and fagots out of the shops and baths; the Jews especially, according to custom, eagerly assisting them in it. And when the funeral pile was ready, Polycarp, laying aside all his garments, and loosing his girdle, sought also to take off his sandals,--a thing he was not accustomed to do, inasmuch as every one of the faithful was always eager who should first touch his skin. For, on account of his holy life, he was, even before his martyrdom, adorned with every kind of good. Immediately then they surrounded him with those substances which had been prepared for the funeral pile. But when they were about also to fix him with nails, he said, "*Leave me as I am; for He that giveth me strength to endure the fire, will also enable me, without your securing me by nails, to remain without moving in the pile.*"

The Prayer Of Polycarp. They did not nail him then, but simply bound him. And he, placing his hands behind him, and being bound like a distinguished ram [*taken*] out of a great flock for sacrifice, and prepared to be an acceptable burnt-offering unto God, looked up to heaven, and said, "*O Lord God Almighty, the Father of thy beloved and blessed Son Jesus Christ, by whom we have received the knowledge of Thee, the God of angels and powers, and of every creature, and of the whole race of the righteous who live before thee, I give Thee thanks that Thou hast counted me, worthy of this day and this hour, that I should have a part in the number of Thy martyrs, in the cup of thy Christ, to the resurrection of eternal life, both of soul and body, through the incorruption [imparted] by the Holy Ghost. Among whom may I be accepted this day before Thee as a fat and acceptable sacrifice, according as Thou, the ever-truthful God, hast fore-ordained, hast revealed beforehand to me, and now hast fulfilled. Wherefore also I praise Thee for all things, I bless Thee, I glorify Thee, along with the everlasting and heavenly Jesus Christ, Thy beloved Son, with whom, to Thee, and the Holy Ghost, be glory both now and to all coming ages. Amen.*"

Polycarp Is Not Injured By The Fire. When he had pronounced this amen, and so finished his prayer, those who were appointed for the purpose kindled the fire. And as the flame blazed forth in great fury, we, to whom it was given to witness it, beheld a great miracle, and have been preserved that we might report to others what then took place. For the fire, shaping itself into the form of an arch, like the sail of a ship when filled with the wind, encompassed as by a circle the body of the martyr. And he appeared within not like flesh which is burnt, but as bread that is baked, or as gold and silver glowing in a furnace. Moreover, we perceived such a sweet odour [*coming from the pile*], as if frankincense or some such precious spices had been smoking there.

Polycarp Is Pierced By A Dagger. At length, when those wicked men perceived that his body could not be consumed by the fire, they commanded an executioner to go near and pierce him through with a dagger. And on his doing this, there came forth a dove, and a great quantity of blood, so that the fire was extinguished; and all the people wondered that there should be such a difference between the unbelievers and the elect, of whom this most admirable Polycarp was one, having in our own times been an apostolic and prophetic teacher, and bishop of the Catholic Church which is in Smyrna. For every word that went out of his mouth either has been or shall yet be accomplished.

The Christians Are Refused Polycarp's Body. But when the adversary of the race of the righteous, the envious, malicious, and wicked one, perceived the impressive nature of his martyrdom, and [*considered*] the blameless life he had led from the beginning, and how he was now crowned with the wreath of immortality, having beyond dispute received his reward, he did his utmost that not the least memorial of him should be taken away by us, although many desired to do this, and to become possessors of his holy flesh. For this end he suggested it to Nicetes, the father of Herod and brother of Alce, to go and entreat the governor not to give up his body to be buried, *"lest,"* said he, *"forsaking Him that was crucified, they begin to worship this one."* This he said at the suggestion and urgent persuasion of the Jews, who also watched us, as we sought to take him out of the fire, being ignorant of this, that it is neither possible for us ever to forsake Christ, who suffered for the salvation of such as shall be saved throughout the whole world (*the blameless one for sinners*), nor to worship any other. For Him indeed, as being the Son of God, we adore; but the martyrs, as disciples and followers of the Lord, we worthily love on account of their extraordinary affection towards their own King and Master, of whom may we also be made companions and fellow-disciples!

The Body Of Polycarp Is Burned. The centurion then, seeing the strife excited by the Jews, placed the body in the midst of the fire, and consumed it. Accordingly, we afterwards took up his bones, as being more precious than the most exquisite jewels, and more purified than gold, and deposited them in a fitting place, whither, being gathered together, as opportunity is allowed us, with joy and rejoicing, the Lord shall grant us to celebrate the anniversary of his martyrdom, both in memory of those who have already finished their course, and for the exercising and preparation of those yet to walk in their steps.

Praise Of The Martyr Polycarp. This, then, is the account of the blessed Polycarp, who, being the twelfth that was martyred in Smyrna (*reckoning those also of Philadelphia*), yet occupies a place of his own in the memory of all men, insomuch that he is everywhere spoken of by the heathen themselves. He was not merely an illustrious teacher, but also a pre-eminent martyr, whose martyrdom all desire to imitate, as having been altogether consistent with the Gospel of Christ. For, having through patience overcome the unjust governor, and thus acquired the crown of immortality, he now, with the apostles and all the righteous[in heaven], rejoicingly glorifies God, even the Father, and blesses our Lord Jesus Christ, the Saviour of our souls, the Governor of our bodies, and the Shepherd of the Catholic Church throughout the world.

This Epistle Is To Be Transmitted To The Brethren. Since, then, ye requested that we would at large make you acquainted with what really took place, we have for the present sent you this summary account through our brother Marcus. When, therefore, ye have yourselves read this Epistle, be pleased to send it to the brethren at a greater distance, that they also may glorify the Lord, who makes such choice of His own servants. They that are with us salute you, and Evarestus, who wrote this Epistle, with all his house.

The Date Of The Martyrdom. Now, the blessed Polycarp suffered martyrdom on the second day of the month Xanthicus just begun, the seventh day before the Kalends of May, on the great Sabbath, at the eighth hour. He was taken by Herod, Philip the Trallian being high priest, Statius Quadratus being proconsul, but Jesus Christ being King for ever, to whom be glory, honour, majesty, and an everlasting throne, from generation to generation. Amen. Salutation. We wish you, brethren, all happiness, while you walk according to the doctrine of the Gospel of Jesus Christ; with whom be glory to God the Father and the Holy Spirit, for the salvation of His holy elect, after whose example the blessed Polycarp suffered, following in whose steps may we too be found in the kingdom of Jesus Christ! These things Caius transcribed from the copy of Irenaeus (*who was a disciple of Polycarp*), having himself been intimate with Irenaeus. And I, Socrates, transcribed them at

Corinth from the copy of Caius. Grace be with you all. And I again, Pionius, wrote them from the previously written copy, having carefully searched into them, and the blessed Polycarp having manifested them to me through a revelation, even as I shall show in what follows. I have collected these things, when they had almost faded away through the lapse of time, that the Lord Jesus Christ may also gather me along with His elect into His heavenly kingdom, to whom, with the Father and the Holy Spirit, be glory for ever and ever. Amen.

Ireneaus of Lyons
(130 – 202 A.D.)

Saint Irenaeus[17], was Bishop of Lugdunum in Gaul, then a part of the Roman Empire (*now Lyons, France*). He was an early Church Father and apologist, and his writings were formative in the early development of Christian theology. He was a hearer of Polycarp, who in turn was traditionally a disciple of John the Evangelist. Irenaeus pointed to Scripture as a proof of orthodox Christianity against heresies, classifying as Scripture not only the Old Testament but most of the books now known as the New Testament, while excluding many works, a large number by Gnostics, that flourished in the 2nd century and claimed scriptural authority.

Irenaeus is also our earliest attestation that the Gospel of John was written by John the apostle, and that the Gospel of Luke was written by Luke, the companion of Paul.In his writing against the Gnostics, who claimed to possess a secret oral tradition from Jesus himself, Irenaeus maintained that the bishops in different cities are known as far back as the Apostles — and none were Gnostic — and that the bishops provided the only safe guide to the interpretation of Scripture.

In a passage that became a locus classicus of Catholic-Protestant polemics, he emphasized the unique position of the bishop of Rome. Irenaeus uses the Logos theology he inherited from Justin Martyr. Irenaeus was a student of Polycarp, who was said to have been tutored by John the Apostle. Before Irenaeus, Christians differed as to which gospel they preferred. The Christians of Asia Minor preferred the Gospel of John. The Gospel of Matthew was the most popular overall Irenaeus asserted that four Gospels, Irenaeus (/aɪrəˈniːəs/; Greek: Εἰρηναῖος) *(2nd century – c. A.D.)* Matthew, Mark, Luke, and John, were canonical scripture.

Irenaeus' best-known book, *Adversus Haereses* or *Against Heresies* (c. 180), is a detailed attack on Gnosticism, which was then a serious threat to the Church, and especially on the system of the Gnostic Valentinus. As one of the first great Christian theologians, he emphasized the traditional elements in the Church, especially

---

[17] http://en.wikipedia.org/wiki/Irenaeus

the episcopate, Scripture, and tradition. Against the Gnostics, who said that they possessed a secret oral tradition from Jesus himself, Irenaeus maintained that the bishops in different cities are known as far back as the Apostles and that the bishops provided the only safe guide to the interpretation of Scripture. His writings, with those of Clement and Ignatius, are taken as among the earliest signs of the developing doctrine of the primacy of the Roman see Irenaeus is the earliest witness to recognition of the canonical character of all four gospels.[

Excerpts of "Fragments from the Lost writings of Irenaeus"

Chapter 1

I Adjure thee, who shalt transcribe this book, by our Lord Jesus Christ, and by His glorious appearing, when He comes to judge the living and the dead, that thou compare what thou hast transcribed, and be careful to set it right according to this copy from which thou hast transcribed; also, that thou in like manner copy down this adjuration, and insert it in the transcript.

[... sections omitted.].

Chapter 7

This [custom], of not bending the knee upon Sunday, is a symbol of the resurrection, through which we have been set free, by the grace of Christ, from sins, and from death, which has been put to death under Him. Now this custom took its rise from apostolic times, as the blessed Irenaeus, the martyr and bishop of Lyons, declares in his treatise On Easter, in which he makes mention of Pentecost also; upon which [feast] we do not bend the knee, because it is of equal significance with the Lord's day, for the reason already alleged concerning it.

Chapter 8

For as the ark [*of the covenant*] was glided within and without with pure gold, so was also the body of Christ pure and resplendent; for it was adorned within by the Word, and shielded without by the Spirit, in order that from both [*materials*] the splendour of the natures might be clearly shown forth.

[... sections omitted.].

Chapter 9

Ever, indeed, speaking well of the deserving, but never ill of the undeserving, we also shall attain to the glory and kingdom of God.

[... sections omitted.].

Chapter 10

It is indeed proper to God, and befitting His character, to show mercy and pity, and to bring salvation to His creatures, even though they be brought under danger of destruction. "For with Him," says the Scripture, "is propitiation."

[... sections omitted.].

Chapter 11

The business of the Christian is nothing else than to be ever preparing for death *meleman amoqnhskein*).

[... sections omitted.].

Chapter 13

For when the Greeks, having arrested the slaves of Christian catechumens, then used force against them, in order to learn from them some secret thing [practised] among Christians, these slaves, having nothing to say that would meet the wishes of their tormentors, except that they had heard from their masters that the divine communion was the body and blood of Christ, and imagining that it was actually flesh and blood, gave their inquisitors answer to that effect.

Then these latter, assuming such to be the case with regard to the practices of Christians, gave information regarding it to other Greeks, and sought to compel the martyrs Sanctus and Blandina to confess, under the influence of torture, [that the allegation was correct]. To these men Blandina replied very admirably in these words "How should those persons endure such *[accusations]*, who, for the sake of the practice [*of piety*], did not avail themselves even of the flesh that was permitted [*them to eat*]?"

[... sections omitted.].

Chapter 15

When, in times of old, Balaam spake these things in parables, he was not acknowledged; and now, when Christ has appeared and fulfilled them, He was not believed. Wherefore [*Balaam*], foreseeing this, and wondering at it, exclaimed, "Alas! alas! who shall live when God brings these things to pass?"

[... sections omitted.].

Chapter 16

Expounding again the law to that generation which followed those who were in in the wilderness, he published Deuteronomy; not as giving to them a different law from that which had been appointed for their fathers, but as recapitulating this latter, in order that they, by hearing what had happened to their fathers, might fear God with their whole heart.

[... sections omitted.].

Chapter 17

By these Christ was typified, and acknowledged, and brought into the world; for He was prefigured in Joseph then from Levi and

Judah He was descended according to the flesh, as King and Priest; and He was acknowledged by Simeon in the temple through Zebulon He was believed in among the Gentiles, as says the prophet, "*the land of Zabulon;*" and through Benjamin [that is, Paul] He was glorified, by being preached throughout all the world.

Chapter 18

And this was not without meaning; but that by means of the number of the ten men, he (*Gideon*) might appear as having Jesus for a helper, as [is indicated] by the compact entered into with them. And when he did not choose to partake with them in their idol-worship, they threw the blame upon him for "Jerubbaal" signifies the judgment-seat of Baal.

[... sections omitted.].

Chapter 19

"Take unto thee Joshua ('I*hsoun*) the son of Nun." For it was proper that Moses should lead the people out of Egypt, but that Jesus (Joshua) should lead them into the inheritance. Also that Moses, as was the case with the law, should cease to be, but that Joshua ('I*hsoun*), as the word, and no untrue type of the Word made flesh (*enupostatou*), should be a preacher to the people. Then again, [it was fit] that Moses should give manna as food to the fathers, but Joshua wheat; as the first-fruits of life, a type of the body of Christ, as also the Scripture declares that the manna of the Lord ceased when the people had eaten wheat from the land.

Chapter 20

"And he laid his hands upon him." The countenance of Joshua was also glorified by the imposition of the hands of Moses, but not to the same degree [*as that of Moses*]. Inasmuch, then, as he had obtained a certain degree of grace, [the Lord] said, "And thou shall confer upon him of thy glory." For [*in this case*] the thing given does not cease to belong to the giver.

Chapter 21

But he does not give, as Christ did, by means of breathing, because he is not the fount of the Spirit.

[… sections omitted.].

Chapter 22

"Thou shall not go with them, neither shalt thou curse the people." He does not hint at anything with regard to the people, for they all lay before his view, but [he refers] to the mystery of Christ pointed out beforehand. For as He was to be born of the fathers according to the flesh, the Spirit gives instructions to the man (*Balaam*) beforehand, lest, going forth in ignorance, he might pronounce a curse upon the people. Not, indeed, that [his curse] could take any effect contrary to the will of God; but [this was done] as an exhibition of the providence of God which He exercised towards them on account of their forefathers.

Chapter 23

"And he mounted upon his ass." The ass was the type of the body of Christ, upon whom all men, resting from their labours, are borne as in a chariot. For the Saviour has taken up the burden of our sins. Now the angel who appeared to Balaam was the Word Himself; and in His hand He held a sword, to indicate the power which He had from above.

[… sections omitted.].

Chapter 26

Know thou that every man is either empty or full. For if he has not the Holy Spirit, he has no knowledge of the Creator; he has not received Jesus Christ the Life; he knows not the Father who is in heaven; if he does not live after the dictates of reason, after the heavenly law, he is not a sober-minded person, nor does he act uprightly such an one is empty. If, on the other hand, he receives God, who says, *"I will dwell with them, and walk in them, and I will be their God,"* such an one is not empty, but full.

Chapter 27

The little boy, therefore, who guided Samson by the hand, pre-typified John the Baptist, who showed to the people the faith in Christ. And the house in which they were assembled signifies the world, in which dwell the various heathen and unbelieving nations, offering sacrifice to their idols. Moreover, the two pillars are the two covenants. The fact, then, of Samson leaning himself upon the pillars, [*indicates*] this, that the people, when instructed, recognized the mystery of Christ.

Chapter 28

"And the man of God said, Where did it fall? And he showed him the place. And he cut down a tree, and cast it in there, and the iron floated." This was a sign that souls should be borne aloft (*anagwghs yukwn*) through the instrumentality of wood, upon which He suffered who can lead those souls aloft that follow His ascension. This event was also an indication of the fact, that when the holy soul of Christ descended [*to Hades*], many souls ascended and were seen in their bodies. For just as the wood, which is the lighter body, was submerged in the water; but the iron, the heavier one, floated so, when the Word of God became one with flesh, by a physical and hypostatic union, the heavy and terrestrial [*part*], having been rendered immortal, was borne up into heaven, by the divine nature, after the resurrection.

Chapter 29

The Gospel according to Matthew was written to the Jews. For they laid particular stress upon the fact that Christ [should be] of the seed of David. Matthew also, who had a still greater desire [to establish this point], took particular pains to afford them convincing proof that Christ is of the seed of David; and therefore he commences with [*an account of*] His genealogy.

[... sections omitted.].

Chapter 36

True knowledge, then, consists in the understanding of Christ, which Paul terms the wisdom of God hidden in a mystery, which "the natural man receiveth not," the doctrine of the cross; of which if any man "taste," he will not accede to the disputations and quibbles of proud and puffed-up men, who go into matters of which they have no perception. For the truth is unsophisticated (*askhmatistos*); and "the word is nigh thee, in thy mouth and in thy heart," as the same apostle declares, being easy of comprehension to those who are obedient.

For it renders us like to Christ, if we experience "*the power of his resurrection and the fellowship of His sufferings.*" For this is the affinity of the apostolical teaching and the most holy "*faith delivered unto us,*" which the unlearned receive, and those of slender knowledge have taught, not "*giving heed to endless genealogies,*" but studying rather [*to observe*] a straightforward course of life; lest, having been deprived of the Divine Spirit, they fail to attain to the kingdom of heaven. For truly the first thing is to deny one's self and to follow Christ; and those who do this are borne onward to perfection, having fulfilled all their Teacher's will, becoming sons of God by spiritual regeneration, and heirs of the kingdom of heaven; those who seek which first shall not be forsaken.

Chapter 37

Those who have become acquainted with the secondary (*i.e., under Christ)* constitutions of the apostles, are aware that the Lord instituted a new oblation in the new covenant, according to [the declaration of] Malachi the prophet. For, "*from the rising of the sun even to the setting my name has been glorified among the Gentiles, and in every place incense is offered to my name, and a pure sacrifice;*" as John also declares in the Apocalypse "*The incense is the prayers of the saints.* "

Then again, Paul exhorts us "*to present our bodies a living sacrifice, holy, acceptable unto God, which is your reasonable service.* " And again, "*Let us offer the sacrifice of praise, that is, the fruit of the lips.* " Now those oblations are not according to the law, the handwriting of which the Lord took away from the midst by cancelling it; but they are according to the Spirit, for we must worship God "*in spirit and in truth.* " And therefore the oblation of the Eucharist is not a carnal one, but a spiritual; and in this respect it is pure.

For we make an oblation to God of the bread and the cup of blessing, giving Him thanks in that He has commanded the earth to bring forth these fruits for our nourishment. And then, when we have perfected the oblation, we invoke the Holy Spirit, that He may exhibit this sacrifice, both the bread the body of Christ, and the cup the blood of Christ, in order that the receivers of these antitypes may obtain remission of sins and life eternal. Those persons, then, who perform these oblations in remembrance of the Lord, do not fall in with Jewish views, but, performing the service after a spiritual manner, they shall be called sons of wisdom.

Chapter 38

The apostles ordained, that "*we should not judge any one in respect to meat or drink, or in regard to a feast day, or the new moons, or the sabbaths.*" Whence then these contentions? whence these schisms? We keep the feast, but in the leaven of malice and wickedness, cutting in pieces the Church of God; and we preserve what belongs to its exterior, that we may cast away these better things, faith and love. We have heard from the prophetic words that these feasts and fasts are displeasing to the Lord.

Chapter 39

Christ, who was called the Son of God before the ages, was manifested in the fulness of time, in order that He might cleanse us through His blood, who were under the power of sin, presenting us as pure sons to His Father, if we yield ourselves obediently to the chastisement of the Spirit. And in the end of time He shall come to do away with all evil, and to reconcile all things, in order that there may be an end of all impurities.

Chapter 40

"And he found the jaw-bone of an ass." It is to be observed that, after [*Samson had committed*] fornication, the holy Scripture no longer speaks of the things happily accomplished by him in connection with the formula, *"The Spirit of the Lord came upon him."* For thus, according to the holy apostle, the sin of fornication is perpetrated against the body, as involving also sin against the temple of God.

Chapter 41

This indicates the persecution against the Church set on foot by the nations who still continue in unbelief. But he (*Samson*) who suffered those things, trusted that there would be a retaliation against those waging this war. But retaliation through what means? First of all, by his betaking himself to the Rock not cognizable to the senses; secondly, by the finding of the jaw-bone of an ass. Now the type of the jaw-bone is the body of Christ.

[... sections omitted.].

Chapter 48

As therefore seventy tongues are indicated by number, and from dispersion the tongues are gathered into one by means of their interpretation; so is that ark declared a type of the body of Christ, which is both pure and immaculate. For as that ark was gilded with pure gold both within and without, so also is the body of Christ pure and resplendent, being adorned within by the Word, and shielded on the outside by the Spirit, in order that from both [materials] the splendour of the natures might be exhibited together.

[... sections omitted.].

Chapter 52

The sacred books acknowledge with regard to Christ, that as He is the Son of man, so is the same Being not a *[mere]* man; and as He is flesh, so is He also spirit, and the Word of God, and God. And as He was born of Mary in the last times, so did He also proceed from God as the First-begotten of every creature; and as He hungered, so did He satisfy [*others*]; and as He thirsted, so did He of old cause the Jews to drink, for the "*Rock was Christ*" Himself thus does Jesus now give to His believing people power to drink spiritual waters, which spring up to life eternal.

And as He was the son of David, so was He also the Lord of David. And as He was from Abraham, so did He also exist before Abraham. And as He was the servant of God, so is He the Son of God, and Lord of the universe. And as He was spit upon ignominiously, so also did He breathe the Holy Spirit into His disciples. And as He was saddened, so also did He give joy to His people. And as He was capable of being handled and touched, so again did He, in a non-apprehensible form, pass through the midst of those who sought to injure Him, and entered without impediment through closed doors. And as He slept, so did He also rule the sea, the winds, and the storms. And as He suffered, so also is He alive, and life-giving, and healing all our infirmity. And as He died, so is He also the Resurrection of the dead. He suffered shame on earth, while He is higher than all glory and praise in heaven; who, "*though He was crucified through weakness, yet He liveth by divine power;*" who "*descended into the lower parts of the earth,*" and who "*ascended up above the heavens;*" for whom a manger sufficed, yet who filled all things; who was dead, yet who liveth for ever and ever. Amen.

Chapter 53

With regard to Christ, the law and the prophets and the evangelists have proclaimed that He was born of a virgin, that He suffered upon a beam of wood, and that He appeared from the dead; that He also ascended to the heavens, and was glorified by the Father, and is the Eternal King; that He is the perfect Intelligence, the Word of God, who was begotten before the light; that He was the Founder of the universe, along with it (light), and the Maker of man; that He is All in all Patriarch among the patriarchs; Law in the laws; Chief Priest among priests; Ruler among kings; the Prophet among prophets; the Angel among angels; the Man among men; Son in the Father; God in God; King to all eternity. For it is He who sailed [*in the ark*] along with Noah, and who guided Abraham; who was bound along with Isaac, and was a Wanderer with Jacob; the Shepherd of those who are saved, and the Bridegroom of the Church; the Chief also of the cherubim, the Prince of the angelic powers; God of God; Son of the Father; Jesus Christ; King for ever and ever. Amen.

Chapter 54

The law and the prophets and evangelists have declared that Christ was born of a virgin, and suffered on the cross; was raised also from the dead, and taken up to heaven; that He was glorified, and reigns for ever. He is Himself termed the Perfect Intellect, the Word of God. He is the First-begotten, after a transcendent manner, the Creator of man; All in all; Patriarch among the patriarchs; Law in the law; the Priest among priests; among kings Prime Leader; the Prophet among the prophets; the Angel among angels; the Man among men; Son in the Father; God in God; King to all eternity. He was sold with Joseph, and He guided Abraham; was bound along with Isaac, and wandered with Jacob; with Moses He was Leader, and, respecting the people, Legislator.

He preached in the prophets; was incarnate of a virgin; born in Bethlehem; received by John, and baptized in Jordan; was tempted in the desert, and proved to be the Lord. He gathered the apostles together, and preached the kingdom of heaven; gave light to the blind, and raised the dead; was seen in the temple, but was not held by the people as worthy of credit; was arrested by the priests, conducted before Herod, and condemned in the presence of Pilate; He manifested Himself in the body, was suspended upon a beam of wood, and raised from the dead; shown to the apostles, and, having been carried up to heaven, sitteth on the right hand of the Father, and has been glorified by Him as the Resurrection of the dead. Moreover, He is the Salvation of the lost, the Light to those dwelling in darkness, and Redemption to those who have been born; the Shepherd of the saved, and the Bridegroom of the Church; the Charioteer of the cherubim, the Leader of the angelic host; God of God; Jesus Christ our Saviour.

[... sections omitted.].

These things the Saviour told in reference to His sufferings and cross; to these persons He predicted His passion. Nor did He conceal the fact that it should be of a most ignominious kind, at the hands of the chief priests. This woman, however, had attached another meaning to the dispensation of His sufferings. The Saviour was foretelling death; and she asked for the glory of immortality. The Lord was asserting that He must stand arraigned before impious judges; but she, taking no note of that judgment, requested as of the judge "*Grant,*" she said, "*that these my two sons may sit, one on the right hand, and the other on the left, in Thy glory.*"

In the one case the passion is referred to, in the other the kingdom is understood. The Saviour was speaking of the cross, while she had in view the glory which admits no suffering. This woman, therefore, as I have already said, is worthy of our admiration, not merely for what she sought, but also for the occasion of her making the request. She did indeed suffer, not merely as a pious person, but also as a woman. For, having been instructed by His words, she considered and believed that it would come to pass, that the kingdom of Christ should flourish in glory, and walk in its vastness throughout the world, and be increased by the preaching of piety. She understood, as was [in fact] the case, that He who appeared in a lowly guise had delivered and received every promise.

I will inquire upon another occasion, when I come to treat upon this humility, whether the Lord rejected her petition concerning His kingdom. But she thought that the same confidence would not be possessed by her, when, at the appearance of the angels, He should be ministered to by the angels, and receive service from the entire heavenly host. Taking the Saviour, therefore, apart in a retired place, she earnestly desired of Him those things which transcend every human nature.

St. Augustine of Hippo
(354 – 430 A.D.)

Augustine of Hippo, also known as St Augustine, St Austin, or St Augoustinos, was an early Christian theologian whose writings are considered very influential in the development of Western Christianity and Western philosophy. He was bishop of Hippo Regius (*present-day Annaba, Algeria*) located in the Roman province of Africa. Writing during the Patristic Era, he is viewed as one of the most important Church Fathers. Among his most important works are *City of God* and *Confessions*, which continue to be read widely today.

According to his contemporary, Jerome, Augustine "*established anew the ancient Faith.*" In his early years, he was heavily influenced by Manichaeism and afterward by the Neo-Platonism of Plotinus. After his conversion to Christianity and his baptism in 387, Augustine developed his own approach to philosophy and theology, accommodating a variety of methods and different perspectives. He believed that the grace of Christ was indispensable to human freedom and he framed the concepts of original sin and just war.

When the Western Roman Empire began to disintegrate, Augustine developed the concept of the Catholic Church as a spiritual City of God (in a book of the same name), distinct from the material Earthly City. His thoughts profoundly influenced the medieval worldview. Augustine's *City of God* was closely identified with the segment of the Church that adhered to the concept of the Trinity as defined by the Council of Nicaea and the Council of Constantinople.[18]

Augustine was one of the most prolific Latin authors in terms of surviving works, and the list of his works consists of more than one hundred separate titles. They include apologetic works against the heresies of the Arians, Donatists, Manichaeans and Pelagians; texts on Christian doctrine, notably *De Doctrina Christiana* (*On Christian Doctrine*); exegetical works such as commentaries on Book of

---

[18] http://en.wikipedia.org/wiki/Augustine_of_Hippo

Genesis, the Psalms and Paul's Letter to the Romans; many sermons and letters; and the *Retractationes*, a review of his earlier works which he wrote near the end of his life. Apart from those, Augustine is probably best known for his *Confessions*), which is a personal account of his earlier life, and for *De civitate dei* (*The City of God*, consisting of 22 books), which he wrote to restore the confidence of his fellow Christians, which was badly shaken by the sack of Rome by the Visigoths in 410.

His *On the Trinity*, in which he developed what has become known as the 'psychological analogy' of the Trinity, is also among his masterpieces, and arguably one of the greatest theological works of all time. He also wrote *On Free Choice Of The Will* (*De libero arbitrio*), addressing why God gives humans free will that can be used for evil.

Excerpts from "On Christian Doctrine"

[... sections omitted.].

But now as to those who talk vauntingly of Divine Grace, and boast that they understand and can explain Scripture without the aid of such directions as those I now propose to lay down, and who think, therefore, that what I have undertaken to write is entirely superfluous. I would such persons could calm themselves so far as to remember that, however justly they may rejoice in God's great gift, yet it was from human teachers they themselves learnt to read. Now, they would hardly think it right that they should for that reason be held in contempt by the Egyptian monk Antony, a just and holy man, who, not being able to read himself, is said to have committed the Scriptures to memory through hearing them read by others, and by dint of wise meditation to have arrived at a thorough understanding of them; or by that barbarian slave Christianus, of whom I have lately heard from very respectable and trustworthy witnesses, who, without any teaching from man, attained a full knowledge of the art of reading simply through prayer that it might be revealed to him; after three days' supplication obtaining his request that he might read through a book presented to him on the spot by the astonished bystanders.

But if any one thinks that these stories are false, I do not strongly insist on them. For, as I am dealing with Christians who profess to understand the Scriptures without any directions from man (and if the fact be so, they boast of a real advantage, and one of no ordinary kind), they must surely grant that every one of us learnt his own language by hearing it constantly from childhood, and that any other language we have learnt, Greek, or Hebrew, or any of the rest, we have learnt either in the same way, by hearing it spoken, or from a human teacher.

Now, then, suppose we advise all our brethren not to teach their children any of these things, because on the outpouring of the Holy Spirit the apostles immediately began to speak the language of every race; and warn every one who has not had a like experience that he need not consider himself a Christian, or may at least doubt whether he has yet received the Holy Spirit? No, no; rather let us put away false pride and learn whatever can be learnt from man; and let him who teaches another communicate what he has himself received without arrogance and without jealousy.

And do not let us tempt Him in whom we have believed, lest, being ensnared by such wiles of the enemy and by our own perversity, we may even refuse to go to the Churches to hear the gospel itself, or to read a book, or to listen to another reading or preaching, in the hope that we shall be carried up to the third heaven, "whether in the body or out of the body," as the apostle says,(1) and there hear unspeakable words, such as it is not lawful for man to utter, or see the Lord Jesus Christ and hear the gospel from His own lips rather than from those of men.

[… sections omitted.].

Chapter 5 – The Trinity, the True Object of Enjoyment.

The true objects of enjoyment, then, are the Father and the Son and the Holy Spirit, who are at the same time the Trinity, one Being, supreme above all, and common to all who enjoy Him, if He is an object, and not rather the cause of all objects, or indeed even if He is the cause of all. For it is not easy to find a name that will suitably express so great excellence, unless it is better to speak in this way: The Trinity, one God, of whom are all things, through whom are all things, in whom are all things.(1) Thus the Father and the Son and the Holy Spirit, and each of these by Himself, is God, and at the same time they are all one God; and each of them by Himself is a complete substance, and yet they are all one substance. The Father is not the Son nor the Holy Spirit; the Son is not the Father nor the Holy Spirit; the Holy Spirit is not the Father nor the Son: but the Father is only Father, the Son is only Son, and the Holy Spirit is only Holy Spirit. To all three belong the same eternity, the same unchangeableness, the same majesty, the same power. In the Father is unity, in the Son equality, in the Holy Spirit the harmony of unity and equality; and these three attributes are all one because of the Father, all equal because of the Son, and all harmonious because of the Holy Spirit.

Chapter 6 – In what sense God is Ineffable.

Have I spoken of God, or uttered His praise, in any worthy way? Nay, I feel that I have done nothing more than desire to speak; and if I have said anything, it is not what I desired to say. How do I know this, except from the fact that God is unspeakable? But what I have said, if it had been unspeakable, could not have been spoken. And so God is not even to be called "unspeakable," because to say even this is to speak of Him. Thus there arises a curious contradiction of words, because if the unspeakable is what cannot be spoken of, it is not unspeakable if it can be called unspeakable. And this opposition of words is rather to be avoided by silence than to be explained away by speech.

And yet God, although nothing worthy of His greatness can be said of Him, has condescended to accept the worship of men's mouths, and has desired us through the medium of our own words to rejoice in His praise. For on this principle it is that He is called Dues (God). For the sound of those two syllables in itself conveys no true knowledge of His nature; but yet all who know the Latin tongue are led, when that sound reaches their ears, to think of a nature supreme in excellence and eternal in existence.

Chapter 7 – What all Men understand by the term God.

For when the one supreme God of gods is thought of, even by those who believe that there are other gods, and who call them by that name, and worship them as gods, their thought takes the form of an endeavor to reach the conception of a nature, than which nothing more excellent or more exalted exists. And since men are moved by different kinds of pleasures, partly by those which pertain to the bodily senses, partly by those which pertain to the intellect and soul, those of them who are in bondage to sense think that either the heavens, or what appears to be most brilliant in the heavens, or the universe itself, is God of gods: or if they try to get beyond the universe, they picture to themselves something of dazzling brightness, and think of it vaguely as infinite, or of the most beautiful form conceivable; or they represent it in the form of the human body, if they think that superior to all others.

Or if they think that there is no one God supreme above the rest, but that there are many or even innumerable gods of equal rank, still these too they conceive as possessed of shape and form, according to what each man thinks the pattern of excellence. Those, on the other hand, who endeavor by an effort of the intelligence to reach a conception of God, place Him above all visible and bodily natures, and even above all intelligent and spiritual natures that are subject to change. All, however, strive emulously to exalt the excellence of God: nor could any one be found to believe that any being to whom there exists a superior is God. And so all concur in believing that God is that which excels in dignity all other objects.

Chapter 8 – God to be esteemed above all else because He is unchangeable Wisdom.

And since all who think about God think of Him as living, they only can form any conception of Him that is not absurd and unworthy who think of Him as life itself; and, whatever may be the bodily form that has suggested itself to them, recognize that it is by life it lives or does not live, and prefer what is living to what is dead; who understand that the living bodily form itself, however it may outshine all others in splendor, overtop them in size, and excel them in beauty, is quite a distinct thing from the life by which it is quickened; and who look upon the life as incomparably superior in dignity and worth to the mass which is quickened and animated by it. Then, when they go on to look into the nature of the life itself, if they find it mere nutritive life, without sensibility, such as that of plants, they consider it inferior to sentient life, such as that of cattle; and above this, again, they place intelligent life, such as that of men.   And, perceiving that even this is subject to change, they are compelled to place above it, again, that unchangeable life which is not at one time foolish, at another time wise, but on the contrary is wisdom itself. For a wise intelligence, that is, one that has attained to wisdom, was, previous to its attaining wisdom, unwise. But wisdom itself never was unwise, and never can become so. And if men never caught sight of this wisdom, they could never with entire confidence prefer a life which is unchangeably wise to one that is subject to change. This will be evident, if we consider that the very rule of truth by which they affirm the unchangeable life to be the more excellent, is itself unchangeable: and they cannot find such a rule, except by going beyond their own nature; for they find nothing in themselves that is not subject to change.

Chapter 9 – All acknowledge the Superiority of unchangeable Wisdom to that which is Variable.

Now, no one is so egregiously silly as to ask, "*How do you know that a life of unchangeable wisdom is preferable to one of change?*" For that very truth about which he asks, how I know it? is unchangeably fixed in the minds of all men, and presented to their common contemplation. And the man who does not see it is like a blind man in the sun, whom it profits nothing that the splendor of its light, so clear and so near, is poured into his very eye-balls. The man, on the other hand, who sees, but shrinks from this truth, is weak in his mental vision from dwelling long among the shadows of the flesh. And thus men are driven back from their native land by the contrary blasts of evil habits, and pursue lower and less valuable objects in preference to that which they own to be more excellent and more worthy.

Chapter 10 – To see God, the Soul must be purified.

Wherefore, since it is our duty fully to enjoy the truth which lives unchangeably, and since the triune God takes counsel in this truth for the things which He has made, the soul must be purified that it may have power to perceive that light, and to rest in it when it is perceived. And let us look upon this purification as a kind of journey or voyage to our native land. For it is not by change of place that we can come nearer to Him who is in every place, but by cultivation of pure desires and virtuous habits.

Chapter 11 – Wisdom becomes Incarnate, a Pattern to us of Purification.

But of this we should have been wholly incapable, had not Wisdom condescended to adapt Himself to our weakness, and to show us a pattern of holy life in the form of our own humanity. Yet, since we when we come to Him do wisely, He when He came to us was considered by proud men to have done very foolishly. And since we when we come to Him become strong, He when He came to us was looked upon as weak. But "the foolishness of God is wiser than men; and the weakness of God is stronger than men."(1) And thus, though Wisdom was Himself our home, He made Himself also the way by which we should reach our home.

Chapter 12 – In what Sense the Wisdom of God came to us.

And though He is everywhere present to the inner eye when it is sound and clear, He condescended to make Himself manifest to the outward eye of those whose inward sight is weak and dim. "For after that, in the wisdom of God, the world by wisdom knew not God, it pleased God by the foolishness of preaching to save them that believe." (2) Not then in the sense of traversing space, but because He appeared to mortal men in the form of mortal flesh, He is said to have come to us. For He came to a place where He had always been, seeing that "He was in the world, and the world was made by Him." But, because men, who in their eagerness to enjoy the creature instead of the Creator had grown into the likeness of this world, and are therefore most appropriately named "the world," did not recognize Him, therefore the evangelist says, "and the world knew Him not." (3) Thus, in the wisdom of God, the world by wisdom knew not God. Why then did He come, seeing that He was already here, except that it pleased God through the foolishness of preaching to save them that believe?

Chapter 13 –The Word was made Flesh.

In what way did He come but this, "The Word was made flesh, and dwelt among us"?(1) Just as when we speak, in order that what we have in our minds may enter through the ear into the mind of the hearer, the word which we have in our hearts becomes an outward sound and is called speech; and yet our thought does not lose itself in the sound, but remains complete in itself, and takes the form of speech without being modified in its own nature by the change: so the Divine Word, though suffering no change of nature, yet became flesh, that He might dwell among us.

Chapter 14 –How the Wisdom of God healed Man.

Moreover, as the use of remedies is the way to health, so this remedy took up sinners to heal and restore them. And just as surgeons, when they bind up wounds, do it not in a slovenly way, but carefully, that there may be a certain degree of neatness in the binding, in addition to its mere usefulness, so our medicine, Wisdom, was by His assumption of humanity adapted to our wounds, curing some of them by their opposites, some of them by their likes. And just as he who ministers to a bodily hurt in some cases applies contraries, as cold to hot, moist to dry, etc., and in other cases applies likes, as a round cloth to a round wound, or an oblong cloth to an oblong wound, and does not fit the same bandage to all limbs, but puts like to like; in the same way the Wisdom of God in healing man has applied Himself to his cure, being Himself healer and medicine both in one. Seeing, then, that man fell through pride, He restored him through humility. We were ensnared by the wisdom of the serpent: we are set free by the foolishness of God. Moreover, just as the former was called wisdom, but was in reality the folly of those who despised God, so the latter is called foolishness, but is true wisdom in those who overcome the devil. We used our immortality so badly as to incur the penalty of death: Christ used His mortality so well as to restore us to life. The disease was brought in through a woman's corrupted soul: the remedy came through a woman's virgin body. To the same class of opposite remedies it belongs, that our vices are cured by the example of His virtues. On the other hand, the following are, as it were, bandages made in the same shape as the limbs and wounds to which they are applied: He was born of a woman to deliver us who fell through a woman: He came as a man to save us who are men, as a mortal to save us who are mortals, by death to save us who were dead. And those who can follow out the matter more fully, who are not hurried on by the necessity of carrying out a set undertaking, will find many other points of instruction in considering the remedies, whether opposites or likes, employed in the medicine of Christianity.

Chapter 15 – Faith is buttressed by the Resurrection and Ascension of Christ, and is stimulated by His coming to Judgment.

The belief of the resurrection of our Lord from the dead, and of His ascension into heaven, has strengthened our faith by adding a great buttress of hope. For it clearly shows how freely He laid down His life for us when He had it in His power thus to take it up again. With what assurance, then, is the hope of believers animated, when they reflect how great He was who suffered so great things for them while they were still in unbelief! And when men look for Him to come from heaven as the judge of quick and dead, it strikes great terror into the careless, so that they betake themselves to diligent preparation, and learn by holy living to long for His approach, instead of quaking at it on account of their evil deeds. And what tongue can tell, or what imagination can conceive, the reward He will bestow at the last, when we consider that for our comfort in this earthly journey He has given us so freely of His Spirit, that in the adversities of this life we may retain our confidence in, and love for, Him whom as yet we see not; and that He has also given to each gifts suitable for the building up of His Church, that we may do what He points out as right to be done, not only without a murmur, but even with delight?

Chapter 16 – Christ purges His church by Medicinal Afflictions.

For the Church is His body, as the apostle's teaching shows us; (2) and it is even called His spouse.(3) His body, then, which has many members, and all performing different functions, He holds together in the bond of unity and love, which is its true health. Moreover He exercises it in the present time, and purges it with many wholesome afflictions, that when He has transplanted it from this world to the eternal world, He may take it to Himself as His bride, without spot or wrinkle, or any such thing.

Chapter 17 – Christ, by Forgiving our Sins, opened the way to our Home.

Further, when we are on the way, and that not a way that lies through space, but through a change of affections, and one which the guilt of our past sins like a hedge of thorns barred against us, what could He, who was willing to lay Himself down as the way by which we should return, do that would be still gracious and more merciful, except to forgive us all our sins, and by being crucified for us to remove the stern decrees that barred the door against our return?

Chapter 18 – The Keys given to the Church.

He has given, therefore, the keys to His Church, that whatsoever it should bind on earth might be bound in heaven, and whatsoever it should loose on earth might be, loosed in heaven; (1) that is to say, that whosoever in the Church should not believe that his sins are remitted, they should not be remitted to him; but that whosoever should believe and should repent, and turn from his sins, should be saved by the same faith and repentance on the ground of which he is received into the bosom of the Church. For he who does not believe that his sins can be pardoned, falls into despair, and becomes worse as if no greater good remained for him than to be evil, when he has ceased to have faith in the results of his own repentance.

Chapter 19 – Bodily and spiritual Death and Resurrection.

Furthermore, as there is a kind of death of the soul, which consists in the putting away of former habits and former ways of life, and which comes through repentance, so also the death of the body consists in the dissolution of the former principle of life. And just as the soul, after it has put away and destroyed by repentance its former habits, is created anew after a better pattern, so we must hope and believe that the body, after that death which we all owe as a debt contracted through sin, shall at the resurrection be changed into a better form;--not that flesh and blood shall inherit the kingdom of God (for that is impossible), but that this corruptible shall put on incorruption, and this mortal shall put on immortality. (2) And thus the body, being the source of no uneasiness because it can feel no want, shall be animated by a spirit perfectly pure and happy, and shall enjoy unbroken peace.

[… sections omitted.].

Chapter 34 – Christ, the first way to God.

And mark that even when He who is Himself the Truth and the Word, by whom all things were made, had been made flesh that He might dwell among us, the apostle yet says: "*Yea, though we have known Christ after the flesh, yet now henceforth know we Him no more.*" (5) For Christ, desiring not only to give the possession to those who had completed the journey, but also to be Himself the way to those who were just setting out, determined to take a fleshly body. Whence also that expression, "*The Lord created (6) me in the beginning of His way,*" (7) that is, that those who wished to come might begin their journey in Him. The apostle, therefore, although still on the way, and following after God who called him to the reward of His heavenly calling, yet forgetting those things which were behind, and pressing on towards those things which were before,(8) had already passed over the beginning of the way, and had now no further need of it; yet by this way all must commence their journey who desire to attain to the truth, and to rest in eternal life.

For He says: *"I am the way, and the truth, and the life;"* (9) that is, by me men come, to me they come, in me they rest. For when we come to Him, we come to the Father also, because through an equal an equal is known; and the Holy Spirit binds, and as it were seals us, so that we are able to rest permanently in the supreme and unchangeable Good. And hence we may learn how essential it is that nothing should detain us on the way, when not even our Lord Himself, so far as He has condescended to be our way, is willing to detain us, but wishes us rather to press on; and, instead of weakly clinging to temporal things, even though these have been put on and worn by Him for our salvation, to pass over them quickly, and to struggle to attain unto Himself, who has freed our nature from the bondage of temporal things, and has set it down at His Father.

[... sections omitted.].

Chapter 38 – Love never Faileth.

But sight shall displace faith; and hope shall be swallowed up in that perfect bliss to which we shall come: love, on the other hand, shall wax greater when these others fail. For if we love by faith that which as yet we see not, how much more shall we love it when we begin to see! And if we love by hope that which as yet we have not reached, how much more shall we love it when we reach it! For there is this great difference between things temporal and things eternal, that a temporal object is valued more before we possess it, and begins to prove worthless the moment we attain it, because it does not satisfy the soul, which has its only true and sure resting-place in eternity: an eternal object, on the other hand, is loved with greater ardor when it is in possession than while it is still an object of desire, for no one in his longing for it can set a higher value on it than really belongs to it, so as to think it comparatively worthless when he finds it of less value than he thought.; on the contrary, however high the value any man may set upon it.

IV. EARLIEST SELECTED APOCRYPHA

As indicated, approximately 200+ Apocryphal documents, fragments and manuscripts have been found since the earthly ministry of Christ. These discoveries range from complete manuscripts to just a few fragments. Some of the apocryphal documents were completely lost to modern scholarship and we know of their existence through the references made by the early Church fathers such as Clement of Rome, Origen, Eusebius, Tertullian and many others. Excerpts from many of the earliest documents are listed in this section and references are made to other documents which have been lost in time. We have included 19 of the most prominent apocryphal works in this section which were widely known and accepted in the early Church.

It should also be noted that an additional 25+ or so apocryphal documents were unearthed in the times *before* Christ (*ie. Old Testament and/or Inter-Testamental periods*) although, as indicated, these apocryphal documents are not the focus of this book.

The Signs Gospel
(50 – 90 A.D.)

D. Moody Smith comments (*Johannine Christianity*, p. 63): "It is now rather widely agreed that the Fourth Evangelist drew upon a miracle tradition or written source(s) substantially independent of the synoptics, whether or not he had any knowledge of one or more of those gospels. Since the epoch-making commentary of Rudolf Bultmann, the hypothesis of a *semeia-* (or miracle) source has gained rather wide acceptance."On the contents of the Signs Gospel, Fortna states (op. cit., p. 19): "*the following deeds of Jesus, less the Johannine insertions they now contain, would have comprised the bulk of SQ: changing water into wine (2:1-11), healing an official's son (4:46-54) and a lame man (5:2-9), feeding the multitude (6:1-14) - probably together with crossing the sea (6:15-25), giving sight to a blind man (9:1-8), and raising Lazarus (11:1-45). (Some would also include the catch of fish now found at 21:1-14.) An articulated series emerges from the reconstruction, not merely a gather of miracle stories, and a few other passages are also to be included: part of chap. 1 (at least the gathering of the first disciples in vv 35-49) as introduction and, as conclusion, 20:30-31a, and perhaps also parts of 12:37-41.*"

There is considerable debate over whether the Signs Gospel may have contained a passion narrative or instead contained only a collection of seven miracle stories. In the reconstruction offered by Fortna, a passion story is included.

On the dating of the Signs Gospel, there is little to go on. The reference to the Pool of Bethesda as still standing in 5:2, even though it was destroyed by the Romans in 70 CE, suggests a dating before the year 70 CE or not too long afterwards. The latest possible date is set by its incorporation into the Gospel of John.

Robert Fortna writes (*The Anchor Bible Dictionary*, v. 6, p. 19):

As SQ's title indicates, it was first of all the word "sign" that suggested the survival of an older layer in the text of the present gospel. On the one hand, this term - and particularly its connection with faith - is used only rarely and negatively in the Synoptics and there never of the miracles Jesus had performed; and on the other hand, in the Fourth Gospel also "signs-faith" sometimes comes in criticism (e.g., 4:48; 6:26) but at other points - presumably pre-

Johannine - is to be understood in an entirely positive sense. Further, in the first part of the gospel there are what seem to be vestiges of a pattern of numbering the signs (2:11, 4:54). In fact, it is these miracle stories and others now unnumbered, together with Jesus' dialogues and long monologues ("*discourses*") now growing out of them, that alone comprise his public activity. What in the other gospels, and in far more diverse form, has been called his "ministry" can only be described in this gospel as his self-presentation in the performing of signs and in extended talk about them.

Thus, to many scholars there has seemed to lie behind the present text a protogospel that presented only Jesus' signs, and a series of them, and did so wholly affirmatively. They were significations (that is, demonstrations) of his messianic status, on the basis of which his first disciples and then many others believed in him; those who "came and saw" (1:39) immediately recognized him as the one so long hoped for in Jewish expectation.

Summary notation: *Due to it's importance and historical significance to the early Church fathers including Eusebius, Athanasius, Polycarp, Ignatius, Clement and Origen of Alexandria, the* **Signs Gospel** *is presented in it's enitrety. Please note sections missing in the early manuscripts.*

The Manuscript in its Entirety

John 1.

[section missing...]

(6) There was a man sent from God, whose name was John. **(7)** He came as a witness, so that all might believe through him.

[section missing...]

(19) This is the testimony given by John when priests and Levites *came* to ask him, "*Who are you?*"
(20) *He* confessed, "*I am not the Messiah.*"
(21) And they asked him, "*What then? Are you Elijah?*"

He said, "*I am not.*" "Are you the prophet?" He answered, "*No.*"
(22) Then they said to him, "Who are you? What do you say about yourself?"
(23) He said, "I *am the voice of one crying out in the wilderness, 'Make straight the way of the Lord,' *" as the prophet Isaiah said. I baptize with water. Among you stands

[section missing...]

(27) the one who is coming after me; I am not worthy to untie the thong of his sandal."
(28) He saw Jesus coming toward him and declared, "Here is the Lamb of God. I came for this reason, that he might be revealed to Israel. I saw the Spirit descending from heaven like a dove on him. **(34)** And I myself have seen and have testified that this is the Son of God."

[section missing...]

(35) *Now* John was standing with two of his disciples *who* heard him say this, and they followed Jesus. (38) They said to him, "*Rabbi, where are you staying?*"

[section missing...]

(39) He said to them, "Come and see." They came and saw where he was staying, and they remained with him that day. It was about four o'clock in the afternoon.
(40) One of the two who heard John speak and followed him was Andrew. (41) He first found his brother Simon and said to him, "*We have found the Messiah.*"

[section missing...]

(42) He brought Simon to Jesus, who looked at him and said, "*You are Simon son of John. You are to be called Cephas.*"
He found Philip and *Jesus* said to him, "Follow me."

[section missing...]

(44) Now Philip was from Bethsaida, the city of Andrew and Peter.

(45) Philip found Nathanael and said to him, "*We have found him about whom Moses in the law wrote, Jesus son of Joseph from Nazareth.*"

(46) Nathanael said to him, "*Can anything good come out of Nazareth?*" Philip said to him, "*Come and see.*"

(47) When Jesus saw Nathanael coming toward him, he said of him, "Here is truly an Israelite."

(49) Nathanael replied, "Rabbi, you are the Son of God! You are the King of Israel!"

John 2.

(1) There was a wedding in Cana, and the mother of Jesus was there.

(2) Jesus and his disciples had also been invited to the wedding.

(3) When the wine gave out, the mother of Jesus said to the servants, "*Do whatever he tells you.*"

[section missing…]

(6) Now standing there were six stone water jars, each holding twenty or thirty gallons.

(7) Jesus said to them, "*Fill the jars with water.*" And they filled them up to the brim.

(8) He said to them, "*Now draw some out, and take it to the chief steward.*" So they took it.

(9) When the steward tasted the water that had become wine, the steward called the bridegroom

(10) and said to him, "*Everyone serves the good wine first, and then the inferior wine after the guests have become drunk. But you have kept the good wine until now.*"

(11) Jesus did this, the first of his signs; and his disciples believed in him.

(12) After this he went down to Capernaum with his disciples.

[section missing…]

(14) In the temple *Jesus* found people selling cattle, sheep, and doves, and the money changers seated at their tables.

(15) Making a whip of cords, he drove all of them out of the temple, both the sheep and the cattle. He also poured out the coins of the money changers and overturned their tables.

(16) He told those who were selling the doves, "Take these things out of here! Stop making my Father's house a marketplace!"

(18) The Jews then said to him, "*What sign can you show us for doing this?*"

[section missing...]

(19) Jesus answered them, "*Destroy this temple, and in three days I will raise it up.*"

[section missing...]

John 4.

[section missing...]

(46) Now there was a royal official whose son lay ill in Capernaum.

(47) He went and said to him, "*Sir, come down before my little boy dies.*"

(50) Jesus said, "*Go; your son will live.*" The man started on his way.

(51) As he was going down, his slaves met him and told him that his child was alive.

(52) So he asked them the hour when he began to recover, and they said to him, "*Yesterday at one in the afternoon the fever left him.*"

(53) So he himself believed, along with his whole household.

(54) Now this was the second sign that Jesus did.

John 5.

[section missing...]

(2) Now in Jerusalem by the Sheep Gate there is a pool, called in Hebrew Beth-zatha, which has five porticoes.

(3) In these lay many invalids—blind, lame, and paralyzed.

[section missing...]

(5) One man was there who had been ill for thirty-eight years.

(6) When Jesus saw him lying there and knew that he had been there a long time, he said to him, "*Do you want to be made well?*"

(7) The sick man answered him, "*Sir, I have no one to put me into the pool when the water is stirred up; and while I am making my way, someone else steps down ahead of me.*"

(8) Jesus said to him, "*Stand up, take your mat and walk.*"

(9) At once the man was made well, and he took up his mat and began to walk.

John 6.

(1) After this Jesus went to the other side of the Sea of Tiberias.

[section missing...]

(3) *He* went up the mountain and sat down there with his disciples.
[section missing...]

(5) When he looked up and saw a large crowd coming toward him, Jesus said to Philip, "*Where are we to buy bread for these people to eat?*"

[section missing...]

(7) Philip answered him, "*Six months' wages would not buy enough bread for each of them to get a little.*"

(8) One of his disciples said to him,

(9) "*There is a boy here who has five barley loaves and two fish. But what are they among so many people?*"

(10) Jesus said, "*Make the people sit down.*" Now there was a great deal of grass in the place; so they sat down, about five thousand in all.

(11) Then Jesus took the loaves, and when he had given thanks, he distributed them to those who were seated; so also the fish, as much as they wanted.

[section missing...]

(13) And from the fragments of the five barley loaves, left by those who had eaten, they filled twelve baskets.

(14) When the people saw the sign that he had done, they began to say, "*This is indeed the prophet who is to come into the world.*"

(15) *Jesus* withdrew again to the mountain by himself.

(16) When evening came, his disciples went down to the sea,

(17) got into a boat, and started across the sea to Capernaum.

(18) The sea became rough because a strong wind was blowing.

(19) When they had rowed about three or four miles, they saw Jesus walking on the sea, and they were terrified.

(20) But he said to them, "*It is I; do not be afraid.*"

(21) And immediately the boat reached the land toward which they were going.

[section missing...]

John 9.

(1) As he walked along, he saw a man blind from birth.

[section missing...]

(6) He spat on the ground and made mud with the saliva and spread the mud on the man's eyes,

(7) saying to him, "*Go, wash in the pool of Siloam.*" Then he went and washed and came back able to see.

(8) The neighbors and those who had seen him before as a beggar began to ask, "*Is this not the man who used to sit and beg?*"

[section missing...]

John 11.

(1) Now a certain Mary; **(2)** her brother Lazarus was ill.

[section missing...]

(3) *She* sent a message to Jesus, *"Lord, he whom you love is ill."*

[section missing...]

(7) He said to the disciples, *"Our friend Lazarus has fallen asleep. Let us go to him."*

[section missing...]

(17) When Jesus arrived, he found that Lazarus had already been in the tomb four days.

[section missing...]

(32) When Mary saw him, she knelt at his feet and said to him, *"Lord, if you had been here, my brother would not have died."*
(33) When Jesus saw her weeping, he was greatly disturbed in spirit and deeply moved.
(34) He said, *"Where have you laid him?"* They said to him, *"Lord, come and see."*

[section missing...]

(38) Then Jesus came to the tomb. It was a cave, and a stone was lying against it.
(39) Jesus said, *"Take away the stone."* *Then* he cried with a loud voice, *"Lazarus, come out!"*

[section missing...]

(44) The dead man came out, his hands and feet bound with strips of cloth, and his face wrapped in a cloth. Jesus said to them, *"Unbind him, and let him go."*
(45) *Those who* had seen what Jesus did, believed in him.

[section missing...]

(47) So the chief priests called a meeting of the council, and said, *"This man is performing many signs".*

(48) *"If we let him go on like this, everyone will believe in him, and the Romans will come and destroy our nation."*

(49) But one of them, Caiaphas, who was high priest that year, said to them,

(50) *"It is better for you to have one man die for the people than to have the whole nation destroyed."*

[section missing...]

(53) So from that day on they planned to put him to death.

John 12.

(1) Six days before the Passover Jesus came to Bethany, the home of Lazarus, whom he had raised from the dead.

(2) There they gave a dinner for him. Martha served, and Lazarus was one of those at the table with him.

(3) Mary took a pound of costly perfume made of pure nard, anointed Jesus, and wiped them with her hair. The house was filled with the fragrance of the perfume.

(4) But Judas Iscariot, one of his disciples, said,

(5) *"Why was this perfume not sold for three hundred denarii and the money given to the poor?"*

[section missing...]

(7) Jesus said, *"She bought it so that she might keep it for the day of my burial".*

(8) *"You always have the poor with you, but you do not always have me."*

[section missing...]

(12) The next day the great crowd that had come to the festival heard that Jesus was coming to Jerusalem.

(13) So they took branches of palm trees and went out to meet him, shouting, *"Hosanna! Blessed is the one who comes in the name of the Lord— the King of Israel!"*

(14) Jesus found a young donkey and sat on it; as it is written:

(15) *"Do not be afraid, daughter of Zion. Look, your king is coming, sitting on a donkey's colt!"*

[section missing...]

(37) Although he had performed so many signs, they did not believe in him.

(38) This was to fulfill the word spoken by the prophet Isaiah: *"Lord, who has believed our message, and to whom has the arm of the Lord been revealed?"*

(39) And so they could not believe, because Isaiah also said,

(40) *"He has blinded their eyes and hardened their heart, so that they might not look with their eyes, and understand with their heart and turn— and I would heal them."*

John 13.

(1) Now before the festival of the Passover, Jesus knew that his hour had come to depart from this world and go to the Father. Having loved his own who were in the world, he loved them to the end.

(2) The devil had already put it into the heart of Judas son of Simon Iscariot to betray him. And during supper

(3) Jesus, knowing that the Father had given all things into his hands, and that he had come from God and was going to God,

(4) got up from the table, took off his outer robe, and tied a towel around himself.

(5) Then he poured water into a basin and began to wash the disciples' feet and to wipe them with the towel that was tied around him.

6) He came to Simon Peter, who said to him, *"Lord, are you going to wash my feet?"*

(7) Jesus answered, *"You do not know now what I am doing, but later you will understand."*

(8) Peter said to him, *"You will never wash my feet."* Jesus answered, *"Unless I wash you, you have no share with me."*

(9) Simon Peter said to him, *"Lord, not my feet only but also my hands and my head!"*

(10) Jesus said to him, "*One who has bathed does not need to wash, except for the feet, but is entirely clean. And you are clean, though not all of you.*"

(11) For he knew who was to betray him; for this reason he said, "*Not all of you are clean.*"

(12) After he had washed their feet, had put on his robe, and had returned to the table, he said to them, "*Do you know what I have done to you?*

(13) You call me Teacher and Lord—and you are right, for that is what I am.

(14) So if I, your Lord and Teacher, have washed your feet, you also ought to wash one another's feet.

(15) For I have set you an example, that you also should do as I have done to you.

(16) Very truly, I tell you, servants are not greater than their master, nor are messengers greater than the one who sent them.

(17) If you know these things, you are blessed if you do them.

(18) I am not speaking of all of you; I know whom I have chosen. But it is to fulfill the scripture, 'The one who ate my bread has lifted his heel against me.'

(19) I tell you this now, before it occurs, so that when it does occur, you may believe that I am he. (

20) Very truly, I tell you, whoever receives one whom I send receives me; and whoever receives me receives him who sent me."

[section missing…]

John 18.

(1) Jesus went out with his disciples across the Kidron valley to a place where there was a garden.

(2) Now Judas, who betrayed him, also knew the place, because Jesus often met there with his disciples.

(3) So Judas brought a detachment of soldiers together with police from the chief priests, and they came there with lanterns and torches and weapons.

(4) Then Jesus asked them, "*Whom are you looking for?*"

(5) They answered, "*Jesus of Nazareth.*" Jesus replied, "*I am he.*"

[section missing…]

(10) Then Simon Peter, who had a sword, drew it, struck the high priest's slave, and cut off his right ear. The slave's name was Malchus.

(11) Jesus said to Peter, "*Put your sword back into its sheath. Am I not to drink the cup that the Father has given me?"*

(12) So the soldiers, their officer, and the Jewish police arrested Jesus and bound him.

(13) First they took him to Annas, who was the father-in-law of Caiaphas, the high priest that year.

[section missing…]

(15) Simon Peter and another disciple followed Jesus. Since that disciple was known to the high priest, he went with Jesus into the courtyard of the high priest,

(16) but Peter was standing outside at the gate. So the other disciple, who was known to the high priest, went out, spoke to the woman who guarded the gate, and brought Peter in.

(17) The woman said to Peter, "*You are not also one of this man's disciples, are you?"* He said, "*I am not."*

(18) Now the slaves and the police had made a charcoal fire because it was cold, and they were standing around it and warming themselves. Peter also was standing with them and warming himself.

(19) Then the high priest questioned Jesus about his teaching.

(20) Jesus answered, "*I have always taught in the temple, where all come together".*

(21) "*Why do you ask me?"*

(22) When he had said this, one of the police standing nearby struck Jesus on the face, saying, "*Is that how you answer the high priest?"*

[section missing…]

(24) Then Annas sent him bound to Caiaphas the high priest.

(25) They asked him, "*You are not also one of his disciples, are you?*" He denied it and said, "*I am not.*"

(26) One of the slaves of the high priest, a relative of the man whose ear Peter had cut off, asked, "*Did I not see you in the garden with him?*"

(27) Again Peter denied it, and at that moment the cock crowed.

(28) Then they took Jesus from Caiaphas to Pilate's headquarters. It was early in the morning.

(29) Pilate said, "*What accusation do you bring against this man?*"

[section missing...]

(33) Then Pilate summoned Jesus and asked him, "*Are you the King of the Jews?*" Jesus answered, "*You say that I am a king.*"

[section missing...]

(38) He told them, "*I find no case against him.*"

(39) "*But you have a custom that I release someone for you at the Passover. Do you want me to release for you the King of the Jews?*"

(40) They shouted in reply, "*Not this man, but Barabbas!*" Now Barabbas was a bandit.

John 19.

(1) Then Pilate took Jesus and had him flogged.

(2) And the soldiers wove a crown of thorns and put it on his head, and they dressed him in a purple robe.

(3) They kept coming up to him, saying, "*Hail, King of the Jews!*" and striking him on the face.

[section missing...]

(6) And the police saw him, they shouted, "*Crucify him! Crucify him!*" Pilate said to them, "*I find no case against him.*"

[section missing...]

(13) Pilate brought Jesus outside and sat on the judge's bench at a place called The Stone Pavement, or in Hebrew Gabbatha.

(14) Now it was the day of Preparation; and it was about noon.

[section missing...]

(16) Then he handed him over to them to be crucified. So they took Jesus.

(17) He went out to what is called The Place of the Skull, which in Hebrew is called Golgotha.

(18) There they crucified him, and with him two others, one on either side.

(19) And there was written, "*Jesus of Nazareth, the King of the Jews.*"

(20) And it was written in Hebrew, in Latin, and in Greek.

[section missing...]

(23) When the soldiers had crucified Jesus, they took his clothes and divided them into four parts, one for each soldier. They also took his tunic; now the tunic was seamless, woven in one piece from the top.

(24) So they said to one another, "*Let us not tear it, but cast lots for it to see who will get it.*" This was to fulfill what the scripture says, "*They divided my clothes among themselves, and for my clothing they cast lots.*"

(25) And that is what the soldiers did. Meanwhile, standing near the cross of Jesus were his mother, and his mother's sister, Mary the wife of Clopas, and Mary Magdalene.

[section missing...]

(28) After this, he said *(in order to fulfill the scripture)*, "*I am thirsty.*"

(29) A jar full of sour wine was standing there. So they put a sponge full of the wine on a branch of hyssop and held it to his mouth.

(30) When Jesus had received the wine, he said, "*It is finished.*" Then he bowed his head and gave up his spirit.

(31) Since it was the day of Preparation, the Jews did not want the bodies left on the cross during the sabbath. So they asked Pilate to have the legs of the crucified men broken and the bodies removed.

(32) Then the soldiers came and broke the legs of the first and of the other who had been crucified with him.

(33) But when they came to Jesus and saw that he was already dead, they did not break his legs.

(34) Instead, one of the soldiers pierced his side with a spear, and at once blood and water came out.

[section missing...]

(36) These things occurred so that the scripture might be fulfilled, "*None of his bones shall be broken.*"

(37) And again another passage of scripture says, "*They will look on the one whom they have pierced.*"

(38) After these things, Joseph of Arimathea, who was a disciple of Jesus, asked Pilate to let him take away the body of Jesus. Pilate gave him permission; so he came and removed his body and wrapped it with the spices in linen cloths.

[section missing...]

(41) Now there was a garden in the place where he was crucified, and in the garden there was a new tomb in which no one had ever been laid.

(42) And so, because it was the day of Preparation, and the tomb was nearby, they laid Jesus there.

John 20.

(1) Early on the first day of the week, Mary Magdalene came to the tomb and saw that the stone had been removed from the tomb.

(2) So she ran and went to Simon Peter and said, "*They have taken the Lord out of the tomb, and we do not know where they have laid him.*"

(3) Then Peter set out and went toward the tomb and went into the tomb.

[section missing...]

(9) For as yet they did not understand the scripture, that he must rise from the dead.

(10) Then *he* returned to *his* home.

(11) But Mary stood weeping outside the tomb. As she wept, she bent over to look into the tomb;

(12) and she saw two angels in white, sitting where the body of Jesus had been lying, one at the head and the other at the feet.

[section missing...]

(14) She turned around and saw Jesus standing there.

(15) Jesus said to her, "*Whom are you looking for, Mary?*" She said to him in Hebrew, "*Rabbouni!.*"

[section missing...]

(17) Jesus said to her, "*Do not hold on to me. But go to my brothers.*"

(18) Mary Magdalene went and announced to the disciples, "*I have seen the Lord.*"

(19) When it was evening on that day and the doors of the house where the disciples had met were locked, Jesus came and stood among them and said, *"Peace be with you."*

(20) He showed them his hands and his side. Then the disciples rejoiced when they saw the Lord.

[section missing...]

(22) He breathed on them and said to them, "*Receive the Holy Spirit.*"

[section missing...]

(30) Now Jesus did many other signs in the presence of his disciples, which are not written in this book.

(31) But these are written so that you may come to believe that Jesus is the Messiah, the Son of God.

John 21.

[section missing...]

(2) Gathered there together were Simon Peter, Thomas called the

Twin, Nathanael of Cana, the sons of Zebedee.

(3) Simon Peter said to them, *"I am going fishing."* They said to him, *"We will go with you."* They went out and got into the boat, but that night they caught nothing.

(4) Just after daybreak, Jesus stood on the beach.

[section missing...]

(6) He said to them, *"Cast the net to the right side of the boat, and you will find some."* So they cast it, and now they were not able to haul it in because there were so many fish.

(7) Simon Peter put on some clothes and jumped into the sea

(8) for they were not far from the land, only about a hundred yards off.

[section missing...]

(11) So Simon Peter went ashore and hauled the net ashore, full of large fish, a hundred fifty-three of them; and though there were so many, the net was not torn.

[section missing...]

(14) This was now the third sign that Jesus did before the disciples

Didache
(50 – 120 A.D.)

The Didache (/ˈdɪdəkiː/; Koine Greek: Διδαχή) or The Teaching of the Twelve Apostles (*Didachē* means *"Teaching"*) is a brief early Christian treatise, dated by most scholars to the late first or early 2nd century. The first line of this treatise is *"Teaching of the Lord to the Gentiles (or Nations) by the Twelve Apostles"*. The text, parts of which constitute the oldest surviving written catechism, has three main sections dealing with Christian ethics, rituals such as baptism and Eucharist, and Church organization. It is considered the first example of the *genre* of the Church Orders.

Lost for centuries, a Greek manuscript of the Didache was rediscovered in 1873 by Philotheos Bryennios, Metropolitan of Nicomedia in the Codex Hierosolymitanus. A Latin version of the first five chapters was discovered in 1900 by J. Schlecht. The Didache is considered part of the category of second-generation Christian writings known as the Apostolic Fathers.

The *Didache* is mentioned by Eusebius (*c.* 324) as the *Teachings of the Apostles* following the books recognized as canonical: "Let there be placed among the spurious works the *Acts of Paul*, the so-called *Shepherd* and the *Apocalypse of Peter*, and besides these the *Epistle of Barnabas*, and what are called the *Teachings of the Apostles*, and also the *Apocalypse of John*, if this be thought proper; for as I wrote before, some reject it, and others place it in the canon."

Athanasius (*367*) and Rufinus (c. 380) list the *Didache* among Apocrypha. (Rufinus gives the curious alternative title *Judicium Petri*, "Judgment of Peter".) It is rejected by Nicephorus (*c.* 810), Pseudo-Anastasius, and Pseudo-Athanasius in *Synopsis* and the 60 Books canon. It is accepted by the Apostolic Constitutions Canon 85, John of Damascus and the Ethiopian Orthodox Church. The *Adversus Aleatores* by an imitator of Cyprian quotes it by name. Unacknowledged citations are very common, if less certain. The section *Two Ways* shares the same language with the *Epistle of Barnabas*, chapters 18–20, sometimes word for word, sometimes added to, dislocated, or abridged, and Barnabas iv, 9 either derives from *Didache*, 16, 2–3, or vice versa. There can also be seen many

similarities to the Epistles of both *Polycarp* and *Ignatius of Antioch*
The *Shepherd of Hermas* seems to reflect it, and Irenaeus,Clement of
Alexandria, and Origen of Alexandria also seem to use the work,
and so in the West do Optatus and the *Gesta apud Zenophilum*. The
Didascalia Apostolorum are founded upon the *Didache*. The
Apostolic Church-Ordinances has used a part, the Apostolic
Constitutions have embodied the *Didascalia*. There are echoes
in Justin Martyr, Tatian, Theophilus of Antioch, Cyprian,
and Lactantius.[19].

> ***Summary notation:*** *Due to it's importance and historical significance to the early
> Church fathers including Eusebius, Athanasius, Polycarp, Ignatius, Clement and
> Origen of Alexandria, the* **Didache** *is presented in it's enitrety;*

The Manuscript in its Entirety

Chapter 1. The Two Ways and the First Commandment.

There are two ways, one of life and one of death, but a great
difference between the two ways. The way of life, then, is this:
First, you shall love God who made you; second, love your
neighbor as yourself, and do not do to another what you would not
want done to you. And of these sayings the teaching is this: Bless
those who curse you, and pray for your enemies, and fast for those
who persecute you. For what reward is there for loving those who
love you? Do not the Gentiles do the same? But love those who
hate you, and you shall not have an enemy. Abstain from fleshly
and worldly lusts. If someone strikes your right cheek, turn to him
the other also, and you shall be perfect. If someone impresses you
for one mile, go with him two. If someone takes your cloak, give
him also your coat. If someone takes from you what is yours, ask it
not back, for indeed you are not able. Give to every one who asks
you, and ask it not back; for the Father wills that to all should be
given of our own blessings (free gifts). Happy is he who gives
according to the commandment, for he is guiltless. Woe to him
who receives; for if one receives who has need, he is guiltless; but

---

[19] http://en.wikipedia.org/wiki/Didache

he who receives not having need shall pay the penalty, why he received and for what. And coming into confinement, he shall be examined concerning the things which he has done, and he shall not escape from there until he pays back the last penny. And also concerning this, it has been said, Let your alms sweat in your hands, until you know to whom you should give.

Chapter 2. The Second Commandment: Grave Sin Forbidden.

And the second commandment of the Teaching; You shall not commit murder, you shall not commit adultery, you shall not commit pederasty, you shall not commit fornication, you shall not steal, you shall not practice magic, you shall not practice witchcraft, you shall not murder a child by abortion nor kill that which is born. You shall not covet the things of your neighbor, you shall not swear, you shall not bear false witness, you shall not speak evil, you shall bear no grudge. You shall not be double-minded nor double-tongued, for to be double-tongued is a snare of death. Your speech shall not be false, nor empty, but fulfilled by deed. You shall not be covetous, nor rapacious, nor a hypocrite, nor evil disposed, nor haughty. You shall not take evil counsel against your neighbor. You shall not hate any man; but some you shall reprove, and concerning some you shall pray, and some you shall love more than your own life.

Chapter 3. Other Sins Forbidden.

My child, flee from every evil thing, and from every likeness of it. Be not prone to anger, for anger leads to murder. Be neither jealous, nor quarrelsome, nor of hot temper, for out of all these murders are engendered. My child, be not a lustful one. for lust leads to fornication. Be neither a filthy talker, nor of lofty eye, for out of all these adulteries are engendered. My child, be not an observer of omens, since it leads to idolatry. Be neither an enchanter, nor an astrologer, nor a purifier, nor be willing to took at these things, for out of all these idolatry is engendered. My child, be not a liar, since a lie leads to theft. Be neither money-loving, nor vainglorious, for out of all these thefts are engendered. My child, be not a murmurer, since it leads the way to blasphemy. Be neither self-willed nor evil-minded, for out of all these blasphemies are engendered.

Rather, be meek, since the meek shall inherit the earth. Be long-suffering and pitiful and guileless and gentle and good and always trembling at the words which you have heard. You shall not exalt yourself, nor give over-confidence to your soul. Your soul shall not be joined with lofty ones, but with just and lowly ones shall it have its intercourse. Accept whatever happens to you as good, knowing that apart from God nothing comes to pass.

Chapter 4. Various Precepts.

My child, remember night and day him who speaks the word of God to you, and honor him as you do the Lord. For wherever the lordly rule is uttered, there is the Lord. And seek out day by day the faces of the saints, in order that you may rest upon their words. Do not long for division, but rather bring those who contend to peace. Judge righteously, and do not respect persons in reproving for transgressions. You shall not be undecided whether or not it shall be. Be not a stretcher forth of the hands to receive and a drawer of them back to give. If you have anything, through your hands you shall give ransom for your sins. Do not hesitate to give, nor complain when you give; for you shall know who is the good repayer of the hire.

Do not turn away from him who is in want; rather, share all things with your brother, and do not say that they are your own. For if you are partakers in that which is immortal, how much more in things which are mortal? Do not remove your hand from your son or daughter; rather, teach them the fear of God from their youth. Do not enjoin anything in your bitterness upon your bondman or maidservant, who hope in the same God, lest ever they shall fear not God who is over both; for he comes not to call according to the outward appearance, but to them whom the Spirit has prepared. And you bondmen shall be subject to your masters as to a type of God, in modesty and fear. You shall hate all hypocrisy and everything which is not pleasing to the Lord. Do not in any way forsake the commandments of the Lord; but keep what you have received, neither adding thereto nor taking away therefrom. In the Church you shall acknowledge your transgressions, and you shall not come near for your prayer with an evil conscience. This is the way of life.

Chapter 5. The Way of Death.

And the way of death is this: First of all it is evil and accursed: murders, adultery, lust, fornication, thefts, idolatries, magic arts, witchcrafts, rape, false witness, hypocrisy, double-heartedness, deceit, haughtiness, depravity, self-will, greediness, filthy talking, jealousy, over-confidence, loftiness, boastfulness; persecutors of the good, hating truth, loving a lie, not knowing a reward for righteousness, not cleaving to good nor to righteous judgment, watching not for that which is good, but for that which is evil; from whom meekness and endurance are far, loving vanities, pursuing revenge, not pitying a poor man, not laboring for the afflicted, not knowing Him Who made them, murderers of children, destroyers of the handiwork of God, turning away from him who is in want, afflicting him who is distressed, advocates of the rich, lawless judges of the poor, utter sinners. Be delivered, children, from all these.

Chapter 6. Against False Teachers, and Food Offered to Idols.

See that no one causes you to err from this way of the Teaching, since apart from God it teaches you. For if you are able to bear the entire yoke of the Lord, you will be perfect; but if you are not able to do this, do what you are able. And concerning food, bear what you are able; but against that which is sacrificed to idols be exceedingly careful; for it is the service of dead gods.

Chapter 7. Concerning Baptism.

And concerning baptism, baptize this way: Having first said all these things, baptize into the name of the Father, and of the Son, and of the Holy Spirit, in living water. But if you have no living water, baptize into other water; and if you cannot do so in cold water, do so in warm. But if you have neither, pour out water three times upon the head into the name of Father and Son and Holy Spirit. But before the baptism let the baptizer fast, and the baptized, and whoever else can; but you shall order the baptized to fast one or two days before.

Chapter 8. Fasting and Prayer (the Lord's Prayer).

But let not your fasts be with the hypocrites, for they fast on the second and fifth day of the week. Rather, fast on the fourth day and the Preparation (Friday). Do not pray like the hypocrites, but rather as the Lord commanded in His Gospel, like this:

> Our Father who art in heaven, hallowed be Thy name. Thy kingdom come. Thy will be done on earth, as it is in heaven. Give us today our daily (needful) bread, and forgive us our debt as we also forgive our debtors. And bring us not into temptation, but deliver us from the evil one (or, evil); for Thine is the power and the glory for ever.

Pray this three times each day.

Chapter 9. The Eucharist.

Now concerning the Eucharist, give thanks this way. First, concerning the cup: We thank thee, our Father, for the holy vine of David Thy servant, which You madest known to us through Jesus Thy Servant; to Thee be the glory for ever. And concerning the broken bread: We thank Thee, our Father, for the life and knowledge which You madest known to us through Jesus Thy Servant to Thee be the glory for ever. Even as this broken bread was scattered over the hills, and was gathered together and became one, so let Thy Church be gathered together from the ends of the earth into Thy kingdom; for Thine is the glory and the power through Jesus Christ for ever.

But let no one eat or drink of your Eucharist, unless they have been baptized into the name of the Lord; for concerning this also the Lord has said, "Give not that which is holy to the dogs."

Chapter 10. Prayer after Communion.

But after you are filled, give thanks this way: We thank Thee, holy Father, for Thy holy name which You didst cause to tabernacle in our hearts, and for the knowledge and faith and immortality, which You madest known to us through Jesus Thy Servant; to Thee be the glory for ever. Thou, Master almighty, didst create all things for Thy name's sake; Thou gavest food and drink to men for enjoyment, that they might give thanks to Thee; but to us You didst freely give spiritual food and drink and life eternal through Thy Servant.

Before all things we thank Thee that You are mighty; to Thee be the glory for ever. Remember, Lord, Thy Church, to deliver it from all evil and to make it perfect in Thy love, and gather it from the four winds, sanctified for Thy kingdom which Thou have prepared for it; for Thine is the power and the glory for ever. Let grace come, and let this world pass away. Hosanna to the God of David! If any one is holy, let him come; if any one is not so, let him repent. Maranatha. Amen. But permit the prophets to make thanksgiving as much as they desire.

Chapter 11. Concerning Teachers, Apostles, and Prophets.

Whosoever, therefore, comes and teaches you all these things that have been said before, receive him. But if the teacher himself turns and teaches another doctrine to the destruction of this, hear him not. But if he teaches so as to increase righteousness and the knowledge of the Lord, receive him as the Lord. But concerning the apostles and prophets, act according to the decree of the Gospel. Let every apostle who comes to you be received as the Lord. But he shall not remain more than one day; or two days, if there's a need. But if he remains three days, he is a false prophet. And when the apostle goes away, let him take nothing but bread until he lodges.

If he asks for money, he is a false prophet. And every prophet who speaks in the Spirit you shall neither try nor judge; for every sin shall be forgiven, but this sin shall not be forgiven. But not every one who speaks in the Spirit is a prophet; but only if he holds the ways of the Lord. Therefore from their ways shall the false prophet and the prophet be known. And every prophet who orders a meal in the Spirit does not eat it, unless he is indeed a false prophet. And every prophet who teaches the truth, but does not do what he teaches, is a false prophet. And every prophet, proved true, working unto the mystery of the Church in the world, yet not teaching others to do what he himself does, shall not be judged among you, for with God he has his judgment; for so did also the ancient prophets. But whoever says in the Spirit, Give me money, or something else, you shall not listen to him. But if he tells you to give for others' sake who are in need, let no one judge him.

Chapter 12. Reception of Christians.

But receive everyone who comes in the name of the Lord, and prove and know him afterward; for you shall have understanding right and left. If he who comes is a wayfarer, assist him as far as you are able; but he shall not remain with you more than two or three days, if need be. But if he wants to stay with you, and is an artisan, let him work and eat. But if he has no trade, according to your understanding, see to it that, as a Christian, he shall not live with you idle. But if he wills not to do, he is a Christ-monger. Watch that you keep away from such.

Chapter 13. Support of Prophets.

But every true prophet who wants to live among you is worthy of his support. So also a true teacher is himself worthy, as the workman, of his support. Every first-fruit, therefore, of the products of wine-press and threshing-floor, of oxen and of sheep, you shall take and give to the prophets, for they are your high priests. But if you have no prophet, give it to the poor. If you make a batch of dough, take the first-fruit and give according to the commandment. So also when you open a jar of wine or of oil, take the first-fruit and give it to the prophets; and of money (silver) and clothing and every possession, take the first-fruit, as it may seem good to you, and give according to the commandment.

Chapter 14. Christian Assembly on the Lord's Day.

But every Lord's day gather yourselves together, and break bread, and give thanksgiving after having confessed your transgressions, that your sacrifice may be pure. But let no one who is at odds with his fellow come together with you, until they be reconciled, that your sacrifice may not be profaned. For this is that which was spoken by the Lord: "In every place and time offer to me a pure sacrifice; for I am a great King, says the Lord, and my name is wonderful among the nations."

Chapter 15. Bishops and Deacons; Christian Reproof.

Appoint, therefore, for yourselves, bishops and deacons worthy of the Lord, men meek, and not lovers of money, and truthful and proved; for they also render to you the service of prophets and teachers. Therefore do not despise them, for they are your honored ones, together with the prophets and teachers. And reprove one another, not in anger, but in peace, as you have it in the Gospel. But to anyone that acts amiss against another, let no one speak, nor let him hear anything from you until he repents. But your prayers and alms and all your deeds so do, as you have it in the Gospel of our Lord.

Chapter 16. Watchfulness; the Coming of the Lord.

Watch for your life's sake. Let not your lamps be quenched, nor your loins unloosed; but be ready, for you know not the hour in which our Lord will come. But come together often, seeking the things which are befitting to your souls: for the whole time of your faith will not profit you, if you are not made perfect in the last time.

For in the last days false prophets and corrupters shall be multiplied, and the sheep shall be turned into wolves, and love shall be turned into hate; for when lawlessness increases, they shall hate and persecute and betray one another, and then shall appear the world-deceiver as Son of God, and shall do signs and wonders, and the earth shall be delivered into his hands, and he shall do iniquitous things which have never yet come to pass since the beginning. Then shall the creation of men come into the fire of trial, and many shall be made to stumble and shall perish; but those who endure in their faith shall be saved from under the curse itself. And then shall appear the signs of the truth: first, the sign of an outspreading in heaven, then the sign of the sound of the trumpet. And third, the resurrection of the dead -- yet not of all, but as it is said: "The Lord shall come and all His saints with Him." Then shall the world see the Lord coming upon the clouds of heaven.

Gospel of Thomas
(50 – 140 A.D.)

The Gospel According to Thomas, commonly shortened to the Gospel of Thomas, is a well-preserved early Christian, non-canonical sayings-gospel which many scholars believe provides insight into the oral gospel traditions. It was discovered near Nag Hammadi, Egypt, in December 1945, in one of a group of books known as the Nag Hammadi library. The Gospel of Thomas was found among a collection of fifty-two writings that included, in addition to an excerpt from Plato's *Republic*, gospels claiming to have been written by Jesus' disciple Philip. Scholars have speculated that the works were buried in response to a letter from Bishop Athanasius, who for the first time declared a strict canon of Christian scripture.

The Gospel of Thomas is very different in tone and structure from other New Testament Apocrypha and the four Canonical Gospels. Unlike the canonical Gospels, it is not a narrative account of the life of Jesus; instead, it consists of *logia* (sayings) attributed to Jesus, sometimes stand-alone, sometimes embedded in short dialogues or parables.. Since its discovery, many scholars have seen it as evidence in support of the existence of the so-called Q source, which might have been very similar in its form as a collection of sayings of Jesus without any accounts of his deeds or his life and death, a so-called "sayings gospel".

Bishop Eusebius included it among a group of books that he believed to be not only spurious, but "the fictions of heretics". However, it is not clear whether he was referring to this Gospel of Thomas or one of the other texts attributed to Thomas.[20]

Summary notation: The Gospel of Thomas mentions many parables by Jesus. Bishop Eusebius and others believed it to be heretical. It suggests that God and Christ are one and indicates that some are elected. Due to the length of the manuscript, only key excerpts or talking points are presented for discussion. Please note sections omitted in the early manuscript.

:

---

[20] http://en.wikipedia.org/wiki/Gospel_of_Thomas

Excerpts from the Gospel of Thomas

[... sections omitted.].

(19) Jesus said, "Blessed is he who came into being before he came into being. If you become my disciples and listen to my words, these stones will minister to you. For there are five trees for you in Paradise which remain undisturbed summer and winter and whose leaves do not fall. Whoever becomes acquainted with them will not experience death."

[... sections omitted.].

(30) Jesus said, "Where there are three gods, they are gods. Where there are two or one, I am with him."

[... sections omitted.].

(39) Jesus said, "The pharisees and the scribes have taken the keys of knowledge (gnosis) and hidden them. They themselves have not entered, nor have they allowed to enter those who wish to. You, however, be as wise as serpents and as innocent as doves."

[... sections omitted.].

(49) Jesus said, "Blessed are the solitary and elect, for you will find the kingdom. For you are from it, and to it you will return."

[... sections omitted.].

Sophia of Jesus Christ (*Gnostic*)
(50 – 200 A.D.)

The Sophia of Jesus Christ[21] is one of many Gnostic tractates from the Nag Hammadi codices, discovered in Egypt in 1945. The Coptic manuscript itself has been dated to the 4th century, however, it is complemented by a few fragments in Greek dating from the 3rd century, implying an earlier date. The text has strong similarities to the *Epistle of Eugnostos*, which is also found in the Nag Hammadi codices, but with a Christian framing added, and expanding it somewhat. The debate about dating is critical, since some argue that it reflects the "*true, recorded, sayings*" of Jesus, which is possible if they were to be dated as far back as the 1st century. Others argue that they are, in fact, considerably later, and constitute an unreliable secondary source (at best *post facto* hearsay).

Most scholars argue that the text is of Gnostic origin, based on the similarities between the mystical teachings found in the text itself and standard Gnostic themes. Highly mystical, the content of this text concerns creation of gods, angels, and the universe with an emphasis on infinite and metaphysical truth. The translation of "The Sophia of Jesus Christ" (also sometimes titled, "The Wisdom of Jesus Christ") is derived from two separately preserved copies of the text. The first copy is in Nag Hammadi Codex III (NHC III); a second copy of this text was preserved in the *Berlin Gnostic Codex*. A third fragment of the text in Greek was also found among the *Oxyrhynchus papyrus* documents. Thus we have three distinct copies of this scripture attested from three separate ancient sources, two in Coptic, one in Greek.

Summary notation: *The **Sophia of Jesus Christ** was condemned by the early Church. They believed that its Gnostic teachings and feminist wording were heretical. Only key excerpts or talking points are presented for discussion. Please note sections omitted in the early manuscript.*

---

[21] http://en.wikipedia.org/wiki/Sophia_of_jesus_Christ

Excerpts from Sophia of Jesus Christ

[... sections omitted.].

After he rose from the dead, his twelve disciples and seven women continued to be his followers, and went to Galilee onto the mountain called "Divination and Joy". When they gathered together and were perplexed about the underlying reality of the universe and the plan, and the holy providence, and the power of the authorities, and about everything the Savior is doing with them in the secret of the holy plan, the Savior appeared - not in his previous form, but in the invisible spirit. And his likeness resembles a great angel of light. But his resemblance I must not describe. No mortal flesh could endure it, but only pure, perfect flesh, like that which he taught us about on the mountain called "Of the Olives" in Galilee.

[... sections omitted.].

The Savior said: "He Who Is is ineffable. No principle knew him, no authority, no subjection, nor any creature from the foundation of the world until now, except he alone, and anyone to whom he wants to make revelation through him who is from First Light. From now on, I am the Great Savior. For he is immortal and eternal. Now he is eternal, having no birth; for everyone who has birth will perish. He is unbegotten, having no beginning; for everyone who has a beginning has an end. Since no one rules over him, he has no name; for whoever has a name is the creation of another."

[... sections omitted.].

"And his consort is the Great Sophia, who from the first was destined in him for union by Self-begotten Father, from Immortal Man, who appeared as First and divinity and kingdom, for the Father, who is called 'Man, Self-Father', revealed this. And he created a great aeon, whose name is 'Ogdoad', for his own majesty.

[... sections omitted.].

The Holy One said to him: "I want you to know that First Man is called 'Begetter, Self-perfected Mind'. He reflected with Great Sophia, his consort, and revealed his first-begotten, androgynous son. His male name is designated 'First Begetter, Son of God', his female name, 'First Begettress Sophia, Mother of the Universe'. Some call her 'Love'. Now First-begotten is called 'Christ'. Since he has authority from his father, he created a multitude of angels without number for retinue from Spirit and Light."

[... sections omitted.].

The perfect Savior said: "Whoever has ears to hear, let him hear. The first aeon is that of Son of Man, who is called 'First Begetter', who is called 'Savior', who has appeared. The second aeon (is) that of Man, who is called 'Adam, Eye of Light'. That which embraces these is the aeon over which there is no kingdom, (the aeon) of the Eternal Infinite God, the Self-begotten aeon of the aeons that are in it, (the aeon) of the immortals, whom I described earlier, (the aeon) above the Seventh, that appeared from Sophia, which is the first aeon.

[... sections omitted.].

The Perfect Savior said to them: "I want you to know that Sophia, the Mother of the Universe and the consort, desired by herself to bring these to existence without her male (consort). But by the will of the Father of the Universe, that his unimaginable goodness might be revealed, he created that curtain between the immortals and those that came afterward, that the consequence might follow ... every aeon and chaos - that the defect of the female might appear, and it might come about that Error would contend with her. And these became the curtain of spirit. From the aeons above the emanations of Light, as I have said already, a drop from Light and Spirit came down to the lower regions of Almighty in chaos, that their molded forms might appear from that drop, for it is a judgment on him, Arch-Begetter, who is called 'Yaldabaoth'.

That drop revealed their molded forms through the breath, as a living soul. It was withered and it slumbered in the ignorance of the soul. When it became hot from the breath of the Great Light of the Male, and it took thought, (then) names were received by all who are in the world of chaos, and all things that are in it through that Immortal One, when the breath blew into him. But when this came about by the will of Mother Sophia - so that Immortal Man might piece together the garments there for a judgment on the robbers - he then welcomed the blowing of that breath; but since he was soul-like, he was not able to take that power for himself until the number of chaos should be complete, (that is,) when the time determined by the great angel is complete.

Epistle of Barnabas
(80 – 120 A.D.)

The Epistle of Barnabas (Greek: Επιστολή Βαρνάβα, Hebrew Βαρνάβα, : איגרת בארנבס‎) is a Greek epistle containing twenty-one chapters, preserved complete in the 4th century *Codex Sinaiticus* where it appears at the end of the New Testament. It is traditionally ascribed to Barnabas who is mentioned in the Acts of the Apostles, although some ascribe it to another Apostolic Father of the same name, "*Barnabas of Alexandria*", or simply attribute it to an unknown early Christian teacher.

The most complete text is in the *Codex Sinaiticus (=S; 4th century)* and the *Codex Hierosolymitanus (=H; 11th century)*, which are usually in agreement on variant readings. A truncated form of the text in which Polycarp's letter to the Philippians 1.1–9.2 continues with Barnabas 5.7a and following, without any indication of the transition, survives in nine Greek manuscripts *(=G; from 11th century onward)* and often agrees with the old Latin translation *(=L)* against S and H.

Toward the end of the 2nd century Clement of Alexandria cites the *Epistle.* It is also appealed to by Origen of Alexandria. Eusebius, the first major Church historian, however, recorded objection to it in his Antilegomena:[22] It was probably written between the years 70 – 131 and addressed to Christian Gentiles. In 16.3–4, the Epistle reads:

> "Furthermore he says again, 'Behold, those who tore down this temple will themselves build it.' It is happening. For because of their fighting it was torn down by the enemies. And now the very servants of the enemies will themselves rebuild it."

This passage clearly places Barnabas after the destruction of the

---

[22] Written texts whose authenticity or value is disputed including the Epistle of James, the Epistle of Jude, 2 Peter, 2 and 3 John, the Apocalypse of John, the Gospel of the Hebrews, the Apocalypse of Peter, the Acts of Paul, the Shepherd of Hermas, the Epistle of Barnabas and the Didache.

Second Temple in A.D. 70. But it also places Barnabas before the Bar Kochba Revolt of A.D. 132, after which there could have been no hope that the Romans would help to rebuild the temple[23]

In Chapter 19, verse 4, it has a brief comment about the homosexuality and pedophilia which had already been documented in the Church at the time of this writing between approximately 80-120 A.D. where the unknown author states, *"thou shall not corrupt boys"*.

---

*Summary notation: The **Epistle of Barnabas** could have easily been a viable candidate for canonization; however, due to issues from Church fathers such as Eusebius and Origen with its "authenticity" and authorship, it was passed over. Only key excerpts or talking points are presented for discussion. Please note sections omitted in the early manuscript.*

Excerpts from the Epistle of Barnabas

[... sections omitted.].

Chapter 5

1) For to this end the Lord endured to deliver His flesh unto corruption, that by the remission of sins we might be cleansed, which cleansing is through the blood of His sprinkling.

2) For the scripture concerning Him containeth some things relating to Israel, and some things relating to us. And it speaketh thus; He was wounded for your transgressions, and He hath been bruised for our sins; by His stripes we were healed. As a sheep He was led to slaughter, as a lamb is dumb before his shearer.

[... sections omitted.].

6) Understand ye. The prophets, receiving grace from Him, prophesied concerning Him. But He Himself endured that He might destroy death and show forth the resurrection of the dead, for that

---

[23] http://en.wikipedia.org/wiki/Epistle_of_Barnabas

He must needs be manifested in the flesh;

7) that at the same time He might redeem the promise made to the fathers, and by preparing the new people for Himself might show, while He was on earth, that having brought about the resurrection He will Himself exercise judgment.

8) Yea and further, He preached teaching Israel and performing so many wonders and miracles, and He loved him exceedingly.

9) And when He chose His own apostles who were to proclaim His Gospel,who that He might show that He came not to call the righteous but sinners were sinners above every sin, then He manifested Himself to be the Son of God.

10) For if He had not come in the flesh neither would men have looked upon Him and been saved, forasmuch as when they look upon the sun that shall cease to be, which is the work of His own hands, they cannot face its rays.

11) Therefore the Son of God came in the flesh to this end, that He might sum up the complete tale of their sins against those who persecuted and slew His prophets.

12) To this end therefore He endured. For God saith of the wounds of His flesh that they came from them; When they shall smite their own shepherd, then shall the sheep of the flock be lost.

13) But He Himself desired so to suffer; for it was necessary for Him to suffer on a tree. For he that prophesied said concerning Him, Spare My soul form the sword; and, Pierce My flesh with nails, for the congregations of evil-doers have risen up against Me.

14) And again He saith; Behold I have given My back to stripes, and My cheeks to smitings, and My face did I set as a hard rock.

[... sections omitted.].

Chapter 7

[... sections omitted.].

3) But moreover when crucified He had vinegar and gall given Him to drink. Hear how on this matter the priests of the temple have revealed. Seeing that there is a commandment in scripture, Whatsoever shall not observe the fast shall surely die, the Lord commanded, because He was in His own person about to offer the vessel of His Spirit a sacrifice for our sins, that the type also which was given in Isaac who was offered upon the alter should be fulfilled.

[... sections omitted.].

6) Attend ye to the commandments which He gave. Take two goats, fair and alike, and offer them, and let the priest take the one for a whole burnt offering for sins.

[... sections omitted.].

9) What then meaneth this? Give heed. The one at the alter, and the other accursed. And moreover the accursed one crowned. For they shall see Him in that day wearing the long scarlet robe about His flesh, and shall say, Is not this He, Whom once we crucified and set at nought and spat upon; verily this was He, Who then said that He was the Son of God.

[... sections omitted.].

Chapter 12

1) In like manner again He defineth concerning the cross in another prophet, who saith; And when shall these things be accomplished? saith the Lord. Whenever a tree shall be bended and stand upright, and whensoever blood shall drop from a tree. Again thou art taught concerning the cross, and Him that was to be crucified.

[... sections omitted.].

10) Behold again it is Jesus, not a son of man, but the Son of God, and He was revealed in the flesh in a figure. Since then men will say that Christ is the son of David, David himself prophesieth being afraid and understanding the error of sinners; The Lord said unto my Lord, Sit thou on My right hand until I set thine enemies for a footstool under Thy feet.

11) And again thus saith Isaiah; The Lord said unto my Christ the Lord, of whose right hand I laid hold, that the nations should give ear before Him, and I will break down the strength of kings. See how David calleth Him Lord, and calleth Him not Son.

[... sections omitted.].

Chapter 18

[... sections omitted.].

8) Again the prophet saith; Behold I have set Thee to be a light unto the Gentiles, that Thou shouldest be for salvation unto the ends of the earth; thus saith the Lord that ransomed thee, even God.

9) Again the prophet saith; The Spirit of the Lord is upon Me, wherefore He anointed Me to preach good tidings to the humble; He hath sent Me to heal them that are broken-hearted, to preach release to the captives and recovery of sight to the blind, to proclaim the acceptable year of the Lord and the day of recompense, to comfort all that mourn.

[... sections omitted.].

Chapter 19

[... sections omitted.].

2) Thou shalt love Him that made thee, thou shalt fear Him that created thee, thou shalt glorify Him that redeemed thee from death; thou shalt be simple in heart and rich in spirit; thou shalt not cleave to those who walk the way of death; thou shalt hate everything that is not pleasing to God; thou shalt hate all hypocrisy; thou shalt never forsake the commandments of the Lord.

3) Thou shalt not exalt thyself, but shalt be lowly minded in all things. Thou shalt not assume glory to thyself. Thou shalt not entertain a wicked design against thy neighbor; thou shalt not admit boldness into thy soul.

4) Thou shalt not commit fornication, thou shalt not commit adultery, thou shalt not corrupt boys. The word of God shall not come forth from thee where any are unclean. Thou shalt not make a difference in a person to reprove him for a transgression. Thou shalt be meek, thou shalt be quiet, thou shalt be fearing the words which thou hast heard. Thou shalt not bear a grudge against thy brother.

[... sections omitted.]

Gospel of Peter
(100 – 130 A.D.)

The Gospel of Peter[24] (Greek: κατά Πέτρον ευαγγέλιον), or Gospel according to Peter, is one of the non-Canonical gospels which were rejected as apocryphal by the Church Fathers and the Catholic Church's synods of Carthage and Rome, which established the New Testament canon,. A major focus of the surviving fragment of the Gospel of Peter is the passion narrative, which is notable for ascribing responsibility for the crucifixion of Jesus to Herod Antipas rather than to Pontius Pilate. The Gospel of Peter explicitly claims to be the work of the Apostle Peter:

> "And I with my companions was grieved; and being wounded in mind we hid ourselves:" — *GoP*, 7.
> "But I Simon Peter and Andrew my brother took our nets and went to the sea;" — *GoP*, 14.

However scholars generally agree that Gospel of Peter is **pseudepigraphical** (*bearing the name of an author who did not actually compose the text*). The Gospel of Peter was recovered in 1886, by the French archaeologist, Urbain Bouriant, in the modern Egyptian city of Akhmim (*sixty miles north of Nag Hammadi*). The 8th or 9th century manuscript had been respectfully buried with an Egyptian monk. The fragmentary Gospel of Peter was the first non-canonical gospel to have been rediscovered, preserved in the dry sand of Egypt. Publication, delayed by Bouriant until 1892, occasioned intense interest. From the passion sequence that is preserved, it is clear that the gospel was a narrative gospel, but whether a complete narrative similar to the canonical gospels or simply a Passion cannot be said.

One of the chief characteristics of the work is that Pontius Pilate is exonerated of all responsibility for the Crucifixion, the onus being laid upon Herod, the scribes, and other Jews, who pointedly do not "*wash their hands*" like Pilate. The opening leaves of the text are lost, so the Passion begins abruptly with the trial of Jesus before Pilate, after Pilate has washed his hands, and closes with its

---

[24] http://en.wikipedia.org/wiki/Gospel_of_peter

unusual and detailed version of the watch set over the tomb and the resurrection. The Gospel of Peter is more detailed in its account of the events after the Crucifixion than any of the canonical gospels, and it varies from the canonical accounts in numerous details: Herod gives the order for the execution, not Pilate, who is exonerated; Joseph (*of Arimathea, which place is not mentioned*) has been acquainted with Pilate; in the darkness that accompanied the crucifixion, "*many went about with lamps, supposing that it was night, and fell down*".

Christ's cry from the cross, in Matthew given as *Eli, Eli, lama sabachthani?* which Matthew explains as meaning "*My God, my God, why hast thou forsaken me?*" is reported in Peter as "*My power, my power, thou hast forsaken me*". Immediately after, Peter states that "*when he had said it he was taken up*", suggesting that Jesus did not actually die. This, together with the claim that on the cross Jesus "*remained silent, as though he felt no pain*", has led many early Christians to accuse the text of docetism[25].

Summary notation: *Due to it's importance and historical significance to the early Church, the* **Gospel of Peter** *is presented in it's entirety; It* **states that the Jews, not Pilate, was responsible for Christ's death.**

The Manuscript in its Entirety

Chapter 1

… but none of t[he] Jews washed their hands, neither Herod nor [o]ne of his judges. A[nd] since they did [not] want to wash, Pilate sto[o]d up. Then, Herod the king ordered that the Lord be taken away, saying to them, "*Do what I ordered you to do to him.*"

Chapter 2

Joseph, the friend of Pilate and the Lord, was there. And knowing that they were about to crucify him, he went to Pilate and

---

[25]http://web.archive.org/web/20071016164346/http://gospels.net/translations/akhmimpetertranslation.html

requested the body of the Lord for burial. And sending to Herod, Pilate requested the body. And Herod said, "*Brother Pilate, even if nobody had requested him, we would have buried him because the Sabbath is coming on. For it is written in the law, "Do not let the sun go down on the one who is being executed."*" And he delivered him to the people before the day of unleavened bread, their feast.

Chapter 3

Then, taking the Lord and running around him, they pushed him and said, "*Let us push the son of God since we control his freedom.*" And they put a purple robe around him and sat him down on the seat of judgment, saying, "*Judge justly, king of Israel!*" And someone who was carrying a crown of thorns put it on the head of the Lord. And others who were standing around spat in his eyes and others struck his cheeks. Others pierced him and some of them scourged him, saying, "*Let us honor the son of God with this honor!*"

Chapter 4

And they brought along two criminals and crucified the Lord in between them. But he kept silent as though he had no pain. And when they set the cross upright they wrote on it, "This is the king of Israel." And after they had put his clothes in front of him, they divided them and cast lots for them. Then, one of these criminals reprimanded them, saying, "*We have suffered this way because of the wicked things we did, but he, the one who is the savior of humanity, what wrong has he done to you?*" And being angry at him, they ordered that the criminal's legs not be broken so that he would die being tortured.

Chapter 5

Then, it was midday and darkness covered all of Judea. And they became afraid because the sun was no longer shining and he was still alive. <For> it is written for them, "*Do not let the sun go down on the one who is being executed.*" And one of them said, "*Make him drink bile with vinegar.*" And after mixing it, they made him drink. And they fulfilled everything and brought their sins to completion on their heads. Many people were walking around with lamps because they thought it was night <and> they were tripping. And the Lord cried out, saying, "*My power, my power, you have forsaken me.*" And after saying this, he was taken up. And at that same hour, the veil of the temple in Jerusalem was torn in two.

Chapter 6

And then, they pulled the nails out of the hands of the Lord and set him on the ground. And the whole ground shook and great fear came over them. Then, the sun shone <again> and it was found to be the ninth hour. So, the Jews rejoiced and gave his body to Joseph that he might bury it, since he had seen the great things he had done. Taking the Lord, he washed him and wrapped him in linen and took him to his own tomb which is called the garden of Joseph

Chapter 7

Then, the Jews and the elders and priests, knowing what evil they had done to themselves, began to mourn and say, "Curse our sins. The judgment and the end of Jerusalem are near." At the time, I was grieving with my friends. We were hurting and could not understand what had happened. For we were being sought by them as criminals and as people who wanted to burn the temple. We fasted about all these things and sat grieving and crying day and night until the Sabbath.

Chapter 8

Then, the scribes and Pharisees and elders gathered together when they heard that all the people were grumbling and mourning, saying, "*If these great signs took place at his death, see how righteous he was.*" The elders were afraid and went to Pilate, urging him and saying, "*Give us soldiers so that we can guard the tomb for three d[ays], and prevent his disciples from coming and stealing him and causing the people to claim that he was raised from the dead and make trouble for us.*"

Then, Pilate gave them the centurion Petronius with soldiers to guard the tomb. And the elders and scribes went with them to the tomb. And after they had rolled a great stone into place with the centurions and soldiers, everyone there stood at the entrance of the tomb. They put seven seals on it and set up a tent to keep watch.

Chapter 9

When the Sabbath morning dawned, a crowd came from Jerusalem and the surrounding area that they might see that the tomb had been sealed. But during the night in which the Lord's day dawned, while the soldiers were stationed in pairs to keep watch, a great voice came from heaven. And they saw the heavens open and two men descend from there, having a great radiance and approaching the tomb. Then, the same stone which had been put in the entrance rolled away from it and gave way partially. And the tomb was opened and both young men went in.

Chapter 10

Then, seeing this, these soldiers woke up the centurions and elders, for they themselves were all there to keep watch. And while they were describing what they had seen, again they saw three men coming out from the tomb, two supporting the other and a cross following them. The heads of the two reached up to the heavens and the head of the one they were leading by the hand went beyond the heavens. And they heard a voice from heaven saying, "Did you preach to those who sleep?" Obediently, there was heard from the cross, "Yes."

Chapter 11

They then determined with each other to go and reveal these things to Pilate. While they were still considering these things, the heavens opened again and a man appeared, descending and going into the tomb. When those around the centurion that night saw these things, they hurried to Pilate after being sent from the tomb they were guarding. And they explained everything they had seen, being extremely anxious and saying, "*Truly, this was the son of God!*" When Pilate replied, he said, "*I am clean from the blood of the son of God, this was considered by you.*" Then everybody urged him and made him promise to command the centurion and the soldiers not to tell what they had seen. "For it is better for us," they said, "to be guilty of this great sin before God and not to fall into the hands of the people of Judea and be stoned." So Pilate ordered the centurion and the soldiers not to talk.

Chapter 12

Since Mary Magdalene, the disciple of the Lord, was afraid of the Jews who were inflamed with anger, she had not done what women usually do at the tombs of those who have died and are loved by them. At the dawn of the Lord's day, however, she took her friends with her and went to the tomb where he had been put. And they were afraid that the Jews might see. They said, "Even if we were not able to weep and mourn on the day he was crucified, let us now do these things at his tomb. But who will roll away the stone which was placed in the entrance for us, so that we can to go in to him and do the things we should? For the stone is great and we are afraid that someone might see us. And if we cannot go in, let us put what we brought in his memory at the entrance. Let us weep and mourn until we get to our houses."

Chapter 13

When they arrived, they found that the tomb had been opened. And going in, they stooped over and there was a beautiful man sitting <in> the middle of the tomb and he had an extremely bright robe wrapped around him. Whoever he was, he said to them, "Why did you come? Whom are you seeking? Is it not the one who was crucified? He has risen and gone out. If you do not believe, however, bend down and look there at the place he lay because he is not there. For he has risen and gone out there, where he was sent." Then, the terrified women fled.

Chapter 14

It was the last day of the feast of the unleavened bread and many people were going out, returning to their houses since the festival was over. But we, the twelve disciples of the Lord, were weeping and grieving, and although everyone was mourning because of what had happened, each departed for his own house. But I, Simon Peter, and my brother Andrew took our nets and went out to the sea.

Shepherd of Hermas
(100 – 150 A.D.)

The Shepherd of Hermas (Greek: Ποιμὴν τοῦ Ἑρμᾶ; sometimes just called *The Shepherd*) is a Christian literary work of the 2nd century, considered a valuable book by many Christians, and considered canonical scripture by some of the early Church fathers such as Irenaeus.

Textual criticism, the nature of the theology, and the author's apparent familiarity with the *Book of Revelation* and other Johannine texts, are thought to set the date of composition in the 2nd century. However, several ancient witnesses support an early dating and there is internal evidence for the place and date of this work in the language and theology of the work. Since Paul sent greetings to a Hermas, a Christian of Rome (*Romans* 16:14), a minority have followed Origen of Alexandria's opinion that he was the author.

The Shepherd had great authority in the 2nd and 3rd centuries. It was bound as part of the New Testament in the *Codex Sinaiticus*, and it was listed between the Acts of the Apostles and the Acts of Paul in the stichometrical list of the *Codex Claromontanus*. The work comprises five visions, twelve mandates, and ten parables. It relies on allegory and pays special attention to the Church, calling the faithful to repent of the sins that have harmed it. The shepherd is one of the meanings that was probably attached to some figurines of the *Good Shepherd* as well as a symbol for Christ.

In parable 5, the author mentions a *Son of God*, as a virtuous man filled with a Holy "pre-existent spirit" and adopted as the Son. In the 2nd century, adoptionism (the view that Jesus Christ was only a mortal man) was one of two competing doctrines about Jesus' true nature, the other being that he pre-existed as a divine spirit (Logos); Christ's identity with the Logos (Jn 1:1) was affirmed in 325 at theFirst Council of Nicaea.

It has been pointed out that "*It refers to the 'Son of God' (a much older Egyptian and Babylonian and Persian deist concept*) but never uses the word 'Christ,' 'Jesus,' nor 'Christian'. This, at least a hundred and fifty years after the... Christ child.[26]

Summary notation: *Due to it's importance, usage and historical significance to the early Church, **Shepherd of Hermas** is included in some detail but not entirely due to its length. It does reference Christ as the **Son of God** in many passages.. Due to the length of the manuscript, only key excerpts or talking points are presented for discussion. Please note sections omitted in the early manuscript.*

Excerpts from the Shepherd of Hermas

Vision 1

1:1 The master, who reared me, had sold me to one Rhoda in Rome. After many years, I met her again, and began to love her as a sister.

1:2 After a certain time I saw her bathing in the river Tiber; and I gave her my hand, and led her out of the river. So, seeing her beauty, I reasoned in my heart, saying, "*Happy were I, if I had such an one to wife both in beauty and in character.*" I merely reflected on this and nothing more.

1:3 After a certain time, as I was journeying to Cumae, and glorifying God's creatures for their greatness and splendor and power, as I walked I fell asleep. And a Spirit took me, and bore me away through a pathless tract, through which no man could pass: for the place was precipitous, and broken into clefts by reason of the waters. When then I had crossed the river, I came into the level country, and knelt down, and began to pray to the Lord and to confess my sins.

[… sections omitted.].

3:4 Behold, the God of Hosts, Who by His invisible and mighty power and by His great wisdom created the world, and by His glorious purpose clothed His creation with comeliness, and by His strong word fixed the heaven, and founded the earth upon the waters, and by His own wisdom and providence formed His holy

---

[26] http://en.wikipedia.org/wiki/The_Shepherd_of_Hermas

Church, which also He blessed-behold, He removeth the heavens and the mountains and the hills and the seas, and all things are made level for His elect, that He may fulfill to them the promise which He promised with great glory and rejoicing, if so be that they shall keep the ordinances of God, which they received, with great faith.

[... sections omitted.].

2:8 For the Lord swear concerning His Son, that those who denied their Lord should be rejected from their life, even they that are now about to deny Him in the coming days; but to those who denied Him aforetime, to them mercy was given of His great loving kindness.

[... sections omitted.].

2:11 All these things which had taken place his master heard, and again rejoiced greatly at his deed. So the master called together again his friends and his son, and announced to them the deed that he had done with regard to his dainties which he had received; and they still more approved of his resolve, that his servant should be made joint-heir with his son."

[... sections omitted.]

5:2 The estate is this world, and the lord of the estate is He that created all things, and set them in order, and endowed them with power; and the servant is the Son of God, and the vines are this people whom He Himself planted;

5:3 and the fences are the [*holy*] angels of the Lord who keep together His people; and the weeds, which are plucked up from the vineyard, are the transgressions of the servants of God; and the dainties which He sent to him from the feast are the commandments which He gave to His people through His Son; and the friends and advisers are the holy angels which first created; and the absence of the master is the time which remaineth over until His coming."

[... sections omitted.]

6:2 *"Because,"* saith he, God planted the vineyard, that is, He created the people, and delivered them over to His Son. And the Son placed the angels in charge of them, to watch over them; and the Son Himself cleansed their sins, by laboring much and enduring many toils; for no one can dig without toil or labor.

6:3 Having Himself then cleansed the sins of His people, He showed them the paths of life, giving them the law which He received from His Father. Thou seest," saith he, "*that He is Himself Lord of the people, having received all power from His Father.*

6:4 But how that the lord took his son and the glorious angels as advisers concerning the inheritance of the servant, listen.

[... sections omitted.].

11:1 And after he had completed the interpretations of all the rods, he saith unto me; "*Go, and tell all men to repent, and they shall live unto God; for the Lord in His compassion sent me to give repentance to all, though some of them do not deserve it for their deeds; but being long-suffering the Lord willeth them that were called through His Son to be saved.*"

[... sections omitted.]

12:4 *"Didst thou see,"* saith he, "*that the stones which came through the gate have gone to the building of the tower, but those which came not through it were cast away again to their own place?*" "I saw, Sir," say I. "*Thus,*" saith he, "*no one shall enter into the kingdom of God, except he receive the name of His Son.* "

12:5 For if thou wisht to enter into any city, and that city is walled all round and has one gate only, canst thou enter into that city except through the gate which it hath?" "*Why, how*, Sir," say I, "*is it possible otherwise?*" "If then thou canst not enter into the city except through the gate itself, even so," saith he, "a man cannot enter into the kingdom of God except by the name of His Son that is beloved by Him.

12:6 *Didst thou see,"* saith he, "*the multitude that is building the* *tower?"* "I saw it, Sir," say I. *"They,"* saith he, *"are all glorious angels. With these then the Lord is walled around. But the gate is the Son of God; there is this one entrance only to the Lord. No one then shall enter in unto Him otherwise than through His Son".*

[... sections omitted.]

13:5 For this cause thou seest the tower made a single stone with the rock. So also they that have believed in the Lord through His Son and clothe themselves in these spirits, shall become one spirit and one body, and their garments all of one color. But such persons as bear the names of the virgins have their dwelling in the tower."

[... sections omitted.]

The Apocolypse of Peter
(100 – 150 A.D.)

The Apocalypse of **Peter** *(or Revelation of Peter)* is an early Christian text of the 2nd century and an example of apocalyptic literature with Hellenistic literature overtones. It is not in the Bible today, but is mentioned in **the Muratorian fragment, the oldest surviving list of New Testament books,** as no longer being allowed to be read in Church. The text is extant in two incomplete versions of a lost Greek original, one Koine Greek, and an Ethiopic version, which diverge considerably.

The Greek manuscript was unknown until it was discovered during excavations directed by Sylvain Grébaut during the 1886–87 season in a desert necropolis at Akhmim in Upper Egypt. The fragment consisted of parchment leaves of the Greek version that had been carefully deposited in the grave of a Christian monk of the 8th or 9th century. The manuscript is in the Egyptian Museum in Cairo. The Ethiopic version was discovered in 1910.

Before that, the work had been known only through copious quotes in early Christian writings. In addition, some common lost source had been necessary to account for closely parallel passages in such apocalyptic Christian literature as the Apocalypse of Esdras, the Apocalypse of Paul, and the Passion of Saint Perpetua.[27].

The Revelation of Peter affords the earliest embodiment in Christian literature of those pictorial presentations of heaven and hell which have exercised so widespread and enduring an influence. It has, in its imagery, little or no kinship with the Book of Daniel, the Book of Enoch, or the Revelation of S. John.

Its only parallels in canonical scripture, with the notable exception of the Second Epistle of Peter, are to be found in Isaiah lxvi., 24, Mark ix., 44, 48, and the parable of Dives and Lazarus in Luke xvi., 19. It is indeed Judaic in the severity of its morality and even in its phraseology (*cf. the frequent use of the word righteous, and the idea that God and not Christ will come to judge sinners*). The true

---

[27] http://en.wikipedia.org/wiki/Apocalypse_of_Peter

parallels for, if not the sources of, its imagery of the rewards and punishments which await men after death are to be found in Greek beliefs which have left their traces in such passages as the Vision of Er at the end of Plato's *Republic*.[28]

Summary notation: *Due to it's importance and historical significance to the early Church, the **Apocolypse of Peter** is presented in it's entirety; It mentions the lake of fire and the major sins causing men and women to burn including **homosexuality:***

The Manuscript in its Entirety

1 . . . many of them will be false prophets, and will teach divers ways and doctrines of perdition: but these will become sons of perdition.

3. And then God will come unto my faithful ones who hunger and thirst and are afflicted and purify their souls in this life; and he will judge the sons of lawlessness.

4. And furthermore the Lord said: Let us go into the mountain: Let us pray.. And going with him, we, the twelve disciples, begged that he would show us one of our brethren, the righteous who are gone forth out of the world, in order that we might see of what manner of form they are, and having taken courage, might also encourage the men who hear us.

6. And as we prayed, suddenly there appeared two men standing before the Lord towards the East, on whom we were not able to look;

7. for there came forth from their countenance a ray as of the sun, and their raiment was shining, such as eye of man never saw; for no mouth is able to express or heart to conceive the glory with which they were endued, and the beauty of their appearance.

8. And as we looked upon them, we were astounded; for their bodies were whiter than any snow and ruddier than any rose;

9. and the red thereof was mingled with the white, and I am utterly unable to express their beauty;

10. for their hair was curly and bright and seemly both on their face and shoulders, as it were a wreath woven of spikenard and

---

[28] http://www.earlychristianwritings.com/info/apocalypsepeter.html

divers-coloured flowers, or like a rainbow in the sky, such was their seemliness.

11. Seeing therefore their beauty we became astounded at them, since they appeared suddenly.

12. And I approached the Lord and said: Who are these?

13. He saith to me: These are your brethren the righteous, whose forms ye desired to see.

14. And I said to him: And where are all the righteous ones and what is the aeon in which they are and have this glory?

15. And the Lord showed me a very great country outside of this world, exceeding bright with light, and the air there lighted with the rays of the sun, and the earth itself blooming with unfading flowers and full of spices and plants, fair-flowering and incorruptible and bearing blessed fruit.

16. And so great was the perfume that it was borne thence even unto us.

17. And the dwellers in that place were clad in the raiment of shining angels and their raiment was like unto their country; and angels hovered about them there.

18. And the glory of the dwellers there was equal, and with one voice they sang praises alternately to the Lord God, rejoicing in that place.

19. The Lord saith to us: This is the place of your high-priests, the righteous men.

20. And over against that place I saw another, squalid, and it was the place of punishment; and those who were punished there and the punishing angels had their raiment dark like the air of the place.

21. And there were certain there hanging by the tongue: and these were the blasphemers of the way of righteousness; and under them lay fire, burning and punishing them.

22. And there was a great lake, full of flaming mire, in which were certain men that pervert righteousness, and tormenting angels afflicted them.

23. And there were also others, women, hanged by their hair over that mire that bubbled up: and these were they who adorned themselves for adultery; and the men who mingled with them in the defilement of adultery, were hanging by the feet and their heads in that mire. And I said: I did not believe that I should come into this place.

24. And I saw the murderers and those who conspired with them, cast into a certain strait place, full of evil snakes, and smitten by those beasts, and thus turning to and fro in that punishment; and worms, as it were clouds of darkness, afflicted them. And the souls of the murdered stood and looked upon the punishment of those murderers and said: O God, thy judgment is just.

25. And near that place I saw another strait place into which the gore and the filth of those who were being punished ran down and became there as it were a lake: and there sat women having the gore up to their necks, and over against them sat many children who were born to them out of due time, crying; and there came forth from them sparks of fire and smote the women in the eyes: and these were the accursed who conceived and caused abortion.

26. And other men and women were burning up to the middle and were cast into a dark place and were beaten by evil spirits, and their inwards were eaten by restless worms: and these were they who persecuted the righteous and delivered them up.

27. And near those there were again women and men gnawing their own lips, and being punished and receiving a red-hot iron in their eyes: and these were they who blasphemed and slandered the way of righteousness.

28. And over against these again other men and women gnawing their tongues and having flaming fire in their mouths: and these were the false witnesses.

29. And in a certain other place there were pebbles sharper than swords or any spit, red-hot, and women and men in tattered and filthy raiment rolled about on them in punishment: and these were the rich who trusted in their riches and had no pity for orphans and widows, and despised the commandment of God.

30. And in another great lake, full of pitch and blood and mire bubbling up, there stood men and women up to their knees: and these were the usurers and those who take interest on interest.

31. An other men and women were being hurled down from a great cliff and reached the bottom, and again were driven by those who were set over them to climb up upon the cliff, and thence were hurled down again, and had no rest from this punishment: and these were they who defiled their bodies acting as women; and the women who were with them were those who lay with one another as a man with a woman.

32. And alongside of that cliff there was a place full of much fire, and there stood men who with their own hands had made for themselves carven images instead of God. And alongside of these were other men and women, having rods and striking each other and never ceasing from such punishment.

33. And others again near them, women and men, burning and turning themselves and roasting: and these were they that leaving the way of God.

Secret Book of James (*Gnostic*)
(100 – 150 A.D.)

The **Apocryphon of James**, also known by the translation of its title - the **Secret Book of James**, is a pseudonymous text amongst the New Testament Apocrypha. It describes the secret teachings of Jesus to Peter and James, given after the Resurrection but before the Ascension.

Many of the sayings appear to be shared with the canonical Gospels, and the text includes this reference to other sayings: "*It sufficed for some persons to pay attention to the teaching and understand 'The Shepherds' and 'The Seed' and 'The Building' and 'The Lamps of the Virgins' and 'The Wage of the Workers' and 'The Double Drachma' and 'The Woman'.*" The references to salvation through "*the cross*" seem to imply familiarity with Paul's letters, or at least his teachings.

But its introduction says, "*And five hundred and fifty days after he arose from the dead, we said to him: ...*", which is considerably longer than the forty days which Luke's Acts of the Apostles gives for the Ascension. Some have felt that this implies that the relationship of the Apocryphon of James with the canon is through oral tradition, and that the community which wrote it rejected or else did not know Luke-Acts[29].

The Apocryphon (*Secret Book*) of James is probably the earliest example of a long-standing Gnostic tradition that the risen Jesus delivered secret teachings to his disciples. The gospel is framed within the format of a letter from James, the brother of Jesus, to a recipient whose name cannot be determined due to the fragmentary condition of the first page of the papyrus codex (*known as the Jung Codex from the Nag Hammadi library*). The MS is a Coptic translation of a Greek original, though the author claims to have written in Hebrew.

Jesus speaks of the importance of being "*full*" of the Spirit, for with it comes the knowledge (*gnosis*) of God's kingdom necessary to achieve salvation. After the revelation to James and Peter, James sends the apostles off to their missionary destinations, then travels

---

[29] http://en.wikipedia.org/wiki/Apocryphon_of_James

to Jerusalem. Peter is given secondary importance in the dialogue, possibly representative of the developing conflict with the orthodox Church.

Secret James shows a familiarity with the known parables of Jesus, including a list of seven that exist in Matthew and/or Luke. Yet the text betrays no knowledge of the details of the passion accounts, even claiming Jesus to have been buried *"in the sand"* following his crucifixion.

Thus, the body of Secret James likely dates back to the beginning of the second century when, like the Gospel of John, the early Sayings traditions were developed into discourses and dialogues. The narrative framework, consisting of the first two and last two chapters, is most likely a secondary development designed to utilize apostolic authority; the use of the term *"Savior"* in these chapters dates them slightly later than the body of the work. [30]

Summary notation: Due to it's importance and historical significance to the early Church, the Secret Book of James is presented in it's entirety. It was condemned as a Gnostic heresy. Please note sections omitted or missing in the early manuscript.

The Manuscript in its Entirety

James writes to [...]: Peace be with you from Peace, love from Love, grace from Grace, faith from Faith, life from Holy Life!
Since you asked that I send you a secret book which was revealed to me and Peter by the Lord, I could not turn you away or gainsay (?) you; but I have written it in the Hebrew alphabet and sent it to you, and you alone. But since you are a minister of the salvation of the saints, endeavor earnestly and take care not to rehearse this text to many; That the Savior did not wish to tell to all of us, his twelve disciples. But blessed will they be who will be saved through the faith of this discourse.

I also sent you, ten months ago, another secret book which the Savior had revealed to me. Under the circumstances, however, regard that one as revealed to me, James; but this one ...
[untranslatable fragments] ...

---

[30] http://www.maplenet.net/~trowbridge/secjames.htm

the twelve disciples were all sitting together and recalling what the Savior had said to each one of them, whether in secret or openly, and putting it in books. But I was writing that which was in my book - lo, the Savior appeared, after departing from us while we gazed after him. And five hundred and fifty days since he had risen from the dead, we said to him, "*Have you departed and removed yourself from us?*" But Jesus said, "*No, but I shall go to the place from whence I came. If you wish to come with me, come!*"

They all answered and said, "*If you bid us, we come.*" He said, "*Verily I say unto you, no one will ever enter the kingdom of heaven at my bidding, but (only) because you yourselves are full. Leave James and Peter to me, that I may fill them.*" And having called these two, he drew them aside and bade the rest occupy themselves with that which they were about.

The Savior said, "*You have received mercy ...*

[7 lines missing]

Do you not, then, desire to be filled? And your heart is drunken; do you not, then, desire to be sober? Therefore, be ashamed! Henceforth, waking or sleeping, remember that you have seen the Son of Man, and spoken with him in person, and listened to him in person. Woe to those who have seen the Son of Man; blessed will they be who have not seen the man, and they who have not consorted with him, and they who have not spoken with him, and they who have not listened to anything from him; yours is life! Know, then, that he healed you when you were ill, that you might reign. Woe to those who have found relief from their illness, for they will relapse into illness. Blessed are they who have not been ill, and have known relief before falling ill; yours is the kingdom of God. Therefore, I say to you, 'Become full, and leave no space within you empty, for he who is coming can mock you.'"

Then Peter replied, "*Lo, three times you have told us, 'Become full'; but we are full.*" The Savior answered and said, "*For this cause I have said to you, 'Become full,' that you may not be in want. They who are in want, however, will not be saved. For it is good to be full, and bad to be in want. Hence, just as it is good that you be in want and, conversely, bad that you be full, so he who is full is in want, and he who is in want does not* *become full as he who is in want becomes full, and he who has been filled, in turn attains due perfection. Therefore, you must be in want while it is possible to fill you, and be full while it is possible for you to be in want, so that you may be able to fill yourselves the more. Hence, become full of the Spirit, but be in want of reason, for reason <belongs to> the soul; in turn, it is (of the nature of) soul."*

But I answered and said to him, *"Lord, we can obey you if you wish, for we have forsaken our fathers and our mothers and our villages, and followed you. Grant us, therefore, not to be tempted by the devil, the evil one."*

The Lord answered and said, *"What is your merit if you do the will of the Father and it is not given to you from him as a gift while you are tempted by Satan? But if you are oppressed by Satan, and persecuted, and you do his (i.e., the Father's) will, I say that he will love you, and make you equal with me, and reckon you to have become beloved through his providence by your own choice. So will you not cease loving the flesh and being afraid of sufferings? Or do you not know that you have yet to be abused and to be accused unjustly; and have yet to be shut up in prison, and condemned unlawfully, and crucified <without> reason, and buried as I myself, by the evil one? Do you dare to spare the flesh, you for whom the Spirit is an encircling wall? If you consider how long the world existed <before> you, and how long it will exist after you, you will find that your life is one single day, and your sufferings one single hour. For the good will not enter into the world. Scorn death, therefore, and take thought for life! Remember my cross and my death, and you will live!"*

But I answered and said to him, *"Lord, do not mention to us the cross and death, for they are far from you."* The Lord answered and said, *"Verily, I say unto you, none will be saved unless they believe in my cross. But those who have believed in my cross, theirs is the kingdom of God. Therefore, become seekers for death, like the dead who seek for life; for that which they seek is revealed to them. And what is there to trouble them? As for you, when you examine death, it will teach you election. Verily, I say unto you, none of those who fear death will be saved; for the kingdom belongs to those who put themselves to death. Become better than I; make yourselves like the son of the Holy Spirit!"*

"Become earnest about the word! For as to the word, its first part is faith; the second, love; the third, works; for from these comes life. For the word is like a grain of wheat; when someone had sown it, he had faith in it; and

when it had sprouted, he loved it, because he had seen many grains in place of one. And when he had worked, he was saved, because he had prepared it for food, (and) again he left (some) to sow. So also can you yourselves receive the kingdom of heaven; unless you receive this through knowledge, you will not be able to find it. "

"Therefore, I say to you, be sober; do not be deceived! And many times have I said to you all together, and also to you alone, James, have I said, 'Be saved!' And I have commanded you to follow me, and I have taught you what to say before the archons. Observe that I have descended and have spoken and undergone tribulation, and carried off my crown after saving you. For I came down to dwell with you, so that you in turn might dwell with me. And, finding your houses unceiled, I have made my abode in the houses that could receive me at the time of my descent. "

"Therefore, trust in me, my brethren; understand what the great light is. The Father has no need of me, - for a father does not need a son, but it is the son who needs the father - though I go to him. For the Father of the Son has no need of you. " "Hearken to the word, understand knowledge, love life, and no one will persecute you, nor will anyone oppress you, other than you yourselves. "

"O you wretches; O you unfortunates; O you pretenders to the truth; O you falsifiers of knowledge; O you sinners against the Spirit: can you still bear to listen, when it behooved you to speak from the first? Can you still bear to sleep, when it behooved you to be awake from the first, so that the kingdom of heaven might receive you? Verily, I say unto you, had I been sent to those who listen to me, and had I spoken with them, I would never have come down to earth. So, then, be ashamed for these things. "

"Behold, I shall depart from you and go away, and do not wish to remain with you any longer, just as your yourselves have not wished it. Now, therefore, follow me quickly. This is why I say unto you, 'For your sakes I came down.' You are the beloved; you are they who will be the cause of life in many. Invoke the Father, implore God often, and he will give to you. Blessed is he who has seen you with Him when He was proclaimed among the angels, and glorified among the saints; yours is life. Rejoice, and be glad, as sons of God. Keep his will, that you may be saved; accept reproof from me and save yourselves. I intercede on your behalf with the Father, and he will forgive you much. "

And when we had heard these words, we became glad, for we had been grieved at the words we have mentioned before. But when he saw us rejoicing, he said, *"Woe to you who lack an advocate! Woe to you who stand in need of grace! Blessed will they be who have spoken out and obtained grace for themselves. Liken yourselves to foreigners; of what sort are they in the eyes of your city? Why are you disturbed when you cast yourselves away of your own accord and separate yourselves from your city? Why do you abandon your dwelling place of your own accord, making it ready for those who want to dwell in it? O you outcasts and fugitives, woe to you, for you will be caught! Or do you perhaps think that the Father is a lover of mankind, or that he is won over without prayers, or that he grants remission to one on another's behalf, or that he bears with one who asks? - For he knows the desire, and also what it is that the flesh needs! - (Or do you think) that it is not this (flesh) that desires the soul? For without the soul, the body does not sin, just as the soul is not saved without the spirit. But if the soul is saved (when it is) without evil, and the spirit is also saved, then the body becomes free from sin. For it is the spirit that raises the soul, but the body that kills it; that is, it is it (the soul) which kills itself. Verily, I say unto you, he will not forgive the soul the sin by any means, nor the flesh the guilt; for none of those who have worn the flesh will be saved. For do you think that many have found the kingdom of heaven? Blessed is he who has seen himself as a fourth one in heaven!"*

When we heard these words, we were distressed. But when he saw that we were distressed, he said, "*For this cause I tell you this, that you may know yourselves. For the kingdom of heaven is like an ear of grain after it had sprouted in a field. And when it had ripened, it scattered its fruit and again filled the field with ears for another year. You also, hasten to reap an ear of life for yourselves, that you may be filled with the kingdom!*"

"*And as long as I am with you, give heed to me, and obey me; but when I depart from you, remember me. And remember me because when I was with you, you did not know me. Blessed will they be who have known me; woe to those who have heard and have not believed! Blessed will they be who have not seen, yet have believed!*"

"*And once more I prevail upon you, for I am revealed to you building a house which is of great value to you when you find shelter beneath it, just as it will be able to stand by your neighbors' house when it threatens to fall. Verily, I say unto you, woe to those for whose sakes I was sent down to this place; blessed will they be who ascend to the Father! Once more I reprove you, you who are; become like those who are not, that you may be with those who are not. Do not make the kingdom of heaven a desert within you. Do not be proud because of the light that illumines, but be to yourselves as I myself am to you. For your sakes I have placed myself under the curse, that you may be saved."*

But Peter replied to these words and said, *"Sometimes you urge us on to the kingdom of heaven, and then again you turn us back, Lord; sometimes you persuade and draw us to faith and promise us life, and then again you cast us forth from the kingdom of heaven."*

But the Lord answered and said to us, *"I have given you faith many times; moreover, I have revealed myself to you, James, and you (all) have not known me. Now again, I see you rejoicing many times; and when you are elated at the promise of life, are you yet sad, and do you grieve, when you are instructed in the kingdom? But you, through faith and knowledge, have received life. Therefore, disdain the rejection when you hear it, but when you hear the promise, rejoice the more. Verily, I say unto you, he who will receive life and believe in the kingdom will never leave it, not even if the Father wishes to banish him. These are the things that I shall tell you so far; now, however, I shall ascend to the place from whence I came. But you, when I was eager to go, have cast me out, and instead of accompanying me, you have pursued me. But pay heed to the glory that awaits me, and, having opened your heart, listen to the hymns that await me up in the heavens; for today I must take (my place at) the right hand of the Father. But I have said (my) last word to you, and I shall depart from you, for a chariot of spirit has borne me aloft, and from this moment on, I shall strip myself, that I may clothe myself. But give heed; blessed are they who have proclaimed the Son before his descent, that when I have come, I might ascend (again). Thrice blessed are they who were proclaimed by the Son before they came to be, that you might have a portion among them."*

Having said these words, he departed. But we bent (our) knee(s), I and Peter, and gave thanks, and sent our heart(s) upwards to heaven. We heard with our ears, and saw with our eyes, the noise of wars, and a trumpet blare, and a great turmoil. And when we had passed beyond that place, we sent our mind(s) farther upwards, and saw with our eyes and heard with our ears hymns, and angelic benedictions, and angelic rejoicing. And heavenly majesties were singing praise, and we, too, rejoiced.

After this again, we wished to send our spirit upward to the Majesty, and after ascending, we were not permitted to see or hear anything, for the other disciples called us and asked us, *"What did you hear from the Master. And what has he said to you? And where did he go?"* But we answered them, *"He has ascended, and has given us a pledge, and promised life to us all, and revealed to us children (?) who are to come after us, after bidding us love them, as we would be saved for their sakes."*

Gospel of Mary (*Gnostic*)
(120 – 180 A.D.)

The Gospel of Mary is often interpreted as a Gnostic text. According to Pheme Perkins, on the basis of thirteen works, the Gospel follows a format similar to other known Gnostic dialogues which contain a revelation discourse framed by narrative elements. The dialogues are generally concerned with the idea of the Savior as reminder to human beings of their bond with God and true identity, as well as the realization of the believer that redemption consists of the return to God and liberty from matter after death. The Gospel of Mary contains two of these discourses (*7.1–9.4 and 10.10–17.7*) including addresses to New Testament characters (*Peter, Mary, Andrew and Levi*) and an explanation of a sin of adultery (encouragement toward an ascetic lifestyle) which also suit a Gnostic interpretation. Scholars do not always agree which of the New Testament people named Mary is the central character of the *Gospel of Mary.* Some have suggested that she may represent Mary the mother of Jesus.

Arguments in favor of Mary Magdalene are based on her status as a known follower of Jesus, the tradition of being the first witness of his resurrection, and her appearance in other early Christian writings. She is mentioned as accompanying Jesus on his journeys (*Luke 8:2*) and is listed in the Gospel of Matthew as being present at his crucifixion (*Matthew 27:56*). In the Gospel of John, she is recorded as the first witness of Jesus' resurrection (*John 20:14–16*); (*Mark 16:9 later manuscripts*).[31]

In her introduction in *The Complete Gospels*, Karen King names the manuscripts available for the Gospel of Mary, "Only three fragmentary manuscripts are known to have survived into the modern period, two third-century fragments (*P. Rylands 463 and P. Oxyrhynchus 3525*) published in 1938 and 1983, and a longer fifth-century Coptic translation (*Berolinensis Gnosticus 8052,1*) published in 1955." . . . the Gospel of Mary communicates a vision that the world is passing away, not toward a new creation or a new world order, but toward the dissolution of an illusory chaos of suffering,

---

[31] http://en.wikipedia.org/wiki/Gospel_of_Mary

death, and illegitimate domination. The Savior has come so that each soul might discover its own true spiritual nature, its "root" in the Good, and return to the place of eternal rest beyond the constraints of time, matter, and false morality.[32]

Summary notation: *Due to its short length and reception in the early Church, the* **Gospel of Mary** *is presented in its entirety; However, it was declared heretical due to the Gnostic content. The author claims that the savior said "there is no such thing as sin" and puts mind over spirit.. Please note sections missing in the early manuscript.*

The Manuscript in its Entirety

James writes to [...]: Peace be with you from Peace, love from…

[Pages 1-6 are missing]

"… Will m[a]tter then be utterly [destr]oyed or not?"The Savior replied, "*Every nature, every modeled form, every creature, exists in and with each other. They will dissolve again into their own proper root. For the nature of matter is dissolved into what belongs to its nature. Anyone with two ears able to hear should listen!*"

Then Peter said to him, "*You have been explaining every topic to us; tell us one other thing. What is the sin of the world?*"The Savior replied, "**There is no such thing as sin; rather you yourselves are what produces sin when you act in accordance with the nature of adultery, which is called 'sin.' For this reason, the Good came among you, pursuing (the good) which belongs to every nature. It will set it within its root.**"

Then he continued. He said, "*This is why you get si[c]k and die: because [you love] what de[c]ei[ve]s [you]. [Anyone who] thinks should consider (these matters)! "[Ma]tter gav[e bi]rth to a passion which has no Image because it derives from what is contrary to nature. A disturbing confusion then occurred in the whole body.* That is why I told you, '*Become content at heart, while also remaining discontent and disobedient; indeed become contented and agreeable (only) in the presence of that other*

---

[32] http://www.earlychristianwritings.com/gospelmary.html

Image of nature.' Anyone with two ears capable of hearing should listen!"When the Blessed One had said these things, he greeted them all. *"Peace be with you!"* he said. *"Acquire my peace within yourselves!"*

Be on your guard so that no one deceives you by saying, 'Look over here!' or 'Look over there!' For the child of true Humanity exists within you. Follow it! Those who search for it will find it."Go then, preac[h] the good news about the Realm. [Do] not lay down any rule beyond what I determined for you, nor promulgate law like the lawgiver, or else you might be dominated by it."

After he had said these things, he departed from themBut they were distressed and wept greatly. "How are we going to go out to the rest of the world to announce the good news about the Realm of the child of true Humanity?" they said. "If they did not spare him, how will they spare us?"Then Mary stood up. She greeted them all, addressing her brothers and sisters, "Do not weep and be distressed nor let your hearts be irresolute. For his grace will be with you all and will shelter you. Rather we should praise his greatness, for he has prepared us and made us true Human beings."

When Mary had said these things, she turned their heart [to]ward the Good, and they began to deba[t]e about the wor[d]s of [the Savior].Peter said to Mary, "*Sister, we know that the Savior loved you more than all other women. Tell us the words of the Savior that you remember, the things which you know that we don't because we haven't heard them."Mary responded, "I will teach you about what is hidden from you." And she began to speak these words to them.*

She said, "*I saw the Lord in a vision and I said to him, 'Lord, I saw you today in a vision.'He answered me, 'How wonderful you are for not wavering at seeing me! For where the mind is, there is the treasure.'I said to him, 'So now, Lord, does a person who sees a vision see it <with> the soul <or> with the spirit?'*

The Savior answered, 'A person does not see with the soul or with the spirit. 'Rather the mind, which exists between these two, sees the vision an[d] that is w[hat ...]'

[Pages 11-14 are missing.]

And Desire said, *'I did not see you go down, yet now I see you go up. So why do you lie since you belong to me?'"* The soul answered, *'I saw you. You did not see me nor did you know me. You (mis)took the garment (I wore) for my (true) self. And you did not recognize me.'*"After it had said these things, it left rejoicing greatly"Again, it came to the third Power, which is called 'Ignorance.' [It] examined the soul closely, saying, *'Where are you going? You are bound by wickedness. Indeed you are bound! Do not judge!'*

"And the soul said, *'Why do you judge me, since I have not passed judgement? I have been bound, but I have not bound (anything). They did not recognize me, but I have recognized that the universe is to be dissolved, both the things of earth and those of heaven.'*"When the soul had brought the third Power to naught, it went upward and saw the fourth Power. It had seven forms. The first form is darkness; the second is desire; the third is ignorance; the fourth is zeal for death; the fifth is the realm of the flesh; the sixth is the foolish wisdom of the flesh; the seventh is the wisdom of the wrathful person. These are the **seven Powers of Wrath** "They interrogated the soul, *'Where are you coming from, human-killer, and where are you going, space-conqueror?'*"The soul replied, saying, *'What binds me has been slain, and what surrounds me has been destroyed, and my desire has been brought to an end, and ignorance has died. In a [wor]ld, I was set loose from a world [an]d in a type, from a type which is above, and (from) the chain of forgetfulness which exists in time. From this hour on, for the time of the due season of the aeon, I will receive rest i[n] silence.'* "

After Mary had said these things, she was silent, since it was up to this point that the Savior had spoken to her. Andrew responded, addressing the brothers and sisters, *"Say what you will about the things she has said, but I do not believe that the S[a]vior said these things, f[or] indeed these teachings are strange ideas.'*Peter responded, bringing up similar concerns. He questioned them about the Savior: *"Did he, then, speak with a woman in private without our knowing about it? Are we to turn around and listen to her? Did he choose her over us?"* Then [M]ary wept and said to Peter, *"My brother Peter, what are you imagining? Do you think that I have thought up these things by myself in my heart or that I am telling lies about the Savior?"*

Levi answered, speaking to Peter, *"Peter, you have always been a wrathful person. Now I see you contending against the woman like the Adversaries. For if the Savior made her worthy, who are you then for your part to reject her?*

Assuredly the Savior's knowledge of her is completely reliable. That is why he loved her more than us. "Rather we should be ashamed. We should clothe ourselves with the perfect Human, acquire it for ourselves as he commanded us, and announce the good news, not laying down any other rule or law that differs from what the Savior said. "After [he had said these] things, they started going out [to] teach and to preach.

Dialogue of the Savior (*Gnostic*)
(120 – 180 A.D.)

The Dialogue of the Saviour is one of the New Testament Apocrypha texts that was found within the Nag Hammadi library of predominantly gnostic texts. The text appears only once in a single Coptic codex, and is **heavily damaged**. The surviving portions indicate that the general content is a dialogue with Jesus, in a similar manner to, and possibly based on, the Gospel of Thomas.

The text is somewhat peculiarly constructed, containing also a few large interruptions seemingly out of place within, and only superficially edited into, the dialogue. Starting with a series of questions ultimately concerning esoteric knowledge and its pursuit, the text abruptly turns to a description of the origin of the world, interrupted briefly by a return to dialogue. Having expounded the description of creation, it returns to the gnostic question and answer session about how to achieve salvation via gnosis, but is abruptly interrupted by a *natural history list* of the Four Elements, the powers of heaven and earth, and so forth.

After the history list, there is an *apocalyptic* vision, in which Didymus Judas Thomas, Mary, and Matthew, are shown hell from the safety of the edge of the earth, and an angel announces that the material world was an unintended evil creation (see Yaltabaoth). Finally, the text returns to the question-based dialogue.[33]

Our single surviving copy of the Dialogue of the Savior was discovered within the Coptic library at Nag Hammadi in 1945. Despite its badly damaged state, it represents an important stage of development in the Sayings Gospel tradition. The *"dialogue"* is an expansion of the pure sayings collections like the Gospel of Thomas or *Q*; the teachings of Jesus are narrated in response to questions from his disciples. This trend continued its development in the extended discourses of the Gospel of John. Although the sayings have parallels in all four canonical gospels as well as

---

[33] http://en.wikipedia.org/wiki/Dialogue_of_the_Saviour

Thomas, it is unlikely that the Dialogue is directly dependent upon any of them.

Summary notation: The Dialogue of the Savior was condemned as heretical. It is heavily damaged and, therefore, only key excerpts or talking points are presented for discussion: Note the damaged passages indicateing sections omitted or missing [...]

Excerpts from the Dialogue of the Savior

The Savior said to his disciples, "*Already the time has come, brothers, for us to abandon our labor and stand at rest. For whoever stands at rest will rest forever. And I say to you, be always above [...] time [...] you [...] be afraid of [...] you [...] anger is fearful [...] arouse anger [...] but since you have [...] they accepted these words concerning it with fear and trembling, and it set them up with governors, for from it nothing was forthcoming. But when I came, I opened the path, and I taught them about the passage which they will traverse, the elect and solitary, who have known the Father, having believed the truth and all the praises while you offered praise*".

"*So when you offer praise, do so like this: Hear us, Father, just as you heard your only-begotten son, and received him, and gave him rest from any [...] You are the one whose power [...] your armor [...] is [...] light [...] living [...] touch [...] the word [...] repentance [...] life [...] you. You are the thinking and the entire serenity of the solitary. Again: Hear us just as you heard your elect. Through your sacrifice, these will enter; through their good works, these have saved their souls from these blind limbs, so that they might exist eternally. Amen.*

[... sections omitted.].

Matthew said, "*Lord, I want to see that place of life, [the place] where there is no wickedness, but rather, there is pure light!*"The Lord said, "*Brother Matthew, you will not be able to see it as long as you are carrying flesh around.*" Matthew said, "*Lord, even if I will not be able to see it, let me know it!*" The Lord said, "*Everyone who has known himself has seen it in everything given to him to do, [...] and has come to [...] it in his goodness.*"

Judas responded, saying, "*Tell me, Lord, how it is that [...] which shakes the earth moves.* 'The Lord picked up a stone and held it in his hand, saying *"What am I holding in my hand?"* He said, *"It is a stone."* he said to them, *"That which supports the earth is that which supports the heaven. When a Word comes forth from the Greatness, it will come on what supports the heaven and the earth. For the earth does not move. Were it to move, it would fall. But it neither moves nor falls, in order that the First Word might not fail. For it was that which established the cosmos and inhabited it, and inhaled fragrance from it. For [...] which do not move, I [...] you, all the sons of men. For you are from that place. In the hearts of those who speak out of joy and truth, you exist. Even if it comes forth in the body of the Father among men, and is not received, still it [...] return to its place.*

Whoever does not know the work of perfection, knows nothing. If one does not stand in the darkness, he will not be able to see the light. If one does not understand how fire came into existence, he will burn in it, because he does not know the root of it. If one does not first understand water, he knows nothing. For what use is there for him to be baptized in it? If one does not understand how blowing wind came into existence, he will blow away with it. If one does not understand how body, which he bears, came into existence, he will perish with it. And how will someone who does not know the Son know the Father? And to someone who will not know the root of all things, they remain hidden. Someone who will not know the root of wickedness is no stranger to it. Whoever will not understand how he came will not understand how he will go, and he is no stranger to this cosmos which will [...], which will be humiliated."

Then he [...] Judas and Matthew and Mary [...] the edge of heaven and earth. And when he placed his hand upon them, they hoped that they might [...] it. Judas raised his eyes and saw an exceedingly high place, and he saw the place of the abyss below. Judas said to Matthew, *"Brother, who will be able to climb up to such a height or down to the bottom of the abyss? For there is a tremendous fire there, and something very fearful!"* At that moment, a Word came forth from it. As it stood there, he saw how it had come down. Then he said to it, *"Why have you come down?"*

And the Son of Man greeted them and said to them, *"A seed from a power was deficient, and it went down to the abyss of the earth. And the Greatness remembered it, and he sent the Word to it. It brought it up into his presence, so that the First Word might not fail."* Then his disciples were amazed at all the things he had said to them, and they accepted them on faith. And they concluded that it is useless to regard wickedness.

[... sections omitted.].

Matthew said, "*Tell me, Lord, how the dead die, and how the living live.*" The Lord said, "*You have asked me about a saying [...] which eye has not seen, nor have I heard it, except from you. But I say to you that when what invigorates a man is removed, he will be called 'dead'. And when what is alive leaves what is dead, what is alive will be called upon.*"

Judas said, "Why else, for the sake of truth, do they <die> and live?" The Lord said, "*Whatever is born of truth does not die. Whatever is born of woman dies.*" Mary said, "*Tell me, Lord, why I have come to this place to profit or to forfeit.*" The Lord said, "*You make clear the abundance of the revealer!*" Mary said to him, "Lord, is there then a place which is [...] or lacking truth?"

The Lord said, "*The place where I am not!*" Mary said, "Lord, you are fearful and wonderful, and [...] those who do not know you." Matthew said, "*Why do we not rest at once?*" The Lord said, "*When you lay down these burdens!*" Matthew said, "*How does the small join itself to the big?*" The Lord said, "*When you abandon the works which will not be able to follow you, then you will rest.*"

Mary said, "*I want to understand all things, just as they are!*"

The Lord said, "*He who will seek out life! For this is their wealth. For the [...] of this cosmos is [...], and its gold and its silver are misleading.*" His disciples said to him, "*What should we do to ensure that our work will be perfect?*" The Lord said to them, "*Be prepared in face of everything. Blessed is the man who has found [...] the contest [...] his eyes. Neither did he kill, nor was he killed, but he came forth victorious.*"

[... sections omitted.].

Judas said, "*Who forgives the works of whom? The works which [...] the cosmos [...] who forgives the works.*" The Lord said, "*Who [...]? It behooves whoever has understood the works to do the will of the Father. And as for you, strive to rid yourselves of anger and jealousy, and to strip yourselves of your [...], and not to*

Infancy Gospel of James
(140 – 170 A.D.)

The **Gospel of James**, also known as the Infancy Gospel of James or the Protoevangelium of James, is an apocryphal Gospel probably written about A.D. 145, which expands backward in time the infancy stories contained in the Gospels of Matthew and Luke, and presents a narrative concerning the birth and upbringing of Mary herself. It is the oldest source to assert the virginity of Mary not only prior to but during (*and after*) the birth of Jesus. The ancient manuscripts that preserve the book have different titles, including "*The Birth of Mary*", "*The Story of the Birth of Saint Mary, Mother of God,*" and "*The Birth of Mary; The Revelation of James.*

The document presents itself as written by James: "*I, James, wrote this history in Jerusalem.*" Thus the purported author is James, brother of Jesus, whom the text claims to be a son of Joseph from a prior marriage. Scholars have established that the work is pseude-pigraphical (not written by the person it is attributed to). That conclusion is based on the style of the language and the fact that the author describes certain activities as contemporary Jewish customs that probably did not exist. For example, the work suggests there were consecrated temple virgins in Judaism, similar to the Vestal Virgins in pagan Rome,[34]

> ***Summary notation:*** *Due to it's importance and historical significance to the early Church, the* ***Infancy Gospel of James*** *is presented in its entirely.*

Excerpts from the Infancy Gospel of James

Chapter 1

In the records of the twelve tribes of Israel was Joachim, a man rich exceedingly; and he brought his offerings double, saying: There shall be of my superabundance to all the people, and there shall be the offering for my forgiveness to the Lord for a propitiation for me.

---

[34] http://en.wikipedia.org/wiki/Gospel_of_James

For the great day of the Lord was at hand, and the sons of Israel were bringing their offerings. And there stood over against him Rubim, saying: It is not meet for thee first to bring thine offerings, because thou hast not made seed in Israel. And Joachim was exceedingly grieved, and went away to the registers of the twelve tribes of the people, saying: I shall see the registers of the twelve tribes of Israel, as to whether I alone have not made seed in Israel. And he searched, and found that all the righteous had raised up seed in Israel. And he called to mind the patriach Abraham, that in the last day God gave him a son Isaac. And Joachim was exceedingly grieved, and did not come into the presence of his wife; but he retired to the desert, and there pitched his tent, and fasted forty days and forty nights, saying in himself: I will not go down either for food or for drink until the Lord my God shall look upon me, and prayer shall be my food and drink.

Chapter 2

And his wife Anna mourned in two mournings, and lamented in two lamentations, saying: I shall bewail my widowhood; I shall bewail my childlessness. And the great day of the Lord was at hand; and Judith her maid-servant said: How long dost thou humiliate thy soul? Behold, the great day of the Lord is at hand, and it is unlawful for thee to mourn. But take this head-band, which the woman that made it gave to me; for it is not proper that I should wear it, because I am a maid-servant, and it has a royal appearance. And Anna said: Depart from me; for I have not done such things, and the Lord has brought me very low. I fear that some wicked person has given it to thee, and thou hast come to make me a sharer in thy sin. And Judith said: Why should I curse thee, seeing that the Lord hath shut thy womb, so as not to give thee fruit in Israel? And Anna was grieved exceedingly, and put off her garments of mourning, and cleaned her head, and put on her wedding garments, and about the ninth hour went down to the garden to walk. And she saw a laurel, and sat under it, and prayed to the Lord, saying: O God of our fathers, bless me and hear my prayer, as Thou didst bless the womb of Sarah, and didst give her a son Isaac.

Chapter 3

And gazing towards the heaven, she saw a sparrow's nest in the laurel, and made a lamentation in herself, saying: Alas! who begot me? and what womb produced me? because I have become a curse in the presence of the sons of Israel, and I have been reproached, and they have driven me in derision out of the temple of the Lord. Alas! to what have I been likened? I am not like the fowls of the heaven, because even the fowls of the heaven are productive before Thee, O Lord. Alas! to what have I been likened? I am not like the beasts of the earth, because even the beasts of the earth are productive before Thee, O Lord. Alas! to what have I been likened? I am not like these waters, because even these waters are productive before Thee, O Lord. Alas! to what have I been likened? I am not like this earth, because even the earth bringeth forth its fruits in season, and blesseth Thee, O Lord.

Chapter 4

And, behold, an angel of the Lord stood by, saying: Anna, Anna, the Lord hath heard thy prayer, and thou shalt conceive, and shall bring forth; and thy seed shall be spoken of in all the world. And Anna said: As the Lord my God liveth, if I beget either male or female, I will bring it as a gift to the Lord my God; and it shall minister to Him in holy things all the days of its life. And, behold, two angels came, saying to her: Behold, Joachim thy husband is coming with his flocks. For an angel of the Lord went down to him, saying: Joachim, Joachim, the Lord God hath heard thy prayer Go down hence; for, behold, thy wife Anna shall conceive. And Joachim went down and called his shepherds, saying: Bring me hither ten she-lambs without spot or blemish, and they shall be for the Lord my God; and bring me twelve tender calves, and they shall be for the priests and the elders; and a hundred goats for all the people. And, behold, Joachim came with his flocks; and Anna stood by the gate, and saw Joachim coming, and she ran and hung upon his neck, saying: Now I know that the Lord God hath blessed me exceedingly; for, behold the widow no longer a widow, and I the childless shall conceive. And Joachim rested the first day in his house.

Chapter 5

And on the following day he brought his offerings, saying in himself: If the Lord God has been rendered gracious to me, the plate on the priest's forehead will make it manifest to me. And Joachim brought his offerings, and observed attentively the priest's plate when he went up to the altar of the Lord, and he saw no sin in himself. And Joachim said: Now I know that the Lord has been gracious unto me, and has remitted all my sins. And he went down from the temple of the Lord justified, and departed to his own house. And her months were fulfilled, and in the ninth month Anna brought forth. And she said to the midwife: What have I brought forth? and she said: A girl. And said Anna: My soul has been magnified this day. And she laid her down. And the days having been fulfilled, Anna was purified, and gave the breast to the child, and called her name Mary.

Chapter 6

And the child grew strong day by day; and when she was six months old, her mother set her on the ground to try whether she could stand, and she walked seven steps and came into her bosom; and she snatched her up, saying: As the Lord my God liveth, thou shall not walk on this earth until I bring thee into the temple of the Lord. And she made a sanctuary in her bed-chamber, and allowed nothing common or unclean to pass through her. And she called the undefiled daughters of the Hebrews, and they led her astray. And when she was a year old, Joachim made a great feast, and invited the priests, and the scribes, and the elders, and all the people of Israel. And Joachim brought the child to the priests; and they blessed her, saying: O God of our fathers, bless this child, and give her an everlasting name to be named in all generations. And all the people said: So be it, so be it, amen. And he brought her to the chief priests; and they blessed her, saying: O God most high, look upon this child, and bless her with the utmost blessing, which shall be for ever. And her mother snatched her up, and took her into the sanctuary of her bed-chamber, and gave her the breast. And Anna made a song to the Lord God, saying: I will sing a song to the Lord my God, for He hath looked upon me, and hath taken away the reproach of mine enemies; and the Lord hath given the fruit of His righteousness, singular in its kind, and richly endowed before Him. Who will tell the sons of Rubim that Anna gives suck? Hear, hear, ye twelve tribes of Israel, that Anna gives suck. And she laid her to rest in the bed-chamber of her sanctuary, and went out and ministered unto them. And when the supper was ended, they went down rejoicing, and glorifying the God of Israel.

Chapter 7

And her months were added to the child. And the child was two years old, and Joachim said: Let us take her up to the temple of the Lord, that we may pay the vow that we have vowed, lest perchance the Lord send to us, and our offering be not received. And Anna said: Let us wait for the third year, in order that the child may not seek for father or mother. And Joachim said: So let us wait. And the child was three years old, and Joachim said: Invite the daughters of the Hebrews that are undefiled, and let them take each a lamp, and let them stand with the lamps burning, that the child may not turn back, and her heart be captivated from the temple of the Lord. And they did so until they went up into the temple of the Lord. And the priest received her, and kissed her, and blessed her, saying: The Lord has magnified thy name in all generations. In thee, on the last of the days, the Lord will manifest His redemption to the sons of Israel. And he set her down upon the third step of the altar, and the Lord God sent grace upon her; and she danced with her feet, and all the house of Israel loved her.

Chapter 8

And her parents went down marvelling, and praising the Lord God, because the child had not turned back. And Mary was in the temple of the Lord as if she were a dove that dwelt there, and she received food from the hand of an angel. And when she was twelve years old there was held a council of the priests, saying: Behold, Mary has reached the age of twelve years in the temple of the Lord. What then shall we do with her, test perchance she defile the sanctuary of the Lord? And they said to the high priest: Thou standest by the altar of the Lord; go in, and pray concerning her; and whatever the Lord shall manifest unto thee, that also will we do. And the high priest went in, taking the robe with the twelve bells into the holy of holies; and he prayed concerning her. And behold an angel of the Lord stood by him, saying unto him: Zacharias, Zacharias, go out and assemble the widowers of the people, and let them bring each his rod; and to whomsoever the Lord shall show a sign, his wife shall she be. And the heralds went out through all the circuit of Judaea, and the trumpet of the Lord sounded, and all ran.

Chapter 9

And Joseph, throwing away his axe, went out to meet them; and when they had assembled, they went away to the high priest, taking with them their rods. And he, taking the rods of all of them, entered into the temple, and prayed; and having ended his prayer, he took the rods and came out, and gave them to them: but there was no sign in them, and Joseph took his rod last; and, behold, a dove came out of the rod, and flew upon Joseph's head. And the priest said to Joseph, Thou hast been chosen by lot to take into thy keeping the virgin of the Lord. But Joseph refused, saying: I have children, and I am an old man, and she is a young girl. I am afraid lest I become a laughing-stock to the sons of Israel. And the priest said to Joseph: Fear the Lord thy God, and remember what the Lord did to Dathan, and Abiram, and Korah; how the earth opened, and they were swallowed up on account of their contradiction. And now fear, O Joseph, lest the same things happen in thy house. And Joseph was afraid, and took her into his keeping. And Joseph said to Mary: Behold, I have received thee from the temple of the Lord; and now I leave thee in my house, and go away to build my buildings, and I shall come to thee. The Lord will protect thee.

Chapter 10

And there was a council of the priests, saying: Let us make a veil for the temple of the Lord. And the priest said: Call to me the undefiled virgins of the family of David. And the officers went away, and sought, and found seven virgins. And the priest remembered the child Mary, that she was of the family of David, and undefiled before God. And the officers went away and brought her. And they brought them into the temple of the Lord. And the priest said: Choose for me by lot who shall spin the gold, and the white, and the fine linen, and the silk, and the blue, and the scarlet, and the true purple. And the true purple and the scarlet fell to the lot of Mary, and she took them, and went away to her house. And at that time Zacharias was dumb, and Samuel was in his place until the time that Zacharias spake. And Mary took the scarlet, and span it.

Chapter 11

And she took the pitcher, and went out to fill it with water. And, behold, a voice saying: Hail, thou who hast received grace; the Lord is with thee; blessed art thou among women! And she looked round, on the right hand and on the left, to see whence this voice came. And she went away, trembling, to her house, and put down the pitcher; and taking the purple, she sat down on her seat, and drew it out. And, behold, an angel of the Lord stood before her, saying: Fear not, Mary; for thou hast found grace before the Lord of all, and thou shalt conceive, according to His word. And she hearing, reasoned with herself, saying: Shall I conceive by the Lord, the living God? and shall I bring forth as every woman brings forth? And the angel of the Lord said: Not so, Mary; for the power of the Lord shall overshadow thee: wherefore also that holy thing which shall be born of thee shall be called the Son of the Most High. And thou shalt call His name Jesus, for He shall save His people from their sins. And Mary said: Behold, the servant of the Lord before His face: let it be unto me according to thy word.

Chapter 12

And she made the purple and the scarlet, and took them to the priest. And the priest blessed her, and said: Mary, the Lord God hath magnified thy name, and thou shall be blessed in all the generations of the earth. And Mary, with great joy, went away to Elizabeth her kinswoman, and knocked at the door. And when Elizabeth heard her, she threw away the scarlet, and ran to the door, and opened it; and seeing Mary, she blessed her, and said: Whence is this to me, that the mother of my Lord should come to me? for, behold, that which is in me leaped and blessed thee. But Mary had forgotten the mysteries of which the archangel Gabriel had spoken, and gazed up into heaven, and said: Who am I, O Lord, that all the generations of the earth should bless me? And she remained three months with Elizabeth; and day by day she grew bigger. And Mary being afraid, went away to her own house, and hid herself from the sons of Israel. And she was sixteen years old when these mysteries happened.

Chapter 13

And she was in her sixth month; and, behold, Joseph came back from his building, and, entering into his house, he discovered that she was big with child. And he smote his face, and threw himself on the ground upon the sackcloth, and wept bitterly, saying: With what face shall I look upon the Lord my God? and what prayer shall I make about this maiden? because I received her a virgin out of the temple of the Lord, and I have not watched over her. Who is it that has hunted me down? Who has done this evil thing in my house, and defiled the virgin? Has not the history of Adam been repeated in me? For just as Adam was in the hour of his singing praise, and the serpent came, and found Eve alone, and completely deceived her, so it has happened to me also. And Joseph stood up from the sackcloth, and called Mary, and said to her: O thou who hast been cared for by God, why hast thou done this and forgotten the Lord thy God? Why hast thou brought low thy soul, thou that wast brought up in the holy of holies, and that didst receive food from the hand of an angel? And she wept bitterly, saying: I am innocent, and have known no man. And Joseph said to her: Whence then is that which is in thy womb? And she said: As the Lord my God liveth, I do not know whence it is to me.

Chapter 14

And Joseph was greatly afraid, and retired from her, and considered what he should do in regard to her. And Joseph said: If I conceal her sin, I find myself fighting against the law of the Lord; and if I expose her to the sons of Israel, I am afraid lest that which is in her be from an angel, and I shall be found giving up innocent blood to the doom of death. What then shall I do with her? I will put her away from me secretly. And night came upon him; and, behold, an angel of the Lord appears to him in a dream, saying: Be not afraid for this maiden, for that which is in her is of the Holy Spirit; and she will bring forth a Son, and thou shall call His name Jesus, for He will save His people from their sins. And Joseph arose from sleep, and glorified the God of Israel, who had given him this grace; and he kept her.

Chapter 15

And Annas the scribe came to him, and said: Why hast thou not appeared in our assembly? And Joseph said to him: Because I was weary from my journey, and rested the first day. And he turned, and saw that Mary was with child. And he ran away to the priest? and said to him: Joseph, whom thou didst vouch for, has committed a grievous crime. And the priest said: How so? And he said: He has defiled the virgin whom he received out of the temple of the Lord, and has married her by stealth, and has not revealed it to the sons of Israel. And the priest answering, said: Has Joseph done this? Then said Annas the scribe: Send officers, and thou wilt find the virgin with child. And the officers went away, and found it as he had said; and they brought her along with Joseph to the tribunal. And the priest said: Mary, why hast thou done this? and why hast thou brought thy soul low, and forgotten the Lord thy God? Thou that wast reared in the holy of holies, and that didst receive food from the hand of an angel, and didst hear the hymns, and didst dance before Him, why hast thou done this? And she wept bitterly, saying: As the Lord my God liveth, I am pure before Him, and know not a man. And the priest said to Joseph: Why hast thou done this? And Joseph said: As the Lord liveth, I am pure concerning her. Then said the priest: Bear not false witness, but speak the truth. Thou hast married her by stealth, and hast not revealed it to the sons of Israel, and hast not bowed thy head under the strong hand, that thy seed might be blessed. And Joseph was silent.

Chapter 16

And the priest said: Give up the virgin whom thou didst receive out of the temple of the Lord. And Joseph burst into tears. And the priest said: I will give you to drink of the water of the ordeal of the Lord, and He shall make manifest your sins in your eyes. And the priest took the water, and gave Joseph to drink and sent him away to the hill-country; and he returned unhurt. And he gave to Mary also to drink, and sent her away to the hill-country; and she returned unhurt. And all the people wondered that sin did not appear in them. And the priest said: If the Lord God has not made manifest your sins, neither do I judge you. And he sent them away. And Joseph took Mary, and went away to his own house, rejoicing and glorifying the God of Israel.

Chapter 17

And there was an order from the Emperor Augustus, that all in Bethlehem of Judaea should be enrolled. And Joseph said: I shall enrol my sons, but what shall I do with this maiden? How shall I enrol her? As my wife? I am ashamed. As my daughter then? But all the sons of Israel know that she is not my daughter. The day of the Lord shall itself bring it to pass as the Lord will. And he saddled the ass, and set her upon it; and his son led it, and Joseph followed. And when they had come within three miles, Joseph turned and saw her sorrowful; and he said to himself: Likely that which is in her distresses her. And again Joseph turned and saw her laughing. And he said to her: Mary, how is it that I see in thy face at one time laughter, at another sorrow? And Mary said to Joseph: Because I see two peoples with my eyes; the one weeping and lamenting, and the other rejoicing and exulting. And they came into the middle of the road, and Mary said to him: Take me down from off the ass, for that which is in me presses to come forth. And he took her down from off the ass, and said to her: Whither shall I lead thee, and cover thy disgrace? for the place is desert.

Chapter 18

And he found a cave there, and led her into it; and leaving his two sons beside her, he went out to seek a widwife in the district of Bethlehem. And I Joseph was walking, and was not walking; and I looked up into the sky, and saw the sky astonished; and I looked up to the pole of the heavens, and saw it standing, and the birds of the air keeping still. And I looked down upon the earth, and saw a trough lying, and work-people reclining: and their hands were in the trough. And those that were eating did not eat, and those that were rising did not carry it up, and those that were conveying anything to their mouths did not convey it; but the faces of all were looking upwards. And I saw the sheep walking, and the sheep stood still; and the shepherd raised his hand to strike them, and his hand remained up. And I looked upon the current of the river, and I saw the mouths of the kids resting on the water and not drinking, and all things in a moment were driven from their course.

Chapter 19

And I saw a woman coming down from the hill-country, and she said to me: O man, whither art thou going? And I said: I am seeking an Hebrew midwife. And she answered and said unto me: Art thou of Israel? And I said to her: Yes. And she said: And who is it that is bringing forth in the cave? And I said: A woman betrothed to me. And she said to me: Is she not thy wife? And I said to her: It is Mary that was reared in the temple of the Lord, and I obtained her by lot as my wife. And yet she is not my wife, but has conceived of the Holy Spirit. And the widwife said to him: Is this true? And Joseph said to her: Come and see. And the midwife went away with him. And they stood in the place of the cave, and behold a luminous cloud overshadowed the cave. And the midwife said: My soul has been magnified this day, because mine eyes have seen strange things -- because salvation has been brought forth to Israel. And immediately the cloud disappeared out of the cave, and a great light shone in the cave, so that the eyes could not bear it. And in a little that light gradually decreased, until the infant appeared, and went and took the breast from His mother Mary. And the midwife cried out, and said: This is a great day to me, because I have seen this strange sight. And the midwife went forth out of the cave, and Salome met her. And she said to her: Salome, Salome, I have a strange sight to relate to thee: a virgin has brought forth -- a thing which her nature admits not of. Then said Salome: As the Lord my God liveth, unless I thrust in my finger, and search the parts, I will not believe that a virgin has brought forth.

Chapter 20

And the midwife went in, and said to Mary: Show thyself; for no small controversy has arisen about thee. And Salome put in her finger, and cried out, and said: Woe is me for mine iniquity and mine unbelief, because I have tempted the living God; and, behold, my hand is dropping off as if burned with fire. And she bent her knees before the Lord, saying: O God of my fathers, remember that I am the seed of Abraham, and Isaac, and Jacob; do not make a show of me to the sons of Israel, but restore me to the poor; for Thou knowest, O Lord, that in Thy name I have performed my services, and that I have received my reward at Thy hand. And, behold, an angel of the Lord stood by her, saying to her: Salome, Salome, the Lord hath heard thee. Put thy hand to the infant, and carry it, and thou wilt have safety and joy. And Salome went and carried it, saying: I will worship Him, because a great King has been born to Israel. And, behold, Salome was immediately cured, and she went forth out of the cave justified. And behold a voice saying: Salome, Salome, tell not the strange things thou hast seen, until the child has come into Jerusalem.

Chapter 21

And, behold, Joseph was ready to go into Judaea. And there was a great commotion in Bethlehem of Judaea, for Magi came, saying: Where is he that is born king of the Jews? for we have seen his star in the east, and have come to worship him. And when Herod heard, he was much disturbed, and sent officers to the Magi. And he sent for the priests, and examined them, saying: How is it written about the Christ? where is He to be born? And they said: In Bethlehem of Judaea, for so it is written. And he sent them away. And he examined the Magi, saying to them: What sign have you seen in reference to the king that has been born? And the Magi said: We have seen a star of great size shining among these stars, and obscuring their light, so that the stars did not appear; and we thus knew that a king has been born to Israel, and we have come to worship him. And Herod said: Go and seek him; and if you find him, let me know, in order that I also may go and worship him. And the Magi went out. And, behold, the star which they had seen in the east went before them until they came to the cave, and it stood over the top of the cave. And the Magi saw the infant with His mother Mary; and they brought forth from their bag gold, and frankincense, and myrrh. And having been warned by the angel not to go into Judaea, they went into their own country by another road.

Chapter 22

And when Herod knew that he had been mocked by the Magi, in a rage he sent murderers, saying to them: Slay the children from two years old and under. And Mary, having heard that the children were being killed, was afraid, and took the infant and swaddled Him, and put Him into an ox-stall. And Elizabeth, having heard that they were searching for John, took him and went up into the hill-country, and kept looking where to conceal him. And there was no place of concealment. And Elizabeth, groaning with a loud voice, says: O mountain of God, receive mother and child. And immediately the mountain was cleft, and received her. And a light shone about them, for an angel of the Lord was with them, watching over them.

Chapter 23

And Herod searched for John, and sent officers to Zacharias, saying: Where hast thou hid thy son? And he, answering, said to them: I am the servant of God in holy things, and I sit constantly in the temple of the Lord: I do not know where my son is. And the officers went away, and reported all these things to Herod. And Herod was enraged, and said: His son is destined to be king over Israel. And he sent to him again, saying: Tell the truth; where is thy son? for thou knowest that thy life is in my hand. And Zacharias said: I am God's martyr, if thou sheddest my blood; for the Lord will receive my spirit, because thou sheddest innocent blood at the vestibule of the temple of the Lord. And Zacharias was murdered about daybreak. And the sons of Israel did not know that he had been murdered.

Chapter 24

But at the hour of the salutation the priests went away, and Zacharias did not come forth to meet them with a blessing, according to his custom. And the priests stood waiting for Zacharias to salute him at the prayer, and to glorify the Most High. And he still delaying, they were all afraid. But one of them ventured to go in, and he saw clotted blood beside the altar; and he heard a voice saying: Zacharias has been murdered, and his blood shall not be wiped up until his avenger come. And hearing this saying, he was afraid, and went out and told it to the priests. And they ventured in, and saw what had happened; and the fretwork of the temple made a wailing noise, and they rent their clothes from the top even to the bottom. And they found not his body, but they found his blood turned into stone. And they were afraid, and went out and reported to the people that Zacharias had been murdered. And all the tribes of the people heard, and mourned, and lamented for him three days and three nights. And after the three days, the priests consulted as to whom they should put in his place; and the lot fell upon Simeon. For it was he who had been warned by the

Holy Spirit that he should not see death until he should see the Christ in the flesh.

And I James that wrote this history in Jerusalem, a commotion having arisen when Herod died, withdrew myself to the wilderness until the commotion in Jerusalem ceased, glorifying the Lord God, who had given me the gift and the wisdom to write this history. And grace shall be with them that fear our Lord Jesus Christ, to whom be glory to ages of ages. Amen.

Infancy Gospel of Thomas
(140 – 170 A.D.)

The Infancy Gospel of Thomas is a pseudepigraphical (*falsely attributed*) gospel about the childhood of Jesus that is believed to date to the 2nd century. It was part of a popular genre of biblical work, written to satisfy a hunger among early Christians for more miraculous and anecdotal stories of the childhood of Jesus than the Gospel of Luke provided. Later references by Hippolytus of Rome and Origen of Alexandria to a *Gospel of Thomas* are more likely to be referring to this Infancy Gospel than to the wholly different *Gospel of Thomas* with which it is sometimes confused. It would appear to be unrelated to the Canonical Gospels.

The first known probable quotation of its text is from Irenaeus of Lyon, *ca* 185. The earliest possible date of authorship is in the 80s A.D., the approximate date of the Gospel of Luke, from which the author of the Infancy Gospel borrowed the story of Jesus in the temple at age twelve (*see Infancy 19:1-12 and Luke 2:41-52*). Scholars generally agree on a date in the mid- to late-2nd century A.D. There are two 2nd century documents, the *Epistula Apostolorum* and Irenaeus' *Adversus haereses*, which refer to a story of Jesus' tutor telling him, "*Say beta,*" and him replying, "*First tell me the meaning of alpha.*" It is generally agreed that there was at least some period of oral transmission of the text, either wholly or as several different stories before it was first redacted and transcribed, and it is thus entirely possible that both of these documents and the *Infancy Gospel of Thomas* all refer to the oral versions of this story. [35]

---

*Summary notation: Due to it's importance and historical significance to the early Church, the **Infancy Gospel of Thomas** is presented in its entirety. It relates stories about Jesus' childhood and miracles.*

The Manuscript in its Entirety

1. I Thomas, an Israelite, write you this account, that all the

---

[35] http://en.wikipedia.org/wiki/Infancy_Gospel_of_Thomas

brethren from among the heathen may know the miracles of our Lord Jesus Christ in His infancy, which He did after His birth in our country. The beginning of it is as follows:-

2. This child Jesus, when five years old, was playing in the ford of a mountain stream; and He collected the flowing waters into pools, and made them clear immediately, and by a word alone He made them obey Him. And having made some soft clay, He fashioned out of it twelve sparrows. And it was the Sabbath when He did these things. And there were also many other children playing with Him. And a certain Jew, seeing what Jesus was doing, playing on the Sabbath, went off immediately, and said to his father Joseph: Behold, thy son is at the stream, and has taken clay, and made of it twelve birds, and has profaned the Sabbath. And Joseph, coming to the place and seeing, cried out to Him, saying: *"Wherefore doest thou on the Sabbath what it is not lawful to do? And Jesus clapped His hands, and cried out to the sparrows, and said to them: Off you go!* "And the sparrows flew, and went off crying. And the Jews seeing this were amazed, and went away and reported to their chief men what they had seen Jesus doing.

3. And the son of Annas the scribe was standing there with Joseph; and he took a willow branch, and let out the waters which Jesus had collected. And Jesus, seeing what was done, was angry, and said to him: *"O wicked, impious, and foolish! what harm did the pools and the waters do to thee? Behold, even now thou shalt be dried up like a tree, and thou shalt not bring forth either leaves, or root, or fruit".* And straightway that boy was quite dried up. And Jesus departed, and went to Joseph's house. But the parents of the boy that had been dried up took him up, bewailing his youth, and brought him to Joseph, and reproached him because, *said they,* thou hast such a child doing such things.

4. After that He was again passing through the village; and a boy ran up against Him, and struck His shoulder. And Jesus was angry, and said to him: *"Thou shalt not go back the way thou camest".* And immediately he fell down dead. And some who saw what had taken place, said: Whence was this child begotten, that every word of his is certainly accomplished? And the parents of the dead boy went away to Joseph, and blamed him, saying: Since thou hast such a child, it is impossible for thee to live with us in the village; or else teach him to bless, and not to curse: for he is killing our children.

5. And Joseph called the child apart, and admonished Him, saying: Why doest thou such things, and these people suffer, and hate us, and persecute us? And Jesus said: *"I know that these words of thine are not thine own; nevertheless for thy sake I will be silent; but they shall bear their punishment"*. And straightway those that accused Him were struck blind. And those who saw it were much afraid and in great perplexity, and said about Him: Every word which he spoke, whether good or bad, was an act, and became a wonder. And when they saw that Jesus had done such a thing, Joseph rose and took hold of His ear, and pulled it hard. And the child was very angry, and said to him: *"It is enough for thee to seek, and not to find; and most certainly thou hast not done wisely. Knowest thou not that I am thine? Do not trouble me"*.

6. And a certain teacher, Zacchaeus by name, was standing in a certain place, and heard Jesus thus speaking to his father; and he wondered exceedingly, that, being a child, he should speak in such a way. And a few days thereafter he came to Joseph, and said to him: Thou hast a sensible child, and he has some mind. Give him to me, then, that he may learn letters; and I shall teach him along with the letters all knowledge, both how to address all the elders, and to honour them as forefathers and fathers, and how to love those of his own age. And He said to him all the letters from the Alpha even to the Omega, clearly and with great exactness. And He looked upon the teacher Zacchaeus, and said to him: *"Thou who art ignorant of the nature of the Alpha, how canst thou teach others the Beta? Thou hypocrite! first, if thou knowest. teach the A, and then we shall believe thee about the B"*. Then He began to question the teacher about the first letter, and he was not able to answer Him. And in the hearing of many, the child says to Zacchaeus: *"Hear, O teacher, the order of the first letter, and notice here how it has lines, and a middle stroke crossing those which thou seest common; (lines) brought together; the highest part supporting them, and again bringing them under one head; with three points of intersection; of the same kind; principal and subordinate; of equal length. Thou hast the lines of the A"*.

7. And when the teacher Zacchaeus heard the child speaking such and so great allegories of the first letter, he was at a great loss about such a narrative, and about His teaching. And He said to those that were present: *"Alas! I, wretch that I am, am at a loss, bringing shame upon myself by having dragged this child hither. Take him away, then, I beseech thee, brother Joseph. I cannot endure the sternness of his look; I cannot make out his meaning at all. That child does not belong to this earth; he can tame even fire. Assuredly he was born before the creation of the world. What sort of a belly bore him, what sort of a womb nourished him, I do not know. Alas! my friend, he has carried me away; I cannot get at his meaning: thrice wretched that I am, I have deceived myself. I made a struggle to have a scholar, and I was found to have a teacher. My mind is filled with shame, my friends, because I, an old man, have been conquered by a child. There is nothing for me but despondency and death on account of this boy, for I am not able at this hour to look him in the face; and when everybody says that I have been beaten by a little child, what can I say? And how can I give an account of the lines of the first letter that he spoke about? I know not, O my friends; for I can make neither beginning nor end of him. Therefore, I beseech thee, brother Joseph, take him home. What great thing he is, either god or angel, or what I am to say, I know not"*.

8. And when the Jews were encouraging Zacchaeus, the child laughed aloud, and said: Now let thy learning bring forth fruit, and let the blind in heart see. I am here from above, that I may curse them, and call them to the things that are above, as He that sent me on your account has commanded me. And when the child ceased speaking, immediately all were made whole who had fallen under His curse. And no one after that dared to make Him angry, lest He should curse him, and he should be maimed.

9. And some days after, Jesus was playing in an upper room of a certain house, and one of the children that were playing with Him fell down from the house, and was killed. And, when the other children saw this, they ran away, and Jesus alone stood still. And the parents of the dead child coming, reproached...and they threatened Him. And Jesus leaped down from the roof, and stood beside the body of the child, and cried with a loud voice, and said: *"Zeno-for that was his name-stand up, and tell me; did I throw thee down?"* And he stood up immediately, and said: *"Certainly not, my lord; thou didst not throw me down, but hast raised me up. And those that saw this were struck with astonishment"*. And the child's parents glorified God on account of the miracle that had happened, and adored Jesus.

10. A few days after, a young man was splitting wood in the corner, and the axe came down and cut the sole of his foot in two, and he died from loss of blood. And there was a great commotion, and people ran together, and the child Jesus ran there too. And He pressed through the crowd, and laid hold of the young man's wounded foot, and he was cured immediately. And He said to the young man: *"Rise up now, split the wood, and remember me"*. And the crowd seeing what had happened, adored the child, saying: *"Truly the Spirit of God dwells in this child"*.

11. And when He was six years old, His mother gave Him a pitcher, and sent Him to draw water, and bring it into the house. But He struck against some one in the crowd, and the pitcher was broken. And Jesus unfolded the cloak which He had on, and filled it with water, and carried it to His mother. And His mother, seeing the miracle that had happened, kissed Him, and kept within herself the mysteries which she had seen Him doing.

12. And again in seed-time the child went out with His father to sow corn in their land. And while His father was sowing, the child Jesus also sowed one gain of corn. And when He had reaped it, and threshed it, He made a hundred kors; and calling all the poor of the village to the threshing-floor, He gave them the corn, and Joseph took away what was left of the corn. And He was eight years old when He did this miracle.

13. And His father was a carpenter, and at that time made ploughs and yokes. And a certain rich man ordered him to make him a couch. And one of what is called the cross pieces being too short, they did not know what to do. The child Jesus said to His father Joseph: *"Put down the two pieces of wood, and make them even in the middle"*. And Joseph did as the child said to him. And Jesus stood at the other end, and took hold of the shorter piece of wood, and stretched it, and made it equal to the other. And His father Joseph saw it, and wondered, and embraced the child, and blessed Him, saying: *"Blessed am I, because God has given me this child"*.

14. And Joseph, seeing that the child was vigorous in mind and body, again resolved that He should not remain ignorant of the letters, and took Him away, and handed Him over to another teacher. And the teacher said to Joseph: *"I shall first teach him the Greek letters, and then the Hebrew"*. For the teacher was aware of the trial that had been made of the child, and was afraid of Him. Nevertheless he wrote out the alphabet, and gave Him all his attention for a long time, and He made him no answer. And Jesus said to him: *"If thou art really a teacher, and art well acquainted with the letters, tell me the power of the Alpha, and I will tell thee the power of the Beta"*. And the teacher was enraged at this, and struck Him on the head. The child, being in pain, cursed him; and immediately he swooned away, and fell to the ground on his face. And the child returned to Joseph's house; and Joseph was grieved, and gave orders to His mother, saying: *"Do not let him go outside of the door, because those that make him angry die"*.

15. And after some time, another master again, a genuine friend of Joseph, said to him: *"Bring the child to my school; perhaps I shall be able to flatter him into learning his letters"*. And Joseph said: *"If thou hast the courage, brother, take him with thee"*. And he took Him with him in fear and great agony; but the child went along pleasantly. And going boldly into the school, He found a book lying on the reading-desk; and taking it, He read not the letters that were in it, but opening His mouth, He spoke by the Holy Spirit, and taught the law to those that were standing round. And a great crowd having come together, stood by and heard Him, and wondered at the ripeness of His teaching, and the readiness of His words, and that He, child as He was, spoke in such a way. And Joseph hearing of it, was afraid, and ran to the school, in doubt lest his master too should be without experience. And the master said to Joseph: *"Know, brother, that I have taken the child as a scholar, and he is full of much grace and wisdom; but I beseech thee, brother, take him home"*. And when the child heard this, He laughed at him directly, and said: *"Since thou hast spoken aright, and witnessed aright, for thy sake he also that was struck down shall be cured"*. And immediately the other master was cured. And Joseph took the child, and went away home.

16. And Joseph sent his son James to tie up wood and bring it home, and the child Jesus also followed him. And when James was gathering the fagots, a viper bit James' hand. And when he was racked with pain, and at the point of death, Jesus came near and blew upon the bite; and the pain ceased directly, and the beast burst, and instantly James remained safe and sound.

17. And after this the infant of one of Joseph's neighbours fell sick and died, and its mother wept sore. And Jesus heard that there was great lamentation and commotion, and ran in haste, and found the child dead, and touched his breast, and said: "*I say to thee, child, be not dead, but live, and be with thy mother*". And directly it looked up and laughed. And He said to the woman: "*Take it, and give it milk, and remember me*". And seeing this, the crowd that was standing by wondered, and said: "*Truly this child was either God or an angel of God, for every word of his is a certain fact*". And Jesus went out thence, playing with the other children.

18. And some time after there occurred a great commotion while a house was building, and Jesus stood up and went away to the place. And seeing a man lying dead, He took him by the hand, and said: Man, I say to thee, arise, and go on with thy work. And directly he rose up, and adored Him. And seeing this, the crowd wondered, and said: This child is from heaven, for he has saved many souls from death, and he continues to save during all his life.

19. And when He was twelve years old, His parents went as usual to Jerusalem to the feast of the passover with their fellow-travellers. And after the passover they were coming home again. And while they were coming home, the child Jesus went back to Jerusalem. And His parents thought that He was in the company. And having gone one day's journey, they sought for Him among their relations; and not finding Him, they were in great grief, and turned back to the city seeking for Him. And after the third day they found Him in the temple, sitting in the midst of the teachers, both hearing the law and asking them questions. And they were all attending to Him, and wondering that He, being a child, was shutting the mouths of the elders and teachers of the people, explaining the main points of the law and the parables of the prophets. And His mother ,Mary, coming up, said to Him: "*Why hast thou done this to us, child? Behold, we have been seeking for thee in great trouble*". And Jesus said to them: "*Why do you seek me? Do you not know that I must be about my Father's business?*" And the scribes and the Pharisees said: "*Art thou the mother of this child? And she said: I am. And they said to her: Blessed art thou among women, for God hath* *blessed the fruit of thy womb; for such glory, and such virtue and wisdom, we have neither seen nor heard ever"*. And Jesus rose up, and followed His mother, and was subject to His parents. And His mother observed all these things that had happened. And Jesus advanced in wisdom, and stature, and grace. To whom be glory for ever and ever. Amen.

The Gospel of Truth (*Gnostic*)
(140 – 180 A.D.)

The date and place of composition remain obscure. Although the work was composed in Greek before it was translated into Coptic, whether it was written in Egypt or elsewhere is uncertain. Allusions to documents known from the NT, such as Matthew (Tuckett 1984) and certain Pauline Epistles (Menard 1972), place the date well into the 2d century, a period that harmonizes with the rising influence of Valentinus. The richly subtle and sophisticated style and organization of the text, designed to invite readers in an inoffensive way to a certain view of Jesus' salvific role (Attridge 1988), may argue for a later date.

A Valentinian work entitled the "Gospel of Truth" is attested in the *Adversus Haereses* (3.11.9) of Irenaeus. Unfortunately the heresiologist reveals little about the content of the work, except that it differed significantly from the canonical gospels. Given the general Valentinian affinities of the text of Codex I, it is quite possible that it is identical with the work known to Irenaeus. If so, a date of composition in the middle of the second century (between 140 and 180 C.E.) would be established. On the basis of literary and conceptual affinities between this text and the exiguous fragments of Valentinus, some scholars have suggested that the Gnostic teacher himself was the author. That remains a distinct possibility, although it cannot be definitively established.

Summary notation: *Due to it's importance and historical significance to the early Church, the* **Gospel of Truth** *is presented in some detail but not entirely due to its length.. Only key excerpts or talking points are presented for discussion. It was condemned as heretical. Please note sections omitted in the early manuscript.*

Excerpts from the Gospel of Truth

The gospel of truth is joy to those who have received from the Father of truth the gift of knowing him by the power of the Logos, who has come from the Pleroma and who is in the thought and the mind of the Father; he it is who is called "the Savior," since that is the name of the work which he must do for the redemption of those who have not known the Father. For the name of the gospel is the manifestation of hope, since that is the discovery of those who seek him, because the All sought him from whom it had come forth. You see, the All had been inside of him, that illimitable, inconceivable one, who is better than every thought.

[... sections omitted.].

That is the gospel of him whom they seek, which he has revealed to the perfect through the mercies of the Father as the hidden mystery, Jesus the Christ. Through him he enlightened those who were in darkness because of forgetfulness. He enlightened them and gave them a path. And that path is the truth which he taught them. For this reason error was angry with him, so it persecuted him. It was distressed by him, so it made him powerless. He was nailed to a cross. He became a fruit of the knowledge of the Father. He did not, however, destroy them because they ate of it. He rather caused those who ate of it to be joyful because of this discovery.

[... sections omitted.].

This is the book which no one found possible to take, since it was reserved for him who will take it and be slain. No one was able to be manifest from those who believed in salvation as long as that book had not appeared. For this reason, the compassionate, faithful Jesus was patient in his sufferings until he took that book, since he knew that his death meant life for many. Just as in the case of a will which has not yet been opened, for the fortune of the deceased master of the house is hidden, so also in the case of the All which had been hidden as long as the Father of the All was invisible and unique in himself, in whom every space has its source. For this reason Jesus appeared. He took that book as his own. He was nailed to a cross. He affixed the edict of the Father to the cross.
Oh, such great teaching! He abases himself even unto death, though he is clothed in eternal life. Having divested himself of these perishable rags, he clothed himself in incorruptibility, which no one could possibly take from him. Having entered into the empty territory of fears, he passed before those who were stripped by

forgetfulness, being both knowledge and perfection, proclaiming the things that are in the heart of the Father, so that he became the wisdom of those who have received instruction. But those who are to be taught, the living who are inscribed in the book of the living, learn for themselves, receiving instructions from the Father, turning to him again.

Since the perfection of the All is in the Father, it is necessary for the All to ascend to him. Therefore, if one has knowledge, he gets what belongs to him and draws it to himself. For he who is ignorant, is deficient, and it is a great deficiency, since he lacks that which will make him perfect. Since the perfection of the All is in the Father, it is necessary for the All to ascend to him and for each one to get the things which are his. He registered them first, having prepared them to be given to those who came from

[... sections omitted.].

While his wisdom mediates on the logos, and since his teaching expresses it, his knowledge has been revealed. His honor is a crown upon it. Since his joy agrees with it, his glory exalted it. It has revealed his image. It has obtained his rest. His love took bodily form around it. His trust embraced it. Thus the logos of the Father goes forth into the All, being the fruit of his heart and expression of his will. It supports the All. It chooses and also takes the form of the All, purifying it, and causing it to return to the Father and to the Mother, Jesus of the utmost sweetness. The Father opens his bosom, but his bosom is the Holy Spirit. He reveals his hidden self which is his son, so that through the compassion of the Father the Aeons may know him, end their wearying search for the Father and rest themselves in him, knowing that this is rest. After he had filled what was incomplete, he did away with form. The form of it is the world, that which it served. For where there is envy and strife, there is an incompleteness; but where there is unity, there is completeness. Since this incompleteness came about because they did not know the Father, so when they know the Father, incompleteness, from that moment on, will cease to exist. As one's ignorance disappears when he gains knowledge, and as darkness disappears when light appears, so also incompleteness is eliminated by completeness. Certainly, from that moment on, form is no longer manifest, but will be dissolved in fusion with unity. For now their works lie scattered. In time unity will make the spaces complete. By means of unity each one will understand itself. By means of knowledge it will purify itself of diversity with a view towards unity, devouring matter within itself like fire and darkness by light, death by life.

[... sections omitted.].

And the Spirit came to him in haste when it raised him. Having given its hand to the one lying prone on the ground, it placed him firmly on his feet, for he had not yet stood up. He gave them the means of knowing the knowledge of the Father and the revelation of his son. For when they saw it and listened to it, he permitted them to take a taste of and to smell and to grasp the beloved son.
He appeared, informing them of the Father, the illimitable one. He inspired them with that which is in the mind, while doing his will. Many received the light and turned towards him. But material men were alien to him and did not discern his appearance nor recognize him. For he came in the likeness of flesh and nothing blocked his way because it was incorruptible and unrestrainable. Moreover, while saying new things, speaking about what is in the heart of the Father, he proclaimed the faultless word. Light spoke through his mouth, and his voice brought forth life. He gave them thought and understanding and mercy and salvation and the Spirit of strength derived from the limitlessness of the Father and sweetness. He caused punishments and scourgings to cease, for it was they which caused many in need of mercy to astray from him in error and in chains - and he mightily destroyed them and derided them with knowledge. He became a path for those who went astray and knowledge to those who were ignorant, a discovery for those who sought, and a support for those who tremble, a purity for those who were defiled.

[... sections omitted.].

This is the perfection in the thought of the Father and these are the words of his reflection. Each one of his words is the work of his will alone, in the revelation of his Logos. Since they were in the depth of his mind, the Logos, who was the first to come forth, caused them to appear, along with an intellect which speaks the unique word by means of a silent grace. It was called "thought," since they were in it before becoming manifest. It happened, then, that it was the first to come forth - at the moment pleasing to the will of him who desired it; and it is in the will that the Father is at rest and with which he is pleased. Nothing happens without him, nor does anything occur without the will of the Father. But his will is incomprehensible. His will is his mark, but no one can know it, nor is it possible for them to concentrate on it in order to possess it. But that which he wishes takes place at the moment he wishes it - even if the view does not please anyone: it is God`s will. For the Father knows the beginning of them all as well as their end. For when their end arrives, he will question them to their faces. The end, you see, is the recognition of him who is hidden, that is, the Father, from whom the beginning came forth and to whom will return all who have come from him. For they were made manifest for the glory and the joy of his name.

And the name of the Father is the Son. It is he who, in the beginning, gave a name to him who came forth from him - he is the same one - and he begat him for a son. He gave him his name which belonged to him - he, the Father, who possesses everything which exists around him. He possess the name; he has the son. It is possible for them to see him. The name, however, is invisible, for it alone is the mystery of the invisible about to come to ears completely filled with it through the Father`s agency. Moreover, as for the Father, his name is not pronounced, but it is revealed through a son. Thus, then, the name is great.

The Acts of Peter
(150 – 200 A.D.)

The Acts of Peter is one of the earliest of the apocryphal Acts of the Apostles. The majority of the text has survived only in the Latin translation of the Vercelli manuscript, under the title *Actus Petri cum Simone*. It is mainly notable for a description of a miracle contest between Saint Peter and Simon Magus, and as the first record of the tradition that St. Peter was crucified head-down.

The Acts of Peter was originally composed in Greek during the second half of the 2nd century, probably in Asia Minor. Consensus among academics points to its being based on the Acts of John, and traditionally both works were said to be written by Leucius Charinus, whom Epiphanius identifies as the companion of John.

In the text Peter performs miracles such as resurrecting smoked fish, and making dogs talk. Some versions give accounts of stories on the theme of a woman/women who prefer paralysis to sex; sometimes, including in a version from the Berlin Codex, the woman is the daughter of Peter. The text condemns Simon Magus, a figure associated with gnosticism, who appears to have concerned the writer of the text greatly[36]

The Coptic Fragment preserved separately in an early papyrus manuscript (*fourth-fifth century*) now at Berlin; the other contents of it are Gnostic writings which have not yet been published. I follow C. Schmidt's rendering of it. It has a title at the end: The Act of Peter On the first day of the week, that is, on the Lord's day, a multitude gathered together, and they brought unto Peter many sick that he might heal them. And one of the multitude adventured to say unto Peter: Lo, Peter, in our presence thou hast made many blind to see and the deaf to hear and the lame to walk, and hast succoured the weak and given them strength: but wherefore hast thou not succoured thy daughter, the virgin, which grew up beautiful and hath believed in the name of God? For behold, her one side is wholly palsied, and she lieth there stretched out in the corner helpless. We see them that have been healed by thee: thine own daughter thou hast neglected.

---

[36] http://en.wikipedia.org/wiki/Acts_of_Peter

> **Summary notation:** Due to it's importance and historical significance to the early Church, the **Acts of Peter** presented in some detail but not entirely .Due to the length of the manuscript, only key excerpts or talking points are presented for discussion. Please note sections omitted in the early manuscript.

Excerpts from the Acts of Peter

I. The Coptic Fragment

[... sections omitted.].

But Ptolemaeus was not negligent, and bade his servants show him the way and bring him unto me. And when they were come to me, he told me all that had befallen him by the power of our Lord Jesus Christ. Then did he see with the eyes of his flesh, and with the eyes of his soul, and much people believed (*hoped*) in Christ: and he did them good and gave them the gift of God.

Thereafter Ptolemaeus died, departing out of this life, and went unto his Lord: and when he made his will he bequeathed a piece of land in the name of my daughter, because through her he had believed in God and was made whole. But I unto whom the disposition thereof fell, exercised it with great carefulness: I sold the land, and God alone knoweth neither I nor my daughter (*received the price*). I sold the land and kept nought back of the price, but gave all the money unto the poor. Know therefore, thou servant of Jesus Christ, that God directeth them that are his, and prepareth good for every one of them, although we think that God hath forgotten us. Therefore now, brethren, let us be sorrowful and watch and pray, and so shall the goodness of God look upon us, whereon we wait.

And yet further discourse did Peter hold before them all, and glorified the name of Christ the Lord and gave them all of the bread: and when he had distributed it, he rose up and went unto his house.

[... sections omitted.].

III The Vercelli Acts

Chapter 1

At the time when Paul was sojourning in Rome and confirming many in the faith, it came also to pass that one by name Candida, the wife of Quartus that was over the prisons, heard Paul and paid heed to his words and believed. And when she had instructed her husband also and he believed, Quartus suffered Paul to go whither he would away from the city: to whom Paul said: If it be the will of God, he will reveal it unto me. And after Paul had fasted three days and asked of the Lord that which should be profitable for him, he saw a vision, even the Lord saying unto him: *"Arise, Paul, and become a physician in thy body (i.e. by going thither in person) to them that are in Spain"*.

He therefore, having related to the brethren what God had commanded, nothing doubting, prepared himself to set forth from the city. But when Paul was about to depart, there was great weeping throughout all the brotherhood, because they thought that they should see Paul no more, so that they even rent their clothes. For they had in mind also how that Paul had oftentimes contended with the doctors of the Jews and confuted them, saying: Christ, upon whom your fathers laid hands, abolished their sabbaths and fasts and holy-days and circumcision, and the doctrines of men and the rest of the traditions he did abolish. But the brethren lamented *(and adjured)* Paul by the coming of our Lord Jesus Christ, that he should not be absent above a year, saying: *"We know thy love for thy brethren; forget not us when thou art come thither, neither begin to forsake us, as little children without a mother"*. And when they besought him long with tears, there came a sound from heaven, and a great voice saying: *"Paul the servant of God is chosen to minister all the days of his life: by the hands of Nero the ungodly and wicked man shall he be perfected before your eyes"*. And a very great fear fell upon the brethren because of the voice which came from heaven: and they were confirmed yet more in the faith.

Chapter 2

Now they brought unto Paul bread and water for the sacrifice, that he might make prayer and distribute it to every one. Among whom it befell that a woman named Rufina desired, she also, to receive the Eucharist at the hands of Paul: to whom Paul, filled with the spirit of God, said as she drew near: "*Rufina, thou comest not worthily unto the altar of God, arising from beside one that is not thine husband but an adulterer, and assayest to receive the Eucharist of God. For behold Satan shall trouble thine heart and cast thee down in the sight of all them that believe in the Lord, that they which see and believe may know that they have believed in the living God, the searcher of hearts. But if thou repent of thine act, he is faithful that is able to blot out thy sin and set thee free from this sin: but if thou repent not, while thou art yet in the body, devouring fire and outer darkness shall receive thee for ever*". And immediately Rufina fell down, being stricken with palsy from her head unto the nails of her feet, and she had no power to speak (*given her*) for her tongue was bound. And when both they that believed (*in the faith*) and the neophytes saw it, they beat their breasts, remembering their old sins, and mourned and said: "*We know not if God will forgive the former sins which we have committed. Then Paul called for silence and said: Men and brethren which now have begun to believe on Christ, if ye continue not in your former works of the tradition of your fathers, and keep yourselves from all guile and wrath and fierceness and adultery and defilement, and from pride and envy and contempt and enmity, Jesus the living God will forgive you that ye did in ignorance. Wherefore, ye servants of God, arm yourselves every one in your inner man with peace, patience, gentleness, faith, charity, knowledge, wisdom, love of the brethren, hospitality, mercy, abstinence, chastity, kindness, justice: then shall ye have for your guide everlastingly the first-begotten of all creation, and shall have strength in peace with our Lord*". And when they had heard these things of Paul, they besought him to pray for them. And Paul lifted up his voice and said: "*O eternal God, God of the heavens, God of unspeakable majesty (divinity), who hast stablished all things by thy word, who hast bound upon all the world the chain of thy grace, Father of thine holy Son Jesus Christ, we together pray thee through thy Son Jesus Christ, strengthen the souls which were before unbelieving but now are faithful. Once I was a blasphemer, now I am*

blasphemed; once I was a persecutor, now do I suffer persecution of others; once I was the enemy of Christ, now I pray that I may be his friend: for I trust in his promise and in his mercy; I account myself faithful and that I have received forgiveness of my former sins. Wherefore I exhort you also, brethren, to believe in the Lord the Father Almighty, and to put all your trust in our Lord Jesus Christ his Son, believing in him, and no man shall be able to uproot you from his promise. Bow your knees therefore together and commend me unto the Lord, who am about to set forth unto another nation, that his grace may go before me and dispose my journey aright, that he may receive his vessels holy and believing, that they, giving thanks for my preaching of the word of the Lord, may be well grounded in the faith".
But the brethren wept long and prayed unto the Lord with Paul, saying: Be thou, Lord Jesus Christ, with Paul and restore him unto us whole: for we know our weakness which is in us even to this day.

[... sections omitted.].

Chapter 4

Now after a few days there was a great commotion in the midst of the Church, for some said that they had seen wonderful works done by a certain man whose name was Simon, and that he was at Aricia, and they added further that he said he was a great power of God and without God he did nothing. Is not this the Christ? but we believe in him whom Paul preached unto us; for by him have we seen the dead raised, and men. Delivered from divers infirmities: but this man seeketh contention, we know it (*or, but what this contention is, we know not*) for there is no small stir made among us. Perchance also he will now enter into Rome; for yesterday they besought him with great acclamations, saying unto him: Thou art God in Italy, thou art the saviour of the Romans: haste quickly unto Rome. But he spake to the people with a shrill voice, saying: *"Tomorrow about the seventh hour ye shall see me fly over the gate of the city in the form (habit) wherein ye now see me speaking unto you. Therefore, brethren, if it seem good unto you, let us go and await carefully the issue of the matter. They all therefore ran together and came unto the gate".* And when it was the seventh hour, behold suddenly a dust was seen in the sky afar off, like a smoke shining with rays stretching far from it. And when he drew near to the gate, suddenly he was not seen: and thereafter he appeared, standing in the midst of the people; whom they all worshipped, and took knowledge that he was the same that was seen of them the day before.

And the brethren were not a little offended among themselves, seeing, moreover, that Paul was not at Rome, neither Timotheus nor Barnabas, for they had been sent into Macedonia by Paul, and that there was no man to comfort us, to speak nothing of them that had but just become catechumens. And as Simon exalted himself yet more by the works which he did, and many of them daily called Paul a sorcerer, and others a deceiver, of so great a multitude that had been stablished in the faith all fell away save Narcissus the presbyter and two women in the lodging of the Bithynians, and four that could no longer go out of their house, but were shut up (*day and night*): these gave themselves unto prayer (*by day and night*), beseeching the Lord that Paul might return quickly, or some other that should visit his servants, because the devil had made them fall by his wickedness.

Chapter 5

And as they prayed and fasted, God was already teaching Peter at Jerusalem of that which should come to pass. For whereas the twelve years which the Lord Christ had enjoined upon him were fulfilled, he showed him a vision after this manner, saying unto him: *"Peter, that Simon the sorcerer whom thou didst cast out of Judaea, convicting him, hath again come before thee (prevented thee) at Rome. And that shalt thou know shortly (or, and that thou mayest know in few words): for all that did believe in me hath Satan made to fall by his craft and working: whose Power Simon approveth himself to be. But delay thee not: set forth on the morrow, and there shalt thou find a ship ready, setting sail for Italy, and within few days I will show thee my grace which hath in it no grudging. Peter then, admonished by the vision, related it unto the brethren without delay, saying: It is necessary for me to go up unto Rome to fight with the enemy and adversary of the Lord and of our brethren".*

And he went down to Caesarea and embarked quickly in the ship, whereof the ladder was already drawn up, not taking any provision with him. But the governor of the ship whose name was

Theon looked on Peter and said: "*Whatsoever we have, all is thine. For what thank have we, if we take in a man like unto ourselves who is in uncertain case (difficulty) and share not all that we have with thee? but only let us have a prosperous voyage".* But Peter, giving him thanks for that which he offered, himself fasted while he was in the ship, sorrowful in mind and again consoling himself because God accounted him worthy to be a minister in his service.

And after a few days the governor of the ship rose up at the hour of his dinner and asked Peter to eat with him, and said to him: "*O thou, whoever thou art, I know thee not, but as I reckon, I take thee for a servant of God. For as I was steering my ship at midnight I perceived the voice of a man from heaven saying to me: Theon, Theon! And twice it called me by my name and said to me: Among them that sail with thee let Peter be greatly honoured by thee, for by him shalt thou and the rest be preserved safe without any hurt after such a course as thou hopest not for".* And Peter believed that God would vouchsafe to show his providence upon the sea unto them that were in the ship, and thenceforth began Peter to declare unto Theon the mighty works of God, and how the Lord had chosen him from among the apostles, and for what business he sailed unto Italy: and daily he communicated unto him the word of God. And considering him he perceived by his walk that he was of one mind in the faith and a worthy minister (*deacon*).

Now when there was a calm upon the ship in Hadria *(the Adriatic)*, Theon showed it to Peter, saying unto him: "*If thou wilt account me worthy, whom thou mayest baptize with the seal of the Lord thou hast an opportunity".* For all that were in the ship had fallen asleep, being drunken. And Peter went down by a rope and baptized Theon in the name of the Father and the Son and the Holy Ghost: and he came up out of the water rejoicing with great joy, and Peter also was glad because God had accounted Theon worthy of his name. Arid it came to pass when Theon was baptized, there appeared in the same place a youth shining and beautiful, saying unto them: "*Peace be unto you".* And immediately Peter and Theon went up and entered into the cabin; and Peter took bread and gave thanks unto the Lord which had accounted him worthy of his holy ministry, and for that the youth had appeared unto them, saying: Peace be unto you. And he said:

:" *Thou best and alone holy one, it is thou that hast appeared unto us, O God Jesus Christ, and in thy name hath this man now been washed and sealed with thy holy seal. Therefore thy name do I impart unto him thine eucharist, that he may be thy perfect servant without blame for ever"*.

And as they feasted and rejoiced in the Lord, suddenly there came a wind, not vehement but moderate, at the ship's prow, and ceased not for six days and as many nights, until they came unto Puteoli.

Chapter 6

And when they had touched at Puteoli, Theon leapt out of the ship and went unto the inn where he was wont to lodge, to prepare to receive Peter. Now he with whom he lodged was one by name Ariston, which alway feared the Lord, and because of the Name Theon entrusted himself with him (*had dealings with him*). And when he was come to the inn and saw Ariston, Theon said unto him: God who hath accounted thee worthy to serve him hath communicated his grace unto me also by his holy servant Peter, who hath now sailed with me from Judaea, being commanded by our Lord to come unto Italy. And when he heard that, Ariston fell upon Theon's neck and embraced him and besought him to bring him to the ship and show him Peter. For Ariston said that since Paul set forth unto Spain there was no man of the brethren with whom he could refresh himself, and, moreover, a certain Jew had broken into the city, named Simon, and with his charms of sorcery and his wickedness hath he made all the brotherhood fall away this way and that, so that I also fled from Rome, expecting the coming of Peter: For Paul had told us of him, and I also have seen many things in a vision. Now, therefore, I believe in my Lord that he will build up again his ministry, for all this deceit shall be rooted out from among his servants. For our Lord Jesus Christ is faithful, who is able to restore our minds. And when Theon heard these things from Ariston, who wept, his spirit was raised (*increased*) yet more and he was the more strengthened, because he perceived that he had believed on the living God.

But when they came together unto the ship, Peter looked upon them and smiled, being filled with the Spirit; so that Ariston falling

on his face at Peter's feet, said thus: "*Brother and lord, that hast part in the holy mysteries and showest the right way which is in the Lord Jesus Christ our God, who by thee hath shown unto us his coming: we have lost all them whom Paul had delivered unto us, by the working of Satan; but now I trust in the Lord who hath commanded thee to come unto us, sending thee as his messenger, that he hath accounted us worthy to see his great and wonderful works by thy means. I pray thee therefore, make haste unto the city: for I left the brethren which have stumbled, whom I saw fall into the temptation of the devil, and fled hither, saying unto them: Brethren, stand fast in the faith, for it is of necessity that within these two months the mercy of our Lord bring his servant unto you. For I had seen a vision, even Paul, saying unto me: Ariston, flee thou out of the city. And when I heard it, I believed without delay and went forth in the Lord, although I had an infirmity in my flesh, and came hither; and day by day I stood upon the sea-shore asking the sailors: Hath Peter sailed with you? But now through the abundance of the grace of God I entreat thee, let us go up unto Rome without delay, lest the teaching of this wicked man prevail yet further*".
And as Ariston said this with tears, Peter gave him his hand and raised him up from the earth, and Peter also groaning, said with tears: He hath prevented us which tempteth all the world by his angels; but he that hath power to save his servants from all temptations shall quench his deceits and put him beneath the feet of them that have believed in Christ whom we preach.

And, as they entered in at the gate, Theon entreated Peter, saying: "*Thou didst not refresh thyself on any day in so great a voyage (sea): and now after (before) so hard a journey wilt thou set out forthwith from the ship? tarry and refresh thyself, and so shalt thou set forth: for from hence to Rome upon a pavement of flint I fear lest thou be hurt by the shaking*". But Peter answered and said to them: "*What if it come to pass that a millstone were hung upon me, and likewise upon the enemy of our Lord, even as my Lord said unto us of any that offended one of the brethren, and I were drowned in the sea? but it might be not only a millstone, but that which is far worse, even that I which am the enemy of this persecutor of his servants should die afar off from them that have believed on the Lord Jesus Christ* (so Ficker: the sentence is corrupt; the sense is that Peter must at all costs be with his fellow-Christians, or he will incur even worse punishment than that threatened by our Lord's words). And by no exhortation could Theon prevail to persuade him to tarry there even one day.

But Theon himself delivered all that was in the ship to be sold for the price which he thought good, and followed Peter unto Rome; whom Ariston brought unto the abode of Narcissus the presbyter.

Chapter 7

Now the report was noised through the city unto the brethren that were dispersed, because of Simon, that he might show him to be a deceiver and a persecutor of good men. All the multitude therefore ran together to see the apostle of the Lord stay (*himself, or the brethren*) on Christ. And on the first day of the week when the multitude was assembled to see Peter, Peter began to say with a loud voice: "*Ye men here present that trust in Christ, ye that for a little space have suffered temptation, learn for what cause God sent his Son into the world, and wherefore he made him to be born of the Virgin Mary; for would he so have done if not to procure us some grace or dispensation? even because he would take away all offence and all ignorance and all the contrivance of the devil, his attempts (beginnings) and his strength wherewith he prevailed aforetime, before our God shined forth in the world. And whereas men through ignorance fell into death by many and divers infirmities, Almighty God, moved with compassion, sent his Son into the world. With whom I was; and he (or I) walked upon the water, whereof I myself remain awitness, and do testify that he then worked in the world by signs and wonders, all of which he did*".

"*I do confess, dearly-beloved brethren, that I was with him: yet I denied him, even our Lord Jesus Christ, and that not once only, but thrice; for there were evil dogs that were come about me as they did unto the Lord's prophets. And the Lord imputed it not unto me, but turned unto me and had compassion on the infirmity of my flesh, when (or so that) afterward I bitterly bewailed myself, and lamented the weakness of my faith, because I was befooled by the devil and kept not in mind the word of my Lord. And now I say unto you, O men and brethren, which are gathered together in the name of Jesus Christ: against you also hath the deceiver Satan aimed his arrows, that ye might depart out of the way. But faint not, brethren, neither let your spirit fall, but be strong and persevere and doubt not: for if Satan caused me to stumble, whom the Lord had in great honour, so that I denied the light of mine hope, and if he overthrew me and persuaded me to flee as if I had put my trust in a man, what think ye will he do unto you which are but young in the faith? Did ye suppose that he would not turn you away to make you enemies of the kingdom of God, and cast you down into perdition by a new (or the last) deceit? For whomsoever he casteth out from the hope of our Lord Jesus Christ, he is a son of perdition for ever. Turn yourselves, therefore, brethren, chosen of the Lord, and be strong in God Almighty, the Father of our Lord Jesus Christ, whom no man hath seen at any time, neither can see, save he who hath believed in him. And be ye aware whence this temptation hath come upon you. For it is not only by words that I would convince you that this is Christ whom I preach, but also by deeds and exceeding great works of power do I exhort you by the faith that is in Christ Jesus, that none of you look for any other save him that was despised and mocked of the Jews, even this Nazarene which was crucified and died and the third day rose again".*

Chapter 8

And the brethren repented and entreated Peter to fight against Simon: (*who said that he was the power of God, and lodged in the house of Marcellus a senator, whom he had convinced by his charms*) saying: *"Believe us, brother Peter: there was no man among men so wise as this Marcellus. All the widows that trusted in Christ had recourse unto him; all the fatherless were fed by him; and what more, brother? all the poor called Marcellus their patron, and his house was called the house of the strangers and of the poor, and the emperor said unto him: I will keep thee out of every office, lest thou despoil the provinces to give gifts unto the Christians".* And Marcellus answered: *"All my goods are also thine. And Caesar said to him: Mine they would be if thou keptest them for me; but now they are not mine, for thou givest them to whom thou wilt, and I know not to what vile persons. Having this, then, before our eyes, brother Peter, we report it to thee, how the great mercy of this man is turned unto blasphemy; for if he had not turned, neither should we have departed from the holy faith of God our Lord. And now doth this Marcellus in anger repent him of his good deeds, saying: All this substance have I spent in all this time, vainly believing that I gave it for the knowledge of God! So that if any stranger cometh to the door of his house, he smiteth him with a staff and biddeth him be beaten, saying: Would God I had not spent so much money upon these impostors: and yet more doth he say, blaspheming. But if there abide in thee any mercy of our Lord and aught of the goodness of his commandments, do thou succour the error of this man who hath done so many alms-deeds unto the servants of God".*

And Peter, when he perceived this, was smitten with sharp affliction and said: *"O the divers arts and temptations of the devil! O the contrivances and devices of the wicked! he that nourisheth up for himself a mighty fire in the day of wrath, the destruction of simple men, the ravening wolf, the devourer and scatterer of eternal life! Thou didst enmesh the first man in concupiscence and bind him with thine old iniquity and with the chain of the flesh: thou art wholly the exceeding bitter fruit of the tree of bitterness, who sendest divers lusts upon men. Thou didst compel Judas my fellow-disciple and fellow-apostle to do wickedly and deliver up our Lord Jesus Christ, who shall punish thee therefor. Thou didst harden the heart of Herod and didst inflame Pharaoh and compel him to fight against Moses the holy servant of God; thou didst give boldness unto Caiaphas, that he should deliver our Lord Jesus Christ unto the unrighteous multitude; and even until now thou shootest at innocent souls with thy poisonous arrows. Thou wicked one, enemy of all men, be thou accursed from the Church of him the Son of the holy God omnipotent and as a brand cast out of the fire shalt thou be quenched by the servants of our Lord Jesus Christ. Upon thee let thy blackness be turned and upon thy children, an evil seed; upon thee be turned thy wickedness and thy threatenings; upon thee and thine angels be thy temptations, thou beginning of malice and bottomless pit of darkness! Let thy darkness that thou hast be with thee and with thy vessels which thou ownest! Depart from them that shall believe in God, depart from the servants of Christ and from them that desire to be his soldiers. Keep thou to thyself thy garments of darkness! Without cause knockest thou at other men's doors, which are not thine but of Christ Jesus that keepeth them. For thou, ravening wolf, wouldest carry off the sheep that are not thine but of Christ Jesus, who keepeth them with all care and diligence".*

Chapter 9

As Peter spake thus with great sorrow of mind, many were added unto them that believed on the Lord. But the brethren besought Peter to join battle with Simon and not suffer him any longer to vex the people. And without delay Peter went quickly out of the synagogue (*assembly*) and went unto the house of Marcellus, where Simon lodged: and much people followed him. And when he came to the door, he called the porter and said to him: *"Go, say unto Simon: Peter because of whom thou fleddest out of Judaea waiteth for thee at the door"*. The porter answered and said to Peter: *"Sir, whether thou be Peter, I know not: but I have a command; for he had knowledge that yesterday thou didst enter into the city, and said unto me: Whether it be by day or by night, at whatsoever hour he cometh, say that I am not within"*. And Peter said to the young man: *"Thou hast well said in reporting that which he compelled thee to say"*. And Peter turned unto the people that followed him and said: *"Ye shall now see a great and marvellous wonder"*. And Peter seeing a great dog bound with a strong chain, went to him and loosed him, and when he was loosed the dog received a man's voice and said unto Peter: *"What dost thou bid me to do, thou servant of the unspeakable and living God?* " Peter said unto him: *"Go in and say unto Simon in the midst of his company"*: Peter saith unto thee, *"Come forth abroad, for thy sake am I come to Rome, thou wicked one and deceiver of simple souls"*. And immediately the dog ran and entered in, and rushed into the midst of them that were with Simon, and lifted up his forefeet and in a loud voice said: *"Thou Simon, Peter the servant of Christ who standeth at the door saith unto thee: Come forth abroad, for thy sake am I come to Rome, thou most wicked one and deceiver of simple souls"*. And when Simon heard it, and beheld the incredible sight, he lost the words wherewith he was deceiving them that stood by, and all of them were amazed.

Chapter 10

But when Marcellus saw it he went out to the door and cast himself at Peter's feet and said: *"Peter, I embrace thy feet, thou holy servant of the holy God; I have sinned greatly: but exact thou not my sins, if there be in thee the true faith of Christ, whom thou preachest, if thou remember his commandments, to hate no man, to be unkind to no man, as I learned from thy fellow apostle Paul; keep not in mind my faults, but pray for me unto the Lord, the holy Son of God whom I have provoked to wrath -for I have persecuted his servants- that I be not delivered with the sins of Simon unto eternal fire; who so persuaded me, that I set up a statue to him with this inscription: 'To Simon the new (young) God.' If I knew, O Peter, that thou*

*couldest be won with money, I would give thee all my substance, yea I
would give it and despise it, that I might gain my soul. If I had sons, I
would account them as nothing, if only I might believe in the living God.
But I confess that he would not have deceived me save that he said that he
was the power of God; yet will I tell thee, O most gentle (sweet) Peter: I was
not worthy to hear thee, thou servant of God, neither was I stablished in the
faith of God which is in Christ; therefore was I made to stumble. I beseech
thee, therefore, take not ill that which I am about to say, that Christ our
Lord whom thou preachest in truth said unto thy fellow-apostles in thy
presence: If ye have faith as a grain of mustard seed, ye shall say unto this
mountain: Remove thyself: and straightway it shall remove itself. But this
Simon said that thou, Peter, wast without faith when thou didst doubt, in
the waters. And I have heard that Christ said this also: They that are with
me have not understood me. If, then, ye upon whom he laid his hands,
whom also he chose, did doubt, I, therefore, having this witness, repent me,
and take refuge in thy prayers. Receive my soul, who have fallen away from
our Lord and from his promise. But I believe that he will have mercy upon
me that repent. For the Almighty is faithful to forgive me my sins".*

But Peter said with a loud voice: "*Unto thee, our Lord, be glory and
splendour, O God Almighty, Father of our Lord Jesus Christ. Unto thee be
praise and glory and honour, world without end. Amen. Because thou hast
now fully strengthened and stablished us in thee in the sight of all, holy
Lord, confirm thou Marcellus, and send thy peace upon him and upon his
house this day: and whatsoever is lost or out of the way, thou alone canst
turn them all again; we beseech thee, Lord, shepherd of the sheep that once
were scattered, but now shall be gathered in one by thee. So also receive thou
Marcellus as one of thy lambs and suffer him no longer to go astray (revel)
in error or ignorance. Yea, Lord, receive him that with anguish and tears
entreateth thee*".

Chapter 11

And as Peter spake thus and embraced Mareellus, Peter turned
himself unto the multitude that stood by him and saw there one
that laughed *(smiled)*, in whom was a very evil spirit. And Peter said
unto him: "*Whosoever thou art that didst laugh, show thyself openly unto
all that are present*". And hearing this the young man ran into the
court of the house and cried out with a loud voice and dashed

himself against the wall and said: *"Peter, there is a great contention between Simon and the dog whom thou sentest; for Simon saith to the dog: Say that I am not here. Unto whom the dog saith more than thou didst charge him; and when he hath accomplished the mystery which thou didst command him, he shall die at thy feet".* But Peter said: *"And thou also, devil, whosoever thou art, in the name of our Lord Jesus Christ, go out of that young man and hurt him not at all: show thyself unto all that stand here".* When the young man heard it, he ran forth and caught hold on a great statue of marble which was set in the court of the house, and brake it in pieces with his feet. Now it was a statue of Caesar. Which Marcellus beholding smote his forehead and said unto Peter: *"A great crime hath been committed; for if this be made known unto Caesar by some busybody, he will afflict us with sore punishments".* And Peter said to him: *"I see thee not the same that thou wast a little while ago, for thou saidst that thou wast ready to spend all thy substance to save thy soul. But if thou indeed repentest, believing in Christ with thy whole heart, take in thine hands of the water that runneth down, and pray to the Lord, and in his name sprinkle it upon the broken pieces of the statue and it shall be whole as it was before".* And Marcellus, nothing doubting, but believing with his whole heart, before he took the water lifted up his hands and said: *"I believe in thee, O Lord Jesus Christ: for I am now proved by thine apostle Peter, whether I believe aright in thine holy name. Therefore I take water in mine hands, and in thy name do I sprinkle these stones that the statue may become whole as it was before. If, therefore, Lord, it be thy will that I continue in the body and suffer nothing at Caesar's hand, let this stone be whole as it was before".* And he sprinkled the water upon the stones, and the statue became whole, where at Peter exulted that Marcellus had not doubted in asking of the Lord, and Marcellus was exalted in spirit for that such a sign was first wrought by his hands; and he therefore believed with his whole heart in the name of Jesus Christ the Son of God, by whom all things impossible are made possible.

Chapter 12

But Simon within the house said thus to the dog: *"Tell Peter that I am not within".* Whom the dog answered in the presence of Marcellus: *"Thou exceeding wicked and shameless one, enemy of all that live and believe on Christ Jesus, here is a dumb animal sent unto thee which hath received a human voice to confound thee and show thee to be a deceiver and a liar. Hast thou taken thought so long, to say at last: 'Tell him that I am not within?' Art thou not ashamed to utter thy feeble and useless words against Peter the minister and apostle of Christ, as if thou couldst hide thee from him that hath commanded me to speak against thee to thy face: and that not for thy sake but for theirs whom thou wast deceiving and sending unto destruction? Cursed therefore shalt thou be, thou enemy and corrupter of the way of the truth of Christ, who shall prove by fire that dieth not and in outer darkness, thine iniquities that thou hast committed".* And having thus said, the dog went forth and the people followed him, leaving Simon alone. And the dog came unto Peter as he sat with the multitude that was come to see Peter's face, and the dog related what he had done unto Simon. And thus spake the dog unto the angel and apostle of the true God: Peter, thou wilt have a great contest with the enemy of Christ and his servants, and many that have been deceived by him shalt thou turn unto the faith; wherefore thou shalt receive from God the reward of thy work. And when the dog had said this he fell down at the apostle Peter's feet and gave up the ghost. And when the great multitude saw with amazement the dog speaking, they began then, some to throw themselves down at Peter's feet, and some said: *"Show us another sign, that we may believe in thee as the minister of the living God, for Simon also did many signs in our presence and therefore did we follow him"*.

Chapter 13

And Peter turned and saw a herring (*sardine*) hung in a window, and took it and said to the people: *"If ye now see this swimming in the water like a fish, will ye be able to believe in him whom I preach?"* And they said with one voice: *"Verily we will believe thee"*. Then he said *"Now there was a bath for swimming at hand: In thy name, O Jesus Christ, forasmuch as hitherto it is not believed in, in the sight of all these live and swim like a fish"*. And he cast the herring into the bath, and it lived and began to swim. And all the people saw the fish swimming, and it did not so at that hour only, lest it should be said that it was a delusion (*phantasm*), but he made it to swim for a long time, so that they brought much people from all quarters and showed them the herring that was made a living fish, so that certain of the people even cast bread to it; and they saw that it was whole. And seeing this, many followed Peter and believed in the Lord. And they assembled themselves day and night unto the house of Narcissus the presbyter. And Peter discoursed unto them of the scriptures of the prophets and of those things which our Lord Jesus Christ had wrought both in word and in deeds.

Chapter 14

But Marcellus was confirmed daily by the signs which he saw wrought by Peter through the grace of Jesus Christ which he granted unto him. And Marcellus ran upon Simon as he sat in his house in the dining chamber, and cursed him and said unto him: *"Thou most adverse and pestilent of men, corrupter of my soul and my house, who wouldest have made me fall away from my Lord and Saviour Christ!"* and laying hands on him he commanded him to be thrust out of his house. And the servants having received such licence, covered him with reproaches; some buffeted his face, others beat him with sticks, others cast stones, others emptied out vessels full of filth upon his head, even those who on his account had fled from their master and been a long time fettered; and other their fellowservants of whom he had spoken evil to their master reproached him. saying to him: Now by the will of God who hath had mercy on us and on our master, do we recompense thee with a fit reward. And Simon, shrewdly beaten and cast out of the house, ran unto the house where Peter lodged, even the house of Narcissus, and standing at the gate cried out: *"Lo, here am I, Simon: come thou down, Peter, and I will convict thee that thou hast believed on a man which is a Jew and a carpenter's son"*.

Chapter 15

And when it was told Peter that Simon had said this, Peter sent unto him a woman which had a sucking child, saying to her: Go down quickly, and thou wilt find one that seeketh me. For thee there is no need that thou answer him at all, but keep silence and hear what the child whom thou holdest shall say unto him. The woman therefore went down. Now the child whom she suckled was seven months old; and it received a man's voice and said unto Simon: *"O thou abhorred of God and men, and destruction of truth, and evil seed of all corruption, O fruit by nature unprofitable! but only for a short and little season shalt thou be seen, and thereafter eternal punishment is laid up for thee. Thou son of a shameless father, that never puttest forth thy roots for good but for poison, faithless generation void of all hope! thou wast not confounded when a dog reproved thee; I a child am compelled of God to speak, and not even now art thou ashamed. But even against thy will, on the sabbath day that cometh, another shall bring thee into the forum of Julius that it may be shown what manner of man thou art. Depart therefore from the gate wherein walk the feet of the holy; for thou shalt no more corrupt the innocent souls whom thou didst turn out of the way and make sad; in Christ, therefore, shall be shown thine evil nature, and thy devices shall be cut in pieces. And now speak I this last word unto thee: Jesus Christ saith to thee: Be thou stricken dumb in my name, and depart out of Rome until the sabbath that cometh".* And forthwith he became dumb and his speech was bound; and he went out of Rome until the sabbath and abode in a stable. But the woman returned with the child unto Peter and told him and the rest of the brethren what the child had said unto Simon: and they magnified the Lord which had shown these things unto men.

[… sections omitted.].

[Here the Martyrdom proper begins in the Patmos MS. and the versions.]

Chapter 33

Now Peter was in Rome rejoicing in the Lord with the brethren, and giving thanks night and day for the multitude which was brought daily unto the holy name by the grace of the Lord. And there were gathered also unto Peter the concubines of Agrippa the prefect, being four, Agrippina and Nicaria and Euphemia and Doris; and they, hearing the word concerning chastity and all the oracles of the Lord, were smitten in their souls, and agreeing together to remain pure from the bed of Agrippa they were vexed by him.

Now as Agrippa was perplexed and grieved concerning them

and he loved them greatly. He observed and sent men privily to see whither they went, and found that they went unto Peter. He said therefore unto them when they returned: *"That Christian hath taught you to have no dealings with me: know ye that I will both destroy you, and burn him alive".* They, then, endured to suffer all manner of evil at Agrippa's hand, if only they might not suffer the passion of love, being strengthened by the might of Jesus.

Chapter 34

And a certain woman which was exceeding beautiful, the wife of Albinus, Caesar's friend, by name Xanthippe, came, she also, unto Peter, with the rest of the matrons, and withdrew herself, she also, from Albinus. He therefore being mad, and loving Xanthippe, and marvelling that she would not sleep even upon the same bed with him, raged like a wild beast and would have dispatched Peter; for he knew that he was the cause of her separating from his bed. Many other women also, loving the word of chastity, separated themselves from their husbands, because they desired them to worship God in sobriety and cleanness. And whereas there was great trouble in Rome, Albinus made known his state unto Agrippa, saying to him: *"Either do thou avenge me of Peter that hath withdrawn my wife, or I will avenge myself".* And Agrippa said: *"I have suffered the same at his hand, for he hath withdrawn my concubines".* And Albinus said unto him: *"Why then tarriest thou, Agrippa? let us find him and put him to death for a dealer in curious arts, that we may have our wives again, and avenge them also which are not able to put him to death, whose wives also he hath parted from them".*

Chapter 35

And as they considered these things, Xanthippe took knowledge of the counsel of her husband with Agrippa, and sent and showed Peter, that he might depart from Rome. And the rest of the brethren, together with Marcellus, besought him to depart. But Peter said unto them: *"Shall we be runaways, brethren?"* and they said to him: *"Nay, but that thou mayest yet be able to serve the Lord."* And he obeyed the brethren's voice and went forth alone, saying: *"Let none of you come forth with me, but I will go forth alone, having changed the fashion of mine apparel"*. And as he went forth of the city, he saw the Lord entering into Rome. And when he saw him, he said: *"Lord, whither goest thou thus (or here)?"* And the Lord said unto him: *"I go into Rome to be crucified."* And Peter said unto him: *"Lord, art thou (being) crucified again?"* He said unto him: *"Yea, Peter, I am (being) crucified again"*. And Peter came to himself: and having beheld the Lord ascending up into heaven, he returned to Rome, rejoicing, and glorifying the Lord, for that he said: *"I am being crucified":* the which was about to befall Peter.

Chapter 36

He went up therefore again unto the brethren, and told them that which had been seen by him: and they lamented in soul, weeping and saying: *"We beseech thee, Peter, take thought for us that are young"*. And Peter said unto them: *"If it be the Lord's will, it cometh to pass, even if we will it not; but for you, the Lord is able to stablish you in his faith, and will found you therein and make you spread abroad, whom he himself hath planted, that ye also may plant others through him. But I, so long as the Lord will that I be in the flesh, resist not; and again if he take me to him I rejoice and am glad"*.

And while Peter thus spake, and all the brethren wept, behold four soldiers took him and led him unto Agrippa. And he in his madness (*disease*) commanded him to be crucified on an accusation of godlessness.

The whole multitude of the brethren therefore ran together, both of rich and poor, orphans and widows, weak and strong, desiring to see and to rescue Peter, while the people shouted with one voice, and would not be silenced: *"What wrong hath Peter done, O Agrippa? Wherein hath he hurt thee? tell the Romans! And others said: We fear lest if this man die, his Lord destroy us all"*.

And Peter when he came unto the place stilled the people and said: *"Ye men that are soldiers of Christ! ye men that hope in Christ! remember the signs and wonders which ye have seen wrought through me, remember the compassion of God, how many cures he hath wrought for you. Wait for him that cometh and shall reward every man according to his doings. And now be ye not bitter against Agrippa; for he is the minister of his father's working. And this cometh to pass at all events, for the Lord hath manifested unto me that which befalleth. But why delay I and draw not near unto the cross?* "

Chapter 37

And having approached and standing by the cross he began to say: "*O name of the cross, thou hidden mystery! O grace ineffable that is pronounced in the name of the cross! O nature of man, that cannot be separated from God! O love (friendship) unspeakable and inseparable, that cannot be shown forth by unclean lips! I seize thee now, I that am at the end of my delivery hence (or, of my coming hither). I will declare thee, what thou art: I will not keep silence of the mystery of the cross which of old was shut and hidden from my soul. Let not the cross be unto you which hope in Christ, this which appeareth: for it is another thing, different from that which appeareth, even this passion which is according to that of Christ. And now above all, because ye that can hear are able to hear it of me, that am at the last and final hour of my life, hearken: Separate your souls from every thing that is of the senses, from every thing that appeareth, and does not exist in truth. Blind these eyes of yours, close these ears of yours, put away your doings that are seen; and ye shall perceive that which concerneth Christ, and the whole mystery of your salvation: and let thus much be said unto you that hear, as if it had not been spoken. But now it is time for thee, Peter, to deliver up thy body unto them that take it. Receive it then, ye unto whom it belongeth. I beseech you the executioners, crucify me thus, with the head downward and not otherwise: and the reason wherefore, I will tell unto them that hear*".

Chapter 38

And when they had hanged him up after the manner he desired, he began again to say: "*Ye men unto whom it belongeth to hear, hearken to that which I shall declare unto you at this especial time as I hang here. Learn ye the mystery of all nature, and the beginning of all things, what it was. For the first man, whose race I bear in mine appearance (or, of the race of whom I bear the likeness), fell (was borne) head downwards, and showed forth a manner of birth such as was not heretofore: for it was dead, having no motion. He, then, being pulled down who also cast his first state down upon the earth- established this whole disposition of all things, being hanged up an image of the creation (Gk. vocation) wherein he made the things of the right hand into left hand and the left hand into right hand, and changed about all the marks of their nature, so that he thought those things that were not fair to be fair, and those that were in truth evil, to be good. Concerning which the Lord saith in a mystery: Unless ye make the things of the right hand as those of the left, and those of the left as those of the right, and those that are above as those below, and those that are behind as those that are before, ye shall not have knowedge of the kingdom.*

This thought, therefore, have I declared unto you; and the figure wherein ye now see me hanging is the representation of that man that first came unto birth. Ye therefore, my beloved, and ye that hear me and that shall hear, ought to cease from your former error and return back again. For it is right to mount upon the cross of Christ, who is the word stretched out, the one and only, of whom the spirit saith: For what else is Christ, but the word, the sound of God? So that the word is the upright beam whereon I am crucified. And the sound is that which crosseth it, the nature of man. And the nail which holdeth the cross-tree unto the upright in the midst thereof is the conversion and repentance of man. "

Chapter 39

"Now whereas thou hast made known and revealed these things unto me, O word of life, called now by me wood (or, word called now by me the tree of life), I give thee thanks, not with these lips that are nailed unto the cross, nor with this tongue by which truth and falsehood issue forth, nor with this word which cometh forth by means of art whose nature is material, but with that voice do I give thee thanks, O King, which is perceived (understood) in silence, which is not heard openly, which proceedeth not forth by organs of the body, which goeth not into ears of flesh, which is not heard of corruptible substance, which existeth not in the world, neither is sent forth upon earth, nor written in books, which is owned by one and not by another: but with this, O Jesus Christ, do I give thee thanks, with the silence of a voice, wherewith the spirit that is in me loveth thee, speaketh unto thee, seeth thee, and beseecheth thee. Thou art perceived of the spirit only, thou art unto me father, thou my mother, thou my brother, thou my friend, thou my bondsman, thou my steward: thou art the All and the All is in thee: and thou Art, and there is nought else that is save

thee only.

Unto him therefore do ye also, brethren, flee, and if ye learn that in him alone ye exist, ye shall obtain those things whereof he saith unto you: 'which neither eye hath seen nor ear heard, neither have they entered into the heart of man.' We ask, therefore, for that which thou hast promised to give unto us, O thou undefiled Jesu. We praise thee, we give thee thanks, and confess to thee, glorifying thee, even we men that are yet without strength, for thou art God alone, and none other: to whom be glory now and unto all ages. Amen."

Chapter 40

And when the multitude that stood by pronounced the Amen with a great sound, together with the Amen, Peter gave up his spirit unto the Lord.

And Marcellus not asking leave of any, for it was not possible, when he saw that Peter had given up the ghost, took him down from the cross with his own hands and washed him in milk and wine: and cut fine seven minae of mastic, and of myrrh and aloes and indian leaf other fifty, and perfumed (*embalmed*) his body and filled a coffin of marble of great price with Attic honey and laid it in his own tomb. But Peter by night appeared unto Marcellus and said: *"Marcellus, hast thou heard that the Lord saith: Let the dead be buried of their own dead?"* And when Marcellus said: *"Yea"*, Peter said to him: *"That, then, which thou hast spent on the dead, thou hast lost: for thou being alive hast like a dead man cared for the dead. And Marcellus awoke and told the brethren of the appearing of Peter: and he was with them that had been stablished in the faith of Christ by Peter, himself also being stablished yet more until the coming of Paul unto Rome."*

Chapter 41

[This last chapter, and the last sentence of Chapter 40 are thought by Vouaux to be an addition by the author of i-iii, in other words by the compiler of the Greek original of the Vercelli Acts.]

But Nero, learning thereafter that Peter was departed out of this life, blamed the prefect Agrippa, because he had been put to death without his knowledge; for he desired to punish him more sorely and with greater torment, because Peter had made disciples of certain of them that served him, and had caused them to depart from him: so that he was very wrathful and for a long season spake not unto Agrippa: for he sought to destroy all them that had been made disciples by Peter. And he beheld by night one that scourged him and said unto him: Nero, thou canst not now persecute nor destroy the servants of Christ: refrain therefore thine hands from them. And so Nero, being greatly affrighted by such a vision, abstained from harming the disciples at that time when Peter also departed this life.

And thenceforth the brethren were rejoicing with one mind and exulting in the Lord, glorifying the God and Saviour (*Father?*) of our Lord Jesus Christ with the Holy Ghost, unto whom be glory, world without end. Amen.

The Acts of John
(150 – 200 A.D.)

The Acts of John is a collection of narratives and traditions concerning John the Apostle inspired by the *Gospel of John*, long known in fragmentary form. As a description of acts attributed to one of the major apostles who had put their words down into the New Testament, together with the Acts of Paul it is considered one of the most significant of the apostolic Acts in the New Testament Apocrypha.

The traditional author was said to be one Leucius Charinus, a companion of John, who was associated with several 2nd century "*Acts*." Conventionally, the Acts of John was ascribed to Prochorus, one of the Seven Deacons discussed in Acts of the Apostles. "It is difficult to know when the Acts of John was composed, but many scholars locate it to the second half of the second century." It may have originated as a Christianized wonder tale, designed for an urban Hellenic audience accustomed to such things as having one's portrait painted (*the setting for one episode*), living in that part of the province of Asia.

"It is widely recognized that the surviving Acts of John derives from several sources; most scholars recognize that a large portion of the text (*chaps. 87–105, or just 94–102*) as we now have it was interpolated at a later time into the narrative." The Acts of John was eventually rejected by the orthodox Church for its docetic overtones. After this decision made by the Second Council of Nicaea in 787 A.D., most of the existing copies of the apocryphal book were destroyed, undoubtedly destroying most of the copies in existence at the time.

As with the other works of the Acts of the Apostles genre, the text pertains to narratives set within the framework of the years following the crucifixion and subsequent resurrection of Jesus described by early Christian writings and traditions. Specifically, the account narrates two journeys of John, son of Zebedee, to Ephesus, filled with dramatic events, miracles, and teachings attributed to the apostle. [37]

---

[37] http://en.wikipedia.org/wiki/Acts_of_John

Summary notation: *Due to it's importance and historical significance to the early Church, the* **Acts of John** *is presented in some detail but not entirely. .Due to the length of the manuscript, only key excerpts or talking points are presented for discussion. Please note sections omitted in the early manuscript.* :

Excerpts from the Acts of John

Chapter 1

18 Now John was hastening to Ephesus, moved thereto by a vision. Damonicus therefore, and Aristodemus his kinsman, and a certain very rich man Cleobius, and the wife of Marcellus, hardly prevailed to keep him for one day in Miletus, reposing themselves with him. And when very early in the morning they had set forth, and already about four miles of the journey were accomplished, a voice came from heaven in the hearing of all of us, saying: *"John, thou art about to give glory to thy Lord in Ephesus, whereof thou shalt know, thou and all the brethren that are with thee, and certain of them that are there, which shall believe by thy means".* John therefore pondered, rejoicing in himself, what it should be that should befall (*meet*) him at Ephesus, and said: *"Lord, behold I go according to thy will: let that be done which thou desirest".*

[... sections omitted.].

22 And even as John thus cried out, the city of the Ephesians ran together to the house of Lycomedes, hearing that he was dead. And John, beholding the great multitude that was come, said unto the Lord: *"Now is the time of refreshment and of confidence toward thee, O Christ; now is the time for us who are sick to have the help that is of thee, O physician who healest freely; keep thou mine entering in hither safe from derision. I beseech thee, Jesu, succour this great multitude that it may come to thee who art Lord of all things: behold the affliction, behold them that lie here. Do thou prepare, even from them that are assembled for that end, holy vessels for thy service, when they behold thy gift. For thyself hast said, O Christ, 'Ask, and it shall be given you'. We ask therefore of thee, O king, not gold, not silver, not substance, not possessions, nor aught of what is on earth* *and perisheth, but two souls, by whom thou shalt convert them that are here unto thy way, unto thy teaching, unto thy liberty (confidence), unto thy most excellent (or unfailing) promise: for when they perceive thy power in that those that have died are raised, they will be saved, some of them. Do thou thyself, therefore, give them hope in thee: and so go I unto Cleopatra and say: Arise in the name of Jesus Christ".*

23 And he came to her and touched her face and said: *"Cleopatra, He saith, whom every ruler feareth, and every creature and every power, the abyss and all darkness, and unsmiling death, and the height of heaven, and the circles of hell [and the resurrection of the dead, and the sight of the blind], and the whole power of the prince of this world, and the pride of the ruler: Arise, and be not an occasion unto many that desire not to believe, or an affliction unto souls that are able to hope and to be saved".* And Cleopatra straightway cried with a loud voice: *"I arise, master: save thou thine handmaid".*

Now when she had arisen seven days, the city of the Ephesians was moved at the unlooked for sight. And Cleopatra asked concerning her husband Lycomedes, but John said to her: *"Cleopatra, if thou keep thy soul unmoved and steadfast, thou shalt forthwith have Lycomedes thine husband standing here beside thee, if at least thou be not disturbed nor moved at that which hath befallen, having believed on my God, who by my means shall grant him unto thee alive. Come therefore with me into thine other bedchamber, and thou shalt behold him, a dead corpse indeed, but raised again by the power of my God".*

24 And Cleopatra going with John into her bedchamber, and seeing Lycomedes dead for her sake, had no power to speak (*suffered in her voice*), and ground her teeth and bit her tongue, and closed her eyes, raining down tears: and with calmness gave heed to the apostle. But John had compassion on Cleopatra when he saw that she neither raged nor was beside herself, and called upon the perfect and condescending mercy, saying: *"Lord Jesus Christ, thou seest the pressure of sorrow, thou seest the need; thou seest Cleopatra shrieking her soul out in silence, for she constraineth within her the frenzy that cannot be borne; and I know that for Lycomedes' sake she also will die upon his body".* And she said quietly to John: *"That have I in mind, master, and nought else."*

And the apostle went to the couch whereon Lycomedes lay, and taking Cleopatra's hand he said: *"Cleopatra, because of the multitude that is present, and thy kinsfolk that have come in, with strong crying, say thou to thine husband: Arise and glorify the name of God, for he giveth back the dead to the dead".* And she went to her husband and said to him according as she was taught, and forthwith raised him up. And he, when he arose, fell on the floor and kissed John's feet, but he raised him, saying: *"O man, kiss not my feet but the feet of God by whose power ye are both arisen. "*

25 But Lycomedes said to John: *"I entreat and adjure thee by the God in whose name thou hast raised us, to abide with us, together with all them that are with thee".* Likewise Cleopatra also caught his feet and said the same. And John said to them: *"For tomorrow I will be with you".* And they said to him again: *"We shall have no hope in thy God, but shall have been raised to no purpose, if thou abide not with us".* And Cleobius with Aristodemus and Damonicus were touched in the soul and said to John: *"Let us abide with them, that they continue without offence towards the Lord".* So he continued there with the brethren.

26 There came together therefore a gathering of a great multitude on John's account; and as he discoursed to them that were there, Lycomedes, who had a friend who was a skilful painter, went hastily to him and said to him: *"You see me in a great hurry to come to you: come quickly to my house and paint the man whom I show you without his knowing it".* And the painter, giving some one the necessary implements and colours, said to Lycomedes: *"Show him to me, and for the rest have no anxiety".* And Lycomedes pointed out John to the painter, and brought him near him, and shut him up in a room from which the apostle of Christ could be seen. And Lycomedes was with the blessed man, feasting on the faith and the knowledge of our God, and rejoiced yet more in the thought that he should possess him in a portrait.

27 The painter, then, on the first day made an outline of him and went away. And on the next he painted him in with his colours, and so delivered the portrait to Lycomedes to his great joy. And lie took it and set it up in his own bedchamber and hung it with garlands: so that later John, when he perceived it, said to him: *"My beloved child, what is it that thou always doest when thou comest in from the bath into thy bedchamber alone? do not I pray with thee and the rest of the brethren? or is there something thou art hiding from us? "* And as he said this and talked jestingly with him, he went into the bedchamber, and saw the portrait of an old man crowned with garlands, and lamps and altars set before it. And he called him and said: *"Lycomedes, what meanest thou by this matter of the portrait? can it be one of thy gods that is painted here? for I see that thou art still living in heathen fashion".* And Lycomedes answered him: *"My only God is he who raised me up from death with my wife: but if, next to that God, it be right that the men who have benefited us should be called gods it is thou, father, whom I have had painted in that portrait, whom I crown and love and reverence as having become my good guide".*

28 And John who had never at any time seen his own face said to him: *"Thou mockest me, child: am I like that in form, thy Lord? how canst thou persuade me that the portrait is like me? And Lycomedes brought him a mirror".* And when he had seen himself in the mirror and looked earnestly at the portrait, he said: *"As the Lord Jesus Christ liveth, the portrait is like me: yet not like me, child, but like my fleshly image; for if this painter, who hath imitated this my face, desireth to draw me in a portrait, he will be at a loss, the colours that are now given to thee, and boards and plaster and glue and the position of my shape, and old age and youth and all things that are seen with the eye".*

29 *"But do thou become for me a good painter, Lycomedes. Thou hast colours which he giveth thee through me, who painteth all of us for himself, even Jesus, who knoweth the shapes and appearances and postures and dispositions and types of our souls. And the colours wherewith I bid thee paint are these: faith in God, knowledge, godly fear, friendship, communion, meekness, kindness, brotherly love, purity, simplicity, tranquillity, fearlessness, griefiessness, sobriety, and the whole band of colours that painteth the likeness of thy soul, and even now raiseth up thy members that were cast down, and levelleth them that were lifted up, and tendeth thy bruises, and healeth thy wounds, and ordereth thine hair that was disarranged, and washeth thy face, and chasteneth thine eyes, and purgeth thy bowels, and emptieth thy belly, and cutteth off that which is beneath it; and in a word, when the whole company and mingling of such colours is come together, into thy soul, it shall present it to our Lord Jesus Christ undaunted, whole (unsmoothed), and firm of shape. But this that thou hast now done is childish and imperfect: thou hast drawn a dead likeness of the dead".*

[… sections omitted.].

33 "*Ye men of Ephesus, learn first of all wherefore I am visiting in your city, or what is this great confidence which I have towards you, so that it may become manifest to this general assembly and to all of you (or, so that I manifest myself to). I have been sent, then, upon a mission which is not of man's ordering, and not upon any vain journey; neither am I a merchant that make bargains or exchanges; but Jesus Christ whom I preach, being compassionate and kind, desireth by my means to convert all of you who are held in unbelief and sold unto evil lusts, and to deliver you from error; and by his power will I confound even the unbelief of your praetor, by raising up them that lie before you, whom ye all behold, in what plight and in what sicknesses they are. And to do this (to confound Andronicus) is not possible for me if they perish: therefore shall they be healed*".

[… sections omitted.].

45 And John said to them: "*Men (of Ephesus), believe that for your sakes I have continued in Ephesus, and have put off my journey unto Smyrna and to the rest of the cities, that there also the servants of Christ may turn to him. But since I am not yet perfectly assured concerning you, I have continued praying to my God and beseeching him that I should then depart from Ephesus when I have confirmed you in the faith: and whereas I see that this is come to pass and yet more is being fulfilled, I will not leave you until I have weaned you like children from the nurse's milk, and have set you upon a firm rock*".

46 John therefore continued with them, receiving them in the house of Andromeus. And one of them that were gathered laid down the dead body of the priest of Artemis before the door [*of the temple*], for he was his kinsman, and came in quickly with the rest, saying nothing of it. John, therefore, after the discourse to the brethren, and the prayer and the thanksgiving (*eucharist*) and the laying of hands upon every one of the congregation, said by the spirit: "*There is one here who moved by faith in God hath laid down the priest of Artemis before the gate and is come in, and in the yearning of his soul, taking care first for himself, hath thought thus in himself: It is better for me to take thought for the living than for my kinsman that is dead: for I know that if I turn to the Lord and save mine own soul, John will not deny to raise up the dead also. And John arising from his place went to that into which that kinsman of the priest who had so thought was entered, and took him by the hand and said: Hadst thou this thought when thou camest unto* *me, my child? And he, taken with trembling and affright, said: Yes, lord, and cast himself at his feet."* And John said: *"Our Lord is Jesus Christ, who will show his power in thy dead kinsman by raising him up".*

[... sections omitted.].

Then the elder, hearing this and seeing that he was not bidden, but that the apostle of Christ had told him all that was in his heart, fell on his face on the earth and cried aloud, saying: *"Now know I that God dwelleth in thee, O blessed John! for he that tempteth thee tempteth him that cannot be tempted".* And he entreated him to pray for him. And he instructed him and delivered him the rules (*canons*) and let him go to his house, glorifying God that is over all.

Cassian, Collation XXIV. 21, has it thus: It is told that the most blessed Evangelist John, when he was gently stroking a partridge with his hands, suddenly saw one in the habit of a hunter coming to him. He wondered that a man of such repute and fame should demean himself to such small and humble amusements, and said: *"Art thou that John whose eminent and widespread fame hath enticed me also with great desire to know thee? Why then art thou taken up with such mean amusements?"* The blessed John said to him: *"What is that which thou carriest in thy hands?" "A bow",* said he. *"And why",* said he, *"dost thou not bear it about always stretched?"* He answered him: *"I must not, lest by constant bending the strength of its vigour be wrung and grow soft and perish, and when there is need that the arrows be shot with much strength at some beast, the strength being lost by excess of continual tension, a forcible blow cannot be dealt".* *"Just so",* said the blessed John, *"let not this little and brief relaxation of my mind offend thee, young man, for unless it doth sometimes ease and relax by some remission the force of its tension, it will grow slack through unbroken rigour and will not be able to obey the power of the Spirit."*

[The only common point of the two stories is that St. John amuses himself with a partridge, and a spectator thinks it unworthy of him. The two morals differ wholly. The amount of text lost here is of quite uncertain length. It must have told of the doings at Smyrna, and also, it appears, at Laodicea (see the title of the next section). One of the episodes must have been the conversion of a woman of evil life (see below, 'the harlot that was chaste ') Our best manuscript prefixes a title to the next section: From Laodicca to Ephesus the second time.]

58 Now when some long time had passed, and none of the brethren had been at any time grieved by John, they were then grieved because he had said:" *Brethren, it is now time for me to go to Ephesus (for so have I agreed with them that dwell there) lest they become slack, now for a long time having no man to confirm them. But all of you must have your minds steadfast towards God, who never forsaketh us".*

But when they heard this from him, the brethren lamented because they were to be parted from him. And John said: *"Even if I be parted from you, yet Christ is always with you: whom if ye love purely ye will have his fellowship without reproach, for if he be loved, he preventeth (anticipateth) them that love him."*

[... sections omitted.].

75 And John, looking upon the body, said to the venomous beast: *"Get thee away from him that is to be a servant of Jesus Christ";* and stood up and prayed over him thus: *"O God whose name is glorified by us, as of right: O God who subduest every injurious force: O God whose will is accomplished, who alway hearest us: now also let thy gift be accomplished in this young man; and if there be any dispensation to be wrought through him, manifest it unto us when he is raised up. And straightway the young man rose up, and for a whole hour kept silence".*

76 But when he came to his right senses, John asked of him about his entry into the sepulchre, what it meant, and learning from him that which Andronicus had told him, namely, that he was enamoured of Drusiana, John inquired of him again if he had fulfilled his foul intent, to insult a body full of holiness. And he answered him: *"How could I accomplish it when this fearful beast struck down Fortunatus at a blow in my sight: and rightly, since he encouraged my frenzy, when I was already cured of that unreasonable and horrible madness: but me it stopped with affright, and brought me to that plight in which ye saw me before I arose. And another thing yet more wondrous I will tell thee, which yet went nigh to slay and was within a little of making me a corpse. When my soul was stirred up with folly and the uncontrollable malady was troubling me, and I had now torn away the grave-clothes in which she was clad, and I had then come out of the grave and laid them as thou seest, I went again to my unholy work: and I saw a beautiful youth covering her with his mantle, and from his eyes sparks of light came forth unto her eyes; and he uttered words to me, saying: Callimachus, die that* *thou mayest live. Now who he was I knew not, O servant of God; but that now thou hast appeared here, I recognize that he was an angel of God, that I know well; and this I know of a truth that it is a true God that is proclaimed by thee, and of it I am persuaded. But I beseech thee, be not slack to deliver me from this calamity and this fearful crime, and to present me unto thy God as a man deceived with a shameful and foul deceit. Beseeching help therefore of thee, I take hold on thy feet. I would become one of them that hope in Christ, that the voice may prove true which said to me, 'Die that thou mayest live': and that voice hath also fulfilled its effect, for he is dead, that faithless, disorderly, godless one, and I have been raised by thee, I who will be faithful, God-fearing, knowing the truth, which I entreat thee may be shown me by thee".*

77 And John, filled with great gladness and perceiving the whole spectacle of the salvation of man, said: *"What thy power is, Lord Jesus Christ, I know not, bewildered as I am at thy much compassion and boundless long-suffering. O what a greatness that came down into bondage! O unspeakable liberty brought into slavery by us! O incomprehensible glory that is come unto us! thou that hast kept the dead tabernacle safe from insult; that hast redeemed the man that stained himself with blood and chastened the soul of him that would defile the corruptible body; Father that hast had pity and compassion on the man that cared not for thee; We glorify thee, and praise and bless and thank thy great goodness and long-suffering, O holy Jesu, for thou only art God, and none else: whose is the might that cannot be conspired against, now and world without end. Amen".*

78 And when he had said this John took Callimachus and saluted (*kissed*) him, saying: *"Glory be to our God, my child, who hath had mercy on thee, and made me worthy to glorify his power, and thee also by a good course to depart from that thine abominable madness and drunkenness, and hath called thee unto his own rest and unto renewing of life".*

79 But Andronicus, beholding the dead Callimachus raised, besought John, with the brethren, to raise up Drusiana also, saying: *"O John, let Drusiana arise and spend happily that short space (of life) which she gave up through grief about Callimachus, when she thought she had become a stumbling block to him: and when the Lord will, he shall take her again to himself. And John without delay went unto her tomb and took her hand and said: Upon thee that art the only God do I call, the more than* *great, the unutterable, the incomprehensible: unto whom every power of principalities is subjected: unto whom all authority boweth: before whom all pride falleth down and keepeth silence: whom devils hearing of tremble: whom all creation perceiving keepeth its bounds. Let thy name be glorified by us, and raise up Drusiana, that Callimachus may yet more be confirmed unto thee who dispensest that which unto men is without a way and impossible, but to thee only possible, even salvation and resurrection: and that Drusiana may now come forth in peace, having about her not any the least hindrance now that the young man is turned unto thee- in her course toward thee".*

80 And after these words John said unto Drusiana: *"Drusiana, arise".* And she arose and came out of the tomb; and when she saw herself in her shift only, she was perplexed at the thing, and learned the whole accurately from Andronicus, the while John lay upon his face, and Callimachus with voice and tears glorified God, and she also rejoiced, glorifying him in like manner.

81 And when she had clothed herself, she turned and saw Fortunatus lying, and said unto John: *"Father, let this man also rise, even if he did assay to become my betrayer".* But Callimachus, when he heard her say that, said: *"Do not, I beseech thee, Drusiana, for the voice which I heard took no thought of him, but declared concerning thee only, and I saw and believed: for if he had been good, perchance God would have had mercy on him also and would have raised him by means of the blessed John: he knew therefore that the man was come to a bad end [Lat. he judged him worthy to die whom he did not declare worthy to rise again]".* And John said to him: *"We have not learned, my child, to render evil for evil: for God, though we have done much ill and no good toward him, hath not given retribution unto us, but repentance, and though we were ignorant of his name he did not neglect us but had mercy on us, and when we blasphemed him, he did not punish but pitied us, and when we disbelieved him he bore us no grudge, and when we persecuted his brethren he did not recompense us evil but put into our minds repentance and abstinence from evil, and exhorted us to come unto him, as he hath thee also, my son Callimachus, and not remembering thy former evil hath made thee his servant, waiting upon his mercy. Wherefore if thou allowest not me to raise up Fortunatus, it is for Drusiana so to do".*

82 And she, delaying not, went with rejoicing of spirit and soul unto the body of Fortunatus and said: *"Jesus Christ, God of the ages,*

God of truth, that hast granted me to see wonders and signs, and given to me to become partaker of thy name; that didst breathe thyself into me with thy many-shaped countenance, and hadst mercy on me in many ways; that didst protect me by thy great goodness when I was oppressed by Andronicus that was of old my husband; that didst give me thy servant Andronicus to be my brother; that hast kept me thine handmaid pure unto this day; that didst raise me up by thy servant John, and when I was raised didst show me him that was made to stumble free from stumbling; that hast given me perfect rest in thee, and lightened me of the secret madness; whom I have loved and affectioned: I pray thee, O Christ, refuse not thy Drusiana that asketh thee to raise up Fortunatus, even though he assayed to become my betrayer".

83 And taking the hand of the dead man she said: *"Rise up, Fortunatus, in the name of our Lord Jesus Christ"*. And Fortunatus arose, and when he saw John in the sepulchre, and Andronicus, and Drusiana raised from the dead, and Callimachus a believer, and the rest of the brethren glorifying God, he said: *"O, to what have the powers of these clever men attained! I did not want to be raised, but would rather die, so as not to see them. And with these words he fled and went out of the sepulcher"*.

84 And John, when he saw the unchanged mind (*soul*) of Fortunatus, said: *"O nature that is not changed for the better! O fountain of the soul that abideth in foulness! O essence of corruption full of darkness! O death exulting in them that are thine! O fruitless tree full of fire! O tree that bearest coals for fruit! O matter that dwellest with the madness of matter (al. O wood of trees full of unwholesome shoots) and neighbour of unbelief! Thou hast proved who thou art, and thou art always convicted, with thy children. And thou knowest not how to praise the better things: for thou hast them not. Therefore, such as is thy way (?fruit), such also is thy root and thy nature. Be thou destroyed from among them that trust in the Lord: from their thoughts, from their mind, from their souls, from their bodies, from their acts their life, their conversation, from their business, their occupations, their counsel, from the resurrection unto (or rest in) God, from their sweet savour wherein thou wilt share, from their faith, their prayers, from the holy bath, from the eucharist, from the food of the flesh, from drink, from clothing, from love, from care, from abstinence, from righteousness: from all these, thou most unholy Satan, enemy of God, shall Jesus Christ our God and of all that are like thee and have thy character,* *make thee to perish".*

85 And having thus said, John prayed, and took bread and bare it into the sepulchre to break it; and said: *"We glorify thy name, which converteth us from error and ruthless deceit: we glorify thee who hast shown before our eyes that which we have seen: we bear witness to thy loving-kindness which appeareth in divers ways: we praise thy merciful name, O Lord (we thank thee), who hast convicted them that are convicted of thee: we give thanks to thee, O Lord Jesus Christ, that we are persuaded of thy which is unchanging: we give thanks to thee who hadst need of our nature that should be saved: we give thanks to thee that hast given us this sure , for thou art alone, both now and ever. We thy servants give thee thanks, O holy one, who are assembled with intent and are gathered out of the world (or risen from death)."*

86 And having so prayed and given glory to God, he went out of the sepulchre after imparting unto all the brethren of the eucharist of the Lord. And when he was come unto Andronicus' house he said to the brethren: *"Brethren, a spirit within me hath divined that Fortunatus is about to die of blackness (poisoning of the blood) from the bite of the serpent; but let some one go quickly and learn if it is so indeed".* And one of the young men ran and found him dead and the blackness spreading over him, and it had reached his heart: and came and told John that he had been dead three hours. And John said: *Thou hast thy child, O devil.* ... 'John therefore was with the brethren rejoicing in the Lord.'

[This sentence is in the best manuscript. In Bonnet's edition It introduces the last section of the Acts, which follows immediately in the manuscript. It may belong to either episode. The Latin has: And that day he spent joyfully with the brethren. There cannot be much of a gap between this and the next section, which is perhaps the most interesting in the Acts. The greater part of this episode is preserved only in one very corrupt fourteenth-century manuscript at Vienna. Two important passages (93-5 (part) and 97-8 (part)) were read at the Second Nicene Council and are preserved in the Acts thereof: a few lines of the Hymn are also cited in Latin by Augustine (Ep. 237 (253) to Ceretius): he found it current separately among the Priscillianists. The whole discourse is the best popular exposition we have of the Docetic view of our Lord's person.]

87 Those that were present inquired the cause, and were especially perplexed, because Drusiana had said: *"The Lord appeared unto me in the tomb in the likeness of John, and in that of a youth. Forasmuch, therefore, as they were perplexed and were, in a manner, not* *yet stablished in the faith, so as to endure it steadfastly, John said (or John bearing it patiently, said):*

88 *Men and brethren, ye have suffered nothing strange or incredible as concerning your perception of the , inasmuch as we also, whom he chose for himself to be apostles, were tried in many ways: I, indeed, am neither able to set forth unto you nor to write the things which I both saw and heard: and now is it needful that I should fit them for your hearing; and according as each of you is able to contain it I will impart unto you those things whereof ye are able to become hearers, that ye may see the glory that is about him, which was and is, both now and for ever.*

For when he had chosen Peter and Andrew, which were brethren, he cometh unto me and James my brother, saying: I have need of you, come unto me. And my brother hearing that, said: John, what would this child have that is upon the sea-shore and called us? And I said: What child? And he said to me again: That which beckoneth to us. And I answered: Because of our long watch we have kept at sea, thou seest not aright, my brother James; but seest thou not the man that standeth there, comely and fair and of a cheerful countenance? But he said to me: Him I see not, brother; but let us go forth and we shall see what he would have".

89 *"And so when we had brought the ship to land, we saw him also helping along with us to settle the ship: and when we departed from that place, being minded to follow him, again he was seen of me as having rather bald, but the beard thick and flowing, but of James as a youth whose beard was newly come. We were therefore perplexed, both of us, as to what that which we had seen should mean. And after that, as we followed him, both of us were by little and little perplexed as we considered the matter. Yet unto me there then appeared this yet more wonderful thing: for I would try to see him privily, and I never at any time saw his eyes closing (winking), but only open. And oft-times he would appear to me as a small man and uncomely, and then againt as one reaching unto heaven. Also there was in him another marvel: when I sat at meat he would take me upon his own breast; and sometimes his breast was felt of me to be smooth and tender, and sometimes hard like unto stones, so that I was perplexed in myself and said: Wherefore is this so unto me? And as I considered this, he . . "*

90 *"And at another time he taketh with him me and James and Peter unto the mountain where he was wont to pray, and we saw in him a light such as it is not possible for a man that useth corruptible (mortal) speech to describe what it was like. Again in like manner he bringeth us three up into* *the mountain, saying: Come ye with me. And we went again: and we saw him at a distance praying. I, therefore, because he loved me, drew nigh unto him softly, as though he could not see me, and stood looking upon his hinder parts: and I saw that he was not in any wise clad with garments, but was seen of us naked, and not in any wise as a man, and that his feet were whiter than any snow, so that the earth there was lighted up by his feet, and that his head touched the heaven: so that I was afraid and cried out, and he, turning about, appeared as a man of small stature, and caught hold on my beard and pulled it and said to me: John, be not faithless but believing, and not curious. And I said unto him: But what have I done, Lord? And I say unto you, brethren, I suffered so great pain in that place where he took hold on my beard for thirty days, that I said to him: Lord, if thy twitch when thou wast in sport hath given me so great pain, what were it if thou hadst given me a buffet? And he said unto me: Let it be thine henceforth not to tempt him that cannot be tempted".*

91 *"But Peter and James were wroth because I spake with the Lord, and beckoned unto me that I should come unto them and leave the Lord alone. And I went, and they both said unto me: He (the old man) that was speaking with the Lord upon the top of the mount, who was he? for we heard both of them speaking. And I, having in mind his great grace, and his unity which hath many faces, and his wisdom which without ceasing looketh upon us, said: That shall ye learn if ye inquire of him.*

92 *Again, once when all we his disciples were at Gennesaret sleeping in one house, I alone having wrapped myself in my mantle, watched (or watched from beneath my mantle) what he should do: and first I heard him say: John, go thou to sleep. And I thereon feigning to sleep saw another like unto him [sleeping], whom also I heard say unto my Lord: Jesus, they whom thou hast chosen believe not yet on thee (or do they not yet, &c.?). And my Lord said unto him: Thou sayest well: for they are men.*

93 *Another glory also will I tell you, brethren: Sometimes when I would lay hold on him, I met with a material and solid body, and at other times, again, when I felt him, the substance was immaterial and as if it existed not at all. And if at any time he were bidden by some one of the Pharisees and went to the bidding, we went with him, and there was set before each one of us a loaf by them that had bidden us, and with us he also received one; and his own he would bless and part it among us: and of that little every one was filled, and our own loaves were saved whole, so that they which bade him were amazed. And oftentimes when I walked with him, I desired to see* *the print of his foot, whether it appeared on the earth; for I saw him as it were lifting himself up from the earth: and I never saw it. And these things I speak unto you, brethren, for the encouragement of your faith toward him; for we must at the present keep silence concerning his mighty and wonderful works, inasmuch as they are unspeakable and, it may be, cannot at all be either uttered or heard.*

94 *Now before he was taken by the lawless Jews, who also were governed by (had their law from) the lawless serpent, he gathered all of us together and said: Before I am delivered up unto them let us sing an hymn to the Father, and so go forth to that which lieth before us. He bade us therefore make as it were a ring, holding one another's hands, and himself standing in the midst he said: Answer Amen unto me".* He began, then, to sing an hymn and to say:

> *Glory be to thee, Father.*
> *And we, going about in a ring, answered him: Amen.*
> *Glory be to thee, Word: Glory be to thee, Grace. Amen.*
> *Glory be to thee, Spirit: Glory be to thee, Holy One:*
> *Glory be to thy glory. Amen.*
> *We praise thee, O Father; we give thanks to thee, O Light, wherein darkness*
> *dwelleth not. Amen.*
> *95 Now whereas (or wherefore) we give thanks, I say:*
> *I would be saved, and I would save. Amen.*
> *I would be loosed, and I would loose. Amen.*
> *I would be wounded, and I would wound. Amen.*
> *I would be born, and I would bear. Amen.*
> *I would eat, and I would be eaten. Amen.*
> *I would hear, and I would be heard. Amen.*
> *I would be thought, being wholly thought. Amen.*
> *I would be washed, and I would wash. Amen.*
> *Grace danceth. I would pipe; dance ye all. Amen.*
> *I would mourn: lament ye all. Amen.*
> *The number Eight (lit. one ogdoad) singeth praise with us. Amen.*
> *The number Twelve danceth on high. Amen.*
> *The Whole on high hath part in our dancing. Amen.*
> *Whoso danceth not, knoweth not what cometh to pass. Amen.*
> *I would flee, and I would stay. Amen.*
> *I would adorn, and I would be adorned. Amen.*
> *I would be united, and I would unite. Amen.*
> *A house I have not, and I have houses. Amen.*

A place I have not, and I have places. Amen.
A temple I have not, and I have temples. Amen.
A lamp am I to thee that beholdest me. Amen.
A mirror am I to thee that perceivest me. Amen.
A door am I to thee that knockest at me. Amen.
A way am I to thee a wayfarer. .

96 *Now answer thou (or as thou respondest) unto my dancing. Behold thyself in me who speak, and seeing what I do, keep silence about my mysteries.*

Thou that dancest, perceive what I do, for thine is this passion of the manhood, which I am about to suffer. For thou couldest not at all have understood what thou sufferest if I had not been sent unto thee, as the word of the Father. Thou that sawest what I suffer sawest me as suffering, and seeing it thou didst not abide but wert wholly moved, moved to make wise. Thou hast me as a bed, rest upon me. Who I am, thou shalt know when I depart. What now I am seen to be, that I am not. Thou shalt see when thou comest. If thou hadst known how to suffer, thou wouldest have been able not to suffer. Learn thou to suffer, and thou shalt be able not to suffer. What thou knowest not, I myself will teach thee. Thy God am I, not the God of the traitor. I would keep tune with holy souls. In me know thou the word of wisdom. Again with me say thou: Glory be to thee, Father; glory to thee, Word; glory to thee, Holy Ghost. And if thou wouldst know concerning me, what I was, know that with a word did I deceive all things and I was no whit deceived. I have leaped: but do thou understand the whole, and having understood it, say: Glory be to thee, Father. Amen.

97 *Thus, my beloved, having danced with us the Lord went forth. And we as men gone astray or dazed with sleep fled this way and that. I, then, when I saw him suffer, did not even abide by his suffering, but fled unto the Mount of Olives, weeping at that which had befallen. And when he was crucified on the Friday, at the sixth hour of the day, darkness came upon all the earth. And my Lord standing in the midst of the cave and enlightening it, said: John, unto the multitude below in Jerusalem I am being crucified and pierced with lances and reeds, and gall and vinegar is given me to drink. But unto thee I speak, and what I speak hear thou. I put it into thy mind to come up into this mountain, that thou mightest hear those things which it behoveth a disciple to learn from his teacher and a man from his God.*

98 *And having thus spoken, he showed me a cross of light fixed (set up),* and about the cross a great multitude, not having one form: and in it (the cross) was one form and one likenesst [so the MS.; I would read: and therein was one form and one likeness: and in the cross another multitude, not having one form]. And the Lord himself I beheld above the cross, not having any shape, but only a voice: and a voice not such as was familiar to us, but one sweet and kind and truly of God, saying unto me: John, it is needful that one should hear these things from me, for I have need of one that will hear. This cross of light is sometimes called the (or a) word by me for your sakes, sometimes mind, sometimes Jesus, sometimes Christ, sometimes door, sometimes a way, sometimes bread, sometimes seed, sometimes resurrection, sometimes Son, sometimes Father, sometimes Spirit, sometimes life, sometimes truth, sometimes faith, sometimes grace. And by these names it is called as toward men: but that which it is in truth, as conceived of in itself and as spoken of unto you (MS. us), it is the marking-off of all things, and the firm uplifting of things fixed out of things unstable, and the harmony of wisdom, and indeed wisdom in harmony [this last clause in the MS. is joined to the next: 'and being wisdom in harmony']. There are of the right hand and the left, powers also, authorities, lordships and demons, workings, threatenings, wraths, devils, Satan, and the lower root whence the nature of the things that come into being proceeded.

99 This cross, then, is that which fixed all things apart (al. joined all things unto itself) by the (or a) word, and separate off the things that are from those that are below (lit. the things from birth and below it), and then also, being one, streamed forth into all things (or, made all flow forth. I suggested: compacted all into). But this is not the cross of wood which thou wilt see when thou goest down hence: neither am I he that is on the cross, whom now thou seest not, but only hearest his (or a) voice. I was reckoned to be that which I am not, not being what I was unto many others: but they will call me (say of me) something else which is vile and not worthy of me. As, then, the place of rest is neither seen nor spoken of, much more shall I, the Lord thereof, be neither seen ".

100 "Now the multitude of one aspect (al. of one aspect) that is about the cross is the lower nature: and they whom thou seest in the cross, if they have not one form, it is because not yet hath every member of him that came down been comprehended. But when the human nature (or the upper nature) is taken up, and the race which draweth near unto me and obeyeth my voice, he that now heareth me shall be united therewith, and shall no more be that which now he is, but above them, as I also now am. For so *long as thou callest not thyself mine, I am not that which I am (or was): but if thou hear me, thou, hearing, shalt be as I am, and I shall be that which I was, when I thee as I am with myself. For from me thou art that (which I am). Care not therefore for the many, and them that are outside the mystery despise; for know thou that I am wholly with the Father, and the Father with me.*

101 Nothing, therefore, of the things which they will say of me have I suffered: nay, that suffering also which I showed unto thee and the rest in the dance, I will that it be called a mystery. For what thou art, thou seest, for I showed it thee; but what I am I alone know, and no man else. Suffer me then to keep that which is mine, and that which is thine behold thou through me, and behold me in truth, that I am, not what I said, but what thou art able to know, because thou art akin thereto. Thou hearest that I suffered, yet did I not suffer; that I suffered not, yet did I suffer; that I was pierced, yet I was not smitten; hanged, and I was not hanged; that blood flowed from me, and it flowed not; and, in a word, what they say of me, that befell me not, but what they say not, that did I suffer. Now what those things are I signify unto thee, for I know that thou wilt understand. Perceive thou therefore in me the praising (al. slaying al. rest) of the (or a) Word (Logos), the piercing of the Word, the blood of the Word, the wound of the Word, the hanging up of the Word, the suffering of the Word, the nailing (fixing) of the Word, the death of the Word. And so speak I, separating off the manhood. Perceive thou therefore in the first place of the Word; then shalt thou perceive the Lord, and in the third place the man, and what he hath suffered.

102 When he had spoken unto me these things, and others which I know not how to say as he would have me, he was taken up, no one of the multitudes having beheld him. And when I went down I laughed them all to scorn, inasmuch as he had told me the things which they have said concerning him; holding fast this one thing in myself, that the Lord contrived all things symbolically and by a dispensation toward men, for their conversion and salvation.

103 Having therefore beheld, brethren, the grace of the Lord and his kindly affection toward us, let us worship him as those unto whom he hath shown mercy, not with our fingers, nor our mouth, nor our tongue, nor with any part whatsoever of our body, but with the disposition of our soul -even him who became a man apart from this body: and let us watch because (or we shall find that) now also he keepeth ward over prisons for our sake, and over tombs, in bonds and dungeons, in reproaches and insults, by sea and on dry land, in scourgings, condemnations, conspiracies, frauds, punishments, and in a word, he is with all of us, and himself suffereth with us when we suffer, brethren. When he is called upon by each one of us, he endureth not to shut his ears to us, but as being everywhere he hearkeneth to all of us; and now both to me and to Drusiana, -forasmuch as he is the God of them that are shut up bringing us help by his own compassion.

104 *Be ye also persuaded, therefore, beloved, that it is not a man whom I preach unto you to worship, but God unchangeable, God invincible, God higher than all authority and all power, and elder and mightier than all angels and creatures that are named, and all aeons. If then ye abide in him, and are builded up in him, ye shall possess your soul indestructible."*

105 And when he had delivered these things unto the brethren, John departed, with Andronicus, to walk. And Drusiana also followed afar off with all the brethren, that they might behold the acts that were done by him, and hear his speech at all times in the Lord.

[The remaining episode which is extant in the Greek is the conclusion of the book, the Death or Assumption of John. Before it must be placed the stories which we have only in the Latin (of 'Abdias' and another text by 'Mellitus', i.e. Melito), and the two or three isolated fragments.]

[… sections omitted.].

Chapter 14

Now on the next (*or another*) day Craton, a philosopher, had proclaimed in the market-place that he would give an example of the contempt of riches: and the spectacle was after this manner. He had persuaded two young men, the richest of the city, who were brothers, to spend their whole inheritance and buy each of them a jewel, and these they brake in pieces publicly in the sight of the people. And while they were doing this, it happened by chance that the apostle passed by. And calling Craton the philosopher to him, he said: "*That is a foolish despising of the world which is praised by the mouths of men, but long ago condemned by the judgement of God. For as that is a vain medicine whereby the disease is not extirpated, so is it a vain teaching by which the faults of souls and of conduct are not cured. But indeed my master taught a youth who desired to attain to eternal life, in these words; saying that if he would be perfect, he should sell all his goods and give to the poor, and so doing he would gain treasure in heaven and find the life that has no ending.*" And Craton said to him: "*Here the fruit of covetousness is set forth in the midst of men, and hath been broken to pieces. But if God is indeed thy master and willeth this to be, that the sum of the price of these jewels should be given to the poor, cause thou the gems to be restored whole, that what I have done for the praise of men, thou mayest do for the glory of him whom thou callest thy master.*" Then the blessed John gathered together the fragments of the gems, and holding them in his hands, lifted up his eyes to heaven and said: "*Lord Jesus Christ, unto whom nothing is impossible: who when the world was broken by the tree of concupiscence, didst restore it again in thy faithfulness by the tree of the cross: who didst give to one born blind the eyes which nature had denied him, who didst recall Lazarus, dead and buried, after the fourth day unto the light; and has subjected all diseases and all sicknesses unto the word of thy power: so also now do with these precious stones which these, not knowing the fruits of almsgiving, have broken in pieces for the praise of men: recover thou them, Lord, now by the hands of thine angels, that by their value the work of mercy may be fulfilled, and make these men believe in thee the unbegotten Father through thine only-begotten Son Jesus Christ our Lord, with the Holy Ghost the illuminator and sanctifier of the whole Church, world without end.* "And when the faithful who were with the apostle had answered and said "*Amen*", the fragments of the gems were forthwith so joined in one that no mark at all that they had been broken remained in them. And Craton the philosopher, with his disciples, seeing this, fell at the feet of the apostle and believed thenceforth (*or immediately*) and was baptized, with them all, and began himself publicly to preach the faith of our Lord Jesus Christ.

Chapter 15

Those two brothers, therefore, of whom we spake, sold the gems which they had bought by the sale of their inheritance and gave the price to the poor; and thereafter a very great multitude of believers began to be joined to the apostle.

And when all this was done, it happened that after the same

example, two honourable men of the city of the Ephesian sold all their goods and distributed them to the needy, and followed the apostle as he went through the cities preaching the word of God. But it came to pass, when they entered the city of Pergamum, that they saw their servants walking abroad arrayed in silken raiment and shining with the glory of this world: whence it happened that they were pierced with the arrow of the devil and became sad, seeing themselves poor and clad with a single cloak while their own servants were powerful and prosperous. But the apostle of Christ, perceiving these wiles of the devil, said: "*I see that ye have changed your minds and your countenances on this account, that, obeying the teaching of my Lord Jesus Christ, ye have given all ye had to the poor. Now, if ye desire to recover that which ye formerly possessed of gold, silver, and precious stones, bring me some straight rods, each of you a bundle*". And when they had done so, he called upon the name of the Lord Jesus Christ, and they were turned into gold. And the apostle said to them: "*Bring me small stones from the seashore*". And when they had done this also, he called upon the majesty of the Lord, and all the pebbles were turned into gems. Then the blessed John turned to those men and said to them: "*Go about to the goldsmiths and jewellers for seven days, and when ye have proved that these are true gold and true jewels, tell me*". And they went, both of them, and after seven days returned to the apostle, saying: "*Lord, we have gone about the shops of all the goldsmiths, and they have all said that they never saw such pure gold. Likewise the jewellers have said the same, that they never saw such excellent and precious gems*".

Chapter 16

Then the holy John said unto them: "*Go, and redeem to you the lands which ye have sold, for ye have lost the estates of heaven. Buy yourselves silken raiment, that for a time ye may shine like the rose which showeth its fragrance and redness and suddenly fadeth away. For ye sighed at beholding your servants and groaned that ye were become poor. Flourish, therefore, that ye may fade: be rich for the time, that ye may be beggars for ever. Is not the Lord's hand able to make riches overflowing and unsurpassably glorious? but he hath appointed a conflict for souls, that they may believe that they shall have eternal riches, who for his name's sake have refused temporal wealth. Indeed, our master told us concerning a certain rich man who feasted every day and shone with gold and purple, at whose door lay a beggar, Lazarus, who desired to receive even the crumbs that fell from his table, and no man gave unto him. And it came to pass that on one day they died, both of them, and that beggar was taken into the rest which is in Abraham's bosom, but the rich man was cast into flaming fire: out of which he lifted up his eyes and saw Lazarus, and prayed him to dip his finger in water and cool his mouth for he was tormented in the flames. And Abraham answered him and said: Remember, son, that thou receivedst good things in thy life, but this Lazarus likewise evil things. Wherefore rightly is he now comforted while thou art tormented, and besides all this, a great gulf is fixed between you and us, so that neither can they come thence hither, nor hither thence. But he answered: I have five brethren: I pray that some one may go to warn them, that they come not into this flame. And Abraham said to him: They have Moses and the prophets, let them hear them. To that he answered: Lord, unless one rise up again, they will not believe. Abraham said to him: If they believe not Moses and the prophets, neither will they believe, if one rise again. And these words our Lord and Master confirmed by examples of mighty works: for when they said to him: Who hath come hither from thence, that we may believe him? he answered: Bring hither the dead whom ye have. And when they had brought unto him a young man which was dead (Ps.-Mellitus: three dead corpses), he was waked up by him as one that sleepeth, and confirmed all his words".*

"But wherefore should I speak of my Lord, when at this present there are those whom in his name and in your presence and sight I have raised from the dead: in whose name ye have seen palsied men healed, lepers cleansed, blind men enlightened, and many delivered from evil spirits ? But the riches of these mighty works they cannot have who have desired to have earthly wealth. Finally, when ye yourselves went unto the sick and called upon the name of Jesus Christ, they were healed: ye did drive out devils and restore light to the blind. Behold, this grace is taken from you, and ye are become wretched, who were mighty and great. And where as there was such fear of you upon the devils that at your bidding they left the men whom they possessed, now ye will be in fear of the devils. For he that loveth money is the servant of Mammon: and Mammon is the name of a devil who is set over carnal gains, and is the master of them that love the world. But even the lovers of the world do not possess riches, but are possessed of them. For it is out of reason that for one belly there should be laid up so much food as would suffice a thousand, and for one body so many garments as would

furnish clothing for a thousand men. In vain, therefore, is that stored up which cometh not into use, and for whom it is kept, no man knoweth, as the Holy Ghost saith by the prophet: In vain is every man troubled who heapeth up riches and knoweth not for whom he gathereth them. Naked did our birth from women bring us into this light, destitute of food and drink: naked will the earth receive us which brought us forth. We possess in common the riches of the heaven, the brightness of the sun is equal for the rich and the poor, and likewise the light of the moon and the stars, the softness of the air and the drops of rain, and the gate of the Church and the fount of sanctification and the forgiveness of sins, and the sharing in the altar, and the eating of the body and drinking of the blood of Christ, and the anointing of the chrism, and the grace of the giver, and the visitation of the Lord, and the pardon of sin: in all these the dispensing of the Creator is equal, without respect of persons. Neither doth the rich man use these gifts after one manner and the poor after another.

But wretched and unhappy is the man who would have something more than sufficeth him: for of this come heats of fevers rigours of cold, divers pains in all the members of the body, and he can neither be fed with food nor sated with drink, that covetousness may learn that money will not profit it, which being laid up bringeth to the keepers thereof anxiety by day and night, and suffereth them not even for an hour to be quiet and secure. For while they guard their houses against thieves, till their estate, ply the plough, pay taxes, build storehouses, strive for gain, try to baffle the attacks of the strong, and to strip the weak, exercise their wrath on whom they can, and hardly bear it from others, shrink not from playing at tables and from public shows, fear not to defile or to be defiled, suddenly do they depart out of this world, naked, bearing only their own sins with them, for which they shall suffer eternal punishment".

Chapter 17

While the apostle was thus speaking, behold there was brought to him by his mother, who was a widow, a young man who thirty days before had first married a wife. And the people which were waiting upon the burial came with the widowed mother and cast themselves at the apostle's feet all together with groans, weeping, and mourning, and besought him that in the name of his God, as he had done with Drusiana, so he would raise up this young man also. And there was so great weeping of them all that the apostle himself could hardly refrain from crying and tears. He cast himself down, therefore, in prayer, and wept a long time: and rising from prayer spread out his hands to heaven, and for a long space prayed within himself. And when he had so done thrice, he commanded the body which was swathed to be loosed, and said: "*Thou youth Stacteus, who for love of thy flesh hast quickly lost thy soul: thou youth which knewest not thy creator nor perceivedst the Saviour of men, and wast ignorant of thy true friend, and therefore didst fall into the snare of the worst enemy: behold, I have poured out tears and prayers unto my Lord for thine ignorance, that thou mayest rise from the dead, the bands of death being loosed, and declare unto these two, to Atticus and Eugenius, how great glory they have lost, and how great punishment they have incurred. Then Stacteus arose and worshipped the apostle, and began to reproach his disciples, saying: I beheld your angels weeping, and the angels of Satan rejoicing at your overthrow. For now in a little time ye have lost the kingdom that was prepared for you, and the dwelling places builded of shining stones, full of joy, of feasting and delights, full of everlasting life and eternal light: and have gotten yourselves places of darkness, full of dragons, of roaring flames, of torments, and punishments unsurpassable, of pains and anguish, fear and horrible trembling. Ye have lost the places full of unfading flowers, shining, full of the sounds of instruments of music (organs), and have gotten on the other hand places wherein roaring and howling and mourning ceaseth not day nor night. Nothing else remaineth for you save to ask the apostle of the Lord that like as he hath raised me to life, he would raise you also from death unto salvation and bring back your souls which now are blotted out of the book of life.*"

Chapter 18

"*Then both he that had been raised and all the people together with Atticus and Eugenius, cast themselves at the apostle's feet and besought him to intercede for them with the Lord. Unto whom the holy apostle gave this answer: that for thirty days they should offer penitence to God, and in that space pray especially that the rods of gold might return to their nature and likewise the stones return to the meanness wherein they were made. And it came to pass that after thirty days were accomplished, and neither the rods were turned into wood nor the gems into pebbles, Atticus and Eugenius came and said to the apostle: Thou hast always taught mercy, and preached forgiveness, and bidden that one man should spare another. And if God willeth that a man should forgive a man, how much more shall he, as he is God, both forgive and spare men. We are confounded for our sin: and whereas we have cried with our eyes which lusted after the world, we do now repent with eyes that weep. We pray thee, Lord, we pray thee, apostle of God, show in deed that mercy which in word thou hast always promised.*

Then the holy John said unto them as they wept and repented, and all interceded for them likewise: *"Our Lord God used these words when he spake concerning sinners: I will not the death of a sinner, but I will rather that he be converted and live. For when the Lord Jesus Christ taught us concerning the penitent, he said: Verily I say unto you, there is great joy in heaven over one sinner that repenteth and turneth himself from his sins: and there is more joy over him than over ninety and nine which have not sinned. Wherefore I would have you know that the Lord accepteth the repentance of these men. And he turned unto Atticus and Eugenius and said: Go, carry back the rods unto the wood whence ye took them, for now are they returned to their own nature, and the stones unto the sea-shore, for they are become common stones as they were before. And when this was accomplished, they received again the grace which they had lost, so that again they cast out devils as before time and healed the sick and enlightened the blind, and daily the Lord did many mighty works by their means".*

Chapter 19

[... tells shortly the destruction oi the temple of Ephesus and the conversion of 12,000 people. Then follows the episode of the poison-cup in a form which probably represents the story in the Leucian Acts. (We have seen that the late Greek texts place it at the beginning, in the presence of Domitian.)]

Chapter 20

Now when Aristodemus, who was chief priest of all those idols, saw this, filled with a wicked spirit, he stirred up sedition among the people, so that one people prepared themselves to fight against the other. And John turned to him and said: *"Tell me, Aristodemus, what can I do to take away the anger from thy soul?"* And Aristodemus said: *"If thou wilt have me believe in thy God, I will give thee poison to drink, and if thou drink it, and die not, it will appear that thy God is true".* The apostle answered: *"If thou give me poison to drink, when I call on the name of my Lord, it will not be able to harm me.* " Aristodemus said again: "*I will that thou first see others drink it and die straightway that so thy heart may recoil from that cup.* " And the blessed John said: "*I have told thee already that I am prepared to drink it that thou mayest believe on the Lord Jesus Christ when thou seest me whole after the cup of poison.* " Aristodemus therefore went to the proconsul and asked of him two men who were to undergo the sentence of death. And when he had set them in the midst of the market-place before all the people, in the sight of the apostle he made them drink the poison: and as soon as they had drunk it, they gave up the ghost. Then Aristodemus turned to John and said: "*Hearken to me and depart from thy teaching wherewith thou callest away the people from the worship of the gods; or take and drink this, that thou mayest show that thy God is almighty, if after thou hast drunk, thou canst remain whole.* " Then the blessed John, as they lay dead which had drunk the poison, like a fearless and brave man took the cup, and making the sign of the cross, spake thus: "*My God, and the Father of our Lord Jesus Christ, by whose word the heavens were established, unto whom all things are subject, whom all creation serveth, whom all power obeyeth, feareth, and trembleth, when we call on thee for succour: whose name the serpent hearing is still, the dragon fleeth, the viper is quiet, the toad (which is called a frog) is still and strengthless, the scorpion is quenched, the basilisk vanquished, and the phalangia (spider) doth no hurt -in a word, all venomous things, and the fiercest reptiles and noisome beasts, are pierced (or covered with darkness). [Ps.- Mellitus adds: and all roots hurtful to the health of men dry up.] Do thou, I say, quench the venom of this poison, put out the deadly workings thereof, and void it of the strength which it hath in it: and grant in thy sight unto all these whom thou hast created, eyes that they may see, and ears that they may hear and a heart that they may understand thy greatness. And when he had thus said, he armed his mouth and all his body with the sign of the cross and drank all that was in the cup. And after be had drunk, he said: I ask that they for whose sake I have drunk, be turned unto thee, O Lord, and by thine enlightening receive the salvation which is in thee*". And when for the space of three hours the people saw that John was of a cheerful countenance, and that there was no sign at all of paleness or fear in him, they began to cry out with a loud voice: "*He is the one true God whom John worshippeth.* "

Chapter 21

But Aristodemus even so believed not, though the people reproached him: but turned unto John and said: "*This one thing I lack -if thou in the name of thy God raise up these that have died by this poison, my mind will be cleansed of all doubt.*" When he said that, the people rose against Aristodemus saying: "*We will burn thee and thine house if thou goest on to trouble the apostle further with thy words*". John, therefore, seeing that there was a fierce sedition, asked for silence, and said in the hearing of all: "*The first of the virtues of God which we ought to imitate is patience, by which we are able to bear with the foolishness of unbelievers. Wherefore if Aristodemus is still held by unbelief, let us loose the knots of his unbelief. He shall be compelled, even though late, to acknowledge his creator -for I will not cease from this work until a remedy shall bring help to his wounds, and like physicians which have in their hands a sick man needing medicine, so also, if Aristodemus be not yet cured by that which hath now been done, he shall be cured by that which I will now do*". And he called Aristodemus to him, and gave him his coat, and he himself stood clad only in his mantle. And Aristodemus said to him: "*Wherefore hast thou given me thy coat?*" John said to him: "*That thou mayest even so be put to shame and depart from thine unbelief.*" And Aristodemus said: "*And how shall thy coat make me to depart from unbelief?*" The apostle answered: "*Go and cast it upon the bodies of the dead, and thou shalt say thus: The apostle of our Lord Jesus Christ hath sent me that in his name ye may rise again, that all may know that life and death are servants of my Lord Jesus Christ.*" Which when Aristodemus had done, and had seen them rise, he worshipped John, and ran quickly to the proconsul and began to say with a loud voice: "*Hear me, hear me, thou proconsul; I think thou rememberest that I have often stirred up thy wrath against John and devised many things against him daily, wherefore I fear lest I feel his wrath: for he is a god hidden in the form of a man and hath drunk poison, and not only continueth whole, but them also which had died by the poison he hath recalled to life by my means, by the touch of his coat, and they have no mark of death upon them*". Which when the proconsul heard he said: "*And what wilt thou have me to do?*" Aristodemus answered: "*Let us go and fall at his feet and ask pardon, and whatever he commandeth us let us do.*" Then they came together and cast themselves down and besought forgiveness: and he received them and offered prayer and thanksgiving to God, and he ordained them a fast of a week, and when it was fulfilled he baptized them in the name of the Lord Jesus Christ and his Almighty Father and the Holy Ghost the illuminator. And when thev were baptized, with all their house and their servants and their kindred, they brake all their idols and built a Church in the name of Saint John: wherein he himself was taken up, in manner following

[This bracketed sentence, of late complexion, serves to introduce the last episode of the book. [James gives two additional fragments that do not fit in any other place. These fragments are very broken and are not of much use for this present project. However, if there is intrest in them, they can be found on pages 264-6 of the text.] The last episode of these Acts (as is the case with several others of the apocryphal Acts) was preservcd separately for reading in Church on the Saint's day. We have it in at least nine Greck manuscripts, and in many versions: Latin, Syriac, Armenian, Coptic, Ethiopic, Slavonic. }

106 John therefore continued with the brethren, rejoicing in the Lord. And on the morrow, being the Lord's day, and all the brethren being gathered together, he began to say unto them: *"Brethren and fellow-servants and coheirs and partakers with me in the kingdom of the Lord, ye know the Lord, how many mighty works he hath granted you by my means, how many wonders, healings, signs, how great spiritual gifts, teachings, governings, refreshings, ministries, knowledges, glories, graces, gifts, beliefs, communions, all which ye have seen given you by him in your sight, yet not seen by these eyes nor heard by these ears. Be ye therefore stablished in him, remembering him in your every deed, knowing the mystery of the dispensation which hath come to pass towards men, for what cause the Lord hath l accomplished it. He beseecheth you by me, brethren, and entreateth you, desiring to remain without grief, without insult, not conspired against, not chastened: for he knoweth even the insult that cometh of you, he knoweth even dishonour, he knoweth even conspiracy, he knoweth even chastisement, from them that hearken not to his commandments."*

107 *"Let not then our good God be grieved, the compassionate, the merciful, the holy, the pure, the undefiled, the immaterial, the only, the one, the unchangeable, the simple, the guileless, the unwrathful, even our God Jesus Christ, who is above every name that we can utter or conceive, and more exalted. Let him rejoice with us because we walk aright, let him be* *glad because we live purely, let him be refreshed because our conversation is sober. Let him be without care because we live continently, let him be pleased because we communicate one with another, let him smile because we are chaste, let him be merry because we love him. These things I now speak unto you, brethren, because I am hasting unto the work set before me, and already being perfected by the Lord. For what else could I have to say unto you? Ye have the pledge of our God, ye have the earnest of his goodness, ye have his presence that cannot be shunned. If, then, ye sin no more, he forgiveth you that ye did in ignorance: but if after that ye have known him and he hath had mercy on you, ye walk again in the like deeds, both the former will be laid to your charge, and also ye will not have a part nor mercy before him."*

108 And when he had spoken this unto them, he prayed thus: *"O Jesus who hast woven this crown with thy weaving, who hast joined together these many blossoms into the unfading flower of thy countenance, who hast sown in them these words: thou only tender of thy servants, and physician who healest freely: only doer of good and despiser of none, only merciful and lover of men, only saviour and righteous, only seer of all, who art in all and everywhere present and containing all things and filling all things: Christ Jesus, God, Lord, that with thy gifts and thy mercy shelterest them that trust in thee, that knowest clearly the wiles and the assaults of him that is everywhere our adversary, which he deviseth against us: do thou only, O Lord, succour thy servants by thy visitation. Even so, Lord."*

109 And he asked for bread, and gave thanks thus: *"What praise or what offering or what thanksgiving shall we, breaking this bread, name save thee only, O Lord Jesus? We glorify thy name that was said by the Father: we glorify thy name that was said through the Son (or we glorify the name of Father that was said by thee . . . the name of Son that was said by thee): we glorify thine entering of the Door. We glorify the resurrection shown unto us by thee. We glorify thy way, we glorify of thee the seed, the word, the grace, the faith, the salt, the unspeakable (al. chosen) pearl, the treasure, the plough, the net, the greatness, the diadem, him that for us was called Son of man, that gave unto us truth, rest, knowledge, power, the commandment, the confidence, hope, love, liberty, refuge in thee. For thou, Lord, art alone the root of immortality, and the fount of incorruption, and the seat of the ages: called by all these names for us now that calling on thee by them we may make known thy greatness which at the present is invisible unto us, but visible only unto the pure, being portrayed in thy manhood.*

110 And he brake the bread and gave unto all of us, praying over each of the brethren that he might be worthy of the grace of the Lord and of the most holy eucharist. And he partook also himself likewise, and said: *"Unto me also be there a part with you, and: Peace be with you, my beloved. "*

111 After that he said unto Verus: *"Take with thee some two men, with baskets and shovels, and follow me".* And Verus without delay did as he was bidden by John the servant of God. The blessed John therefore went out of the house and walked forth of the gates, having told the more part to depart from him. And when he was come to the tomb of a certain brother of ours he said to the young men: *"Dig, my children".* And they dug and he was instant with them yet more, saying: *"Let the trench be deeper."* And as they dug he spoke unto them the word of God and exhorted them that were come with him out of the house, edifying and perfecting them unto the greatness of God, and praying over each one of us. And when the young men had finished the trench as he desired, we knowing nothing of it, he took off his garments wherein he was clad and laid them as it were for a pallet in the bottom of the trench: and standing in his shift only he stretched his hands upward and prayed thus:

112 *"O thou that didst choose us out for the apostleship of the Gentiles: O God that sentest us into the world: that didst reveal thyself by the law and the prophets: that didst never rest, but alway from the foundation of the world savedst them that were able to be saved: that madest thyself known through all nature: that proclaimedst thyself even among beasts: that didst make the desolate and savage soul tame and quiet: that gavest thyself to it when it was athirst for thy words: that didst appear to it in haste when it was dying: that didst show thyself to it as a law when it was sinking into lawlessness: that didst manifest thyself to it when it had been vanquished by Satan: that didst overcome its adversary when it fled unto thee: that gavest it thine hand and didst raise it up from the things of Hades: that didst not leave it to walk after a bodily sort (in the body): that didst show to it its own enemy: that hast made for it a clear knowledge toward thee: O God, Jesus, the Father of them that are above the heavens, the Lord of them that are in the heavens, the law of them that are in the other, the course of them that are in the air, the keeper of them that are on the earth, the fear of them that are under the earth, the grace of them that are thine own: receive also the* *soul of thy John, which it may be is accounted worthy by thee ".*

113 *"O thou who hast kept me until this hour for thyself and untouched by union with a woman: who when in my youth I desired to marry didst appear unto me and say to me: John I have need of thee: who didst prepare for me also a sickness of the body: who when for the third time I would marry didst forthwith prevent me, and then at the third hour of the day saidst unto me on the sea: John, if thou hadst not been mine, I would have suffered thee to marry: who for two years didst blind me (or afflict mine eyes), and grant me to mourn and entreat thee: who in the third year didst open the eyes of my mind and also grant me my visible eyes: who when I saw clearly didst ordain that it should be grievous to me to look upon a woman: who didst save me from the temporal fantasy and lead me unto that which endureth always: who didst rid me of the foul madness that is in the flesh: who didst take me from the bitter death and establish me on thee alone: who didst muzzle the secret disease of my soul and cut off the open deed: who didst afflict and banish him that raised tumult in me: who didst make my love of thee spotless: who didst make my joining unto thee perfect and unbroken: who didst give me undoubting faith in thee, who didst order and make clear my inclination toward thee: thou who givest unto every man the due reward of his works, who didst put into my soul that I should have no possession save thee only: for what is more precious than thee? Now therefore Lord, whereas I have accomplished the dispensation wherewith I was entrusted, account thou me worthy of thy rest, and grant me that end in thee which is salvation unspeakable and unutterable. "*

114 *"And as I come unto thee, let the fire go backward, let the darkness be overcome, let the gulf be without strength, let the furnace die out, let Gehenna be quenched. Let angels follow, let devils fear, let rulers be broken, let powers fall; let the places of the right hand stand fast, let them of the left hand not remain. Let the devil be muzzled, let Satan be derided, let his wrath be burned out, let his madness be stilled, let his vengeance be ashamed, let his assault be in pain, let his children be smitten and all his roots plucked up. And grant me to accomplish the journey unto thee without suffering insolence or provocation, and to receive that which thou hast promised unto them that live purely and have loved thee only. "*

115 And having sealed himself in every part, he stood and said: *"Thou art with me, O Lord Jesus Christ":* and laid himself down in the trench where he had strown his garments: and having said unto us: Peace be with you, brethren, he gave up his spirit rejoicing.

The Acts of Andrew
(150 – 200 A.D.)

The Acts of Andrew is one of the major works and earliest pseudepigraphal (noncanonical) series from the New Testament also known as apocryphal Acts, an approximate date given to the Acts of Paul is 160 CE. The Acts were first mentioned by Tertullian. **Tertullian found it heretical because it encouraged women to preach and baptize.** The Acts were considered orthodox by Hippolytus, but were eventually regarded as heretical when the Manichaeans started using the texts. The author of the Acts of Paul is unknown and wrote out of respect for Paul, in Asia Minor. The author does not show any dependency on the canonical Acts, but uses oral traditions of Paul's missionary work.

[The discovery of a Coptic version of the text, demonstrated that the text was composed of:

- the Acts of Paul and Thecla
- the Epistle of the Corinthians to Paul
- the Third Epistle to the Corinthians
- the Martyrdom of Paul – his death at the hand of Nero[38]]

A 2d-century Christian writing recounting the missionary career and death of the apostle Paul and classed among the NT Apocrypha. In this work Paul is pictured as traveling from city to city, converting gentiles and proclaiming the need for a life of sexual abstinence and other encratite practices. Though ancient evidence suggests that the Acts of Paul was a relatively lengthy work (*3600 lines according to the Stichometry of Nicephorus*), only about two-thirds of that amount still survives. Individual sections were transmitted separately by the medieval manuscript tradition (*Lipsius 1891*), most importantly by the Acts of Paul and Thekla and the Martyrdom of Paul, both extant in the original Greek and several ancient translations. Manuscript discoveries in the last century have added considerable additional material. The most important of these include a Greek papyrus of the late 3d century, now at

---

[38] http://en.wikipedia.org/wiki/Acts_of_Paul

Hamburg *(10 pages)*, a Coptic papyrus of the 4th or 5th century, now at Heidelberg *(about 80 pages)*, and a Greek papyrus of correspondence between Paul and the Corinthians *(3 Corinthians = Testuz 1959)*, now at Geneva[39]

Summary notation: *Due to it's importance and historical significance to the early Church, the **Acts of Andrew** is presented in some detail but not entirely .Due to the length of the manuscript, only key excerpts or talking points are presented for discussion. Please note sections omitted or missing in the early manuscript.*

Excerpts from the Acts of Andrew

[The first extant page of the Coptie MS. seems to be p.9.]

9. Paul went into *(the house)* at the place where the *(dead)* was. But Phila the wife of Panchares *(Anchares, MS., see below)* was very wroth and said to her husband in *(great anger)*: *"Husband, thou hast gone . . . . the wild beasts, thou hast not begotten . . . . thy son . . . . where is mine?"*

10 *(he hath not)* desired food . . . to bury him. But (Panchares) stood in the sight of all and made his prayer at the ninth hour, until the people of the city came to bear the boy out. When he had prayed, Paul (came) and saw . . . and of Jesus Christ . . . . the boy . . . the prayer.

11 *(a small piece only)* . . . multitude . . . eight days . . . they thought that he raised up the (boy). But when Paul had remained

12. They asked? him? . . . the men listened to him . . . they sent for Panchares . . . and cried out, saying: *"We believe, Panchares, . . . but save the city from . . many things, which they said. Panchares said unto them: Judge ye whether your good deeds."*

13 is not possible . . . but to (testify) . . . God who hath . . . his Son according to . . . salvation, and I also believe that, my brethren, there is no other God, save Jesus Christ the son of the Blessed, unto whom is glory for ever, Amen. But when they saw that he would not turn to them, they pursued Paul, and caught him, and brought

---

him back into the city, ill-using (?) him, and cast stones at him and thrust him out of their city and out of their country. But Panchares would not return evil for evil: he shut the door of his house and went in with his wife . . . fasting . . . But when it was evening Paul came to him and said:

14. *"God hath . . . Jesus Christ."*

[These are the last words of the episode. The situation is a little cleared by a sentence in the Greek Acts of Titus ascribed to Zenas (not earlier than the fifth century?): 'They arrived at Antioch and found Barnabas the son of Panchares, whom Paul raised up.' Barnabas may be a mistake, but Panchares is, I doubt not, right: for the Coptic definite article is p prefixed to the word, and the Coptic translator finding Panchares in his text has confused the initial of it with his own definite article, and cut it out.We have, then, a husband Panchares and wife Phila at Antioch (in Pisidia perhaps: this is disputed), and their son (possibly named Barnabas) is dead. Phila reproaches Panchares with want of parental affection. I take it that he is a believer, and has not mourned over his son, perhaps knowing that Paul was at hand and hoping for his help. Panchares prays till his fellow-townsmen come to carry out the body for burial. Paul arrives: at some point he raises the dead: but the people are irritated and some catastrophe threatens them at Paul's hands.Panchares makes a profession of faith, the result of which is Paul's ill-treatment and banishment. But Paul returns secretly and reassures Panchares.]

Chapter 2

[The next episode is that of Paul and Thecla, in which the Greek text exists, and will be followed. In the Coptic it has a title:After the flight from Antioch, when he would go to Iconium.It is possible that in this episode the author of the Acts may have used a local legend, current in his time, of a real Christian martyr Thecla. It is otherwise difficult to account for the very great popularity of the cult of St. Thecla, which spread over East and West, and made her the most famous of virgin martyrs. Moreover, one historical personage is introduced into the story, namely, Queen Tryphaena, who was the widow, it seems, of Cotys, King of Thrace, and the mother of Polemo II, King of Pontus. She was a great-niece of the Emperor Claudius. Professor W. M. Ramsay has contended that there was a written story of Thecla which was adapted by the author of the Acts: but his view is not generally accepted.]

1 When Paul went up unto Iconium after he fled from Antioch, there journeyed with him Demas and Hermogenes the coppersmith, which were full of hypocrisy, and flattered Paul as though they loved him. But Paul, looking only unto the goodness of Christ, did them no evil, but loved them well, so that he assayed to make sweet unto them all the oracles of the Lord, and of the teaching and the interpretation (*of the Gospel*) and of the birth and resurrection of the Beloved, and related unto them word by word all the great works of Christ, how they were revealed unto him *(Copt. adds: how that Christ was born of Mary the virgin, and of the seed of David)*.

2 And a certain man named Onesiphorus, when he heard that Paul was come to Iconium, went out with his children Simmias and Zeno and his wife Lectra to meet him, that he might receive him into his house: for Titus had told him what manner of man Paul was in appearance; for he had not seen him in the flesh, but only in the spirit.

3 And he went by the king's highway that leadeth unto Lystra and stood expecting him, and looked upon them that came, according to tbe description of Titus. And he saw Paul coming, a man little of stature, thin-haired upon the head, crooked in the legs, of good state of body, with eyebrows joining, and nose somewhat hooked, full of grace: for sometimes he appeared like a man, and sometimes he had the face of an angel.

4 And when Paul saw Onesiphorus he smiled, and Onesiphorus said: Hail, thou servant of the blessed God. And he said: *"Grace be with thee and with thine house."* But Demas and Hermogenes were envious, and stirred up their hypocrisy yet more, so that Demas said: *"Are we not servants of the Blessed, that thou didst not salute us so?"* And Onesiphorus said: *"I see not in you any fruit of righteousness, but if ye be such, come ye also into my house and refresh yourselves."*

5 And when Paul entered into the house of Onesiphorus, there was great joy, and bowing of knees and breaking of bread, and the word of God concerning abstinence (*or continence*) and the resurrection; for Paul said:

> *"Blessed are the pure in heart, for they shall see God.*
> *Blessed are they that keep the flesh chaste, for they shall become the temple*

of God.

Blessed are they that abstain (or the continent), for unto them shall God speak.

Blessed are they that have renounced this world, for they shall be well-pleasing unto God.

Blessed are they that possess their wives as though they had them not, for they shall inherit God.

Blessed are they that have the fear of God, for they shall become angels of God.

6 Blessed are they that tremble at the oracles of God, for they shall be comforted.

Blessed are they that receive the wisdom of Jesus Christ, for they shall be called sons of the Most High.

Blessed are they that have kept their baptism pure, for they shall rest with the Father and with the Son.

Blessed are they that have compassed the understanding of Jesus Christ, for they shall be in light.

Blessed are they that for love of God have departed from the fashion of this world, for they shall judge angels, and shall be blessed at the right hand of the Father.

Blessed are the merciful, for they shall obtain mercy and shall not see the bitter day of judgement. Blessed are the bodies of the virgins, for they shall be well- pleasing unto God and shall not lose the reward of their continence (chastity), for the word of the Father shall be unto them a work of salvation in the day of his Son, and they shall have rest world Without end."

7 And as Paul was saying these things in the midst of the assembly (*Church*) in the house of Onesiphorus, a certain virgin, Thecla, whose mother was Theocleia, which was betrothed to an husband, Thamyris, sat at the window hard by, and hearkened night and day unto the word concerning chastity which was spoken by Paul: and she stirred not from the window, but was led onward (*or pressed onward*) by faith, rejoicing exceedingly: and further, when she saw many women and virgins entering in to Paul, she also desired earnestly to be accounted worthy to stand before Paul's face and to hear the word of Christ; for she had not yet seen the appearance of Paul, but only heard his speech.

[... sections omitted.].

14 And Demas and Hermogenes said: *"Bring him before Castelius the governor as one that persuadeth the multitudes with the new doctrine of the Christians; and so will he destroy him and thou shalt have thy wife Thecla. And we will teach thee of that resurrection which he asserteth, that it is already come to pass in the children which we have, and we rise again when we have come to the knowledge of the true God".*

15 But when Thamyris heard this of them, he was filled with envy and wrath, and rose up early and went to the house of Onesiphorus with the rulers and officers and a great crowd with staves, saying unto Paul: :" *Thou hast destroyed the city of the Iconians and her that was espoused unto me, so that she will not have me: let us go unto Castelius the governor. And all the multitude said: Away with the wizard, for he hath corrupted all our wives. And the multitude rose up together against him".*

16 And Thamyris, standing before the judgement seat, cried aloud and said:*" 0 proconsul, this is the man-we know not whence he is-who alloweth not maidens to marry: let him declare before thee wherefore he teacheth such things."* And Demas and Hermogenes said to Thamyris: *"Say thou that he is a Christian, and so wilt thou destroy him."* But the governor kept his mind steadfast and called Paul, saying unto him: *"Who art thou, and what teachest thou? for it is no light accusation that these bring against thee."*

17 And Paul lifted up his voice and said: *"If I am this day examined what I teach, hearken, 0 proconsul. The living God, the God of vengeance, the jealous God, the God that hath need of nothing, but desireth the salvation of men, hath sent me, that I may sever them from corruption and uncleanness and all pleasure and death, that they may sin no more. Wherefore God hath sent his own Child, whom I preach and teach that men should have hope in him who alone hath had compassion upon the world that was in error; that men may no more be under judgement but have faith and the fear of God and the knowledge of sobriety and the love of truth. If then I teach the things that have been revealed unto me of God, what wrong do I O proconsul?"* And the governor having heard that, commanded Paul to be bound and taken away to prison until he should have leisure to hear him more carefully.

18 But Thecla at night took off her bracelets and gave them to the doorkeeper, and when the door was opened for her she went into the prison, and gave the jailer a mirror of silver and so went in to Paul and sat by his feet and heard the wonderful works of God. And Paul feared not at all, but walked in the confidence of God: and her faith also was increased as she kissed his chains.

19 Now when Thecla was sought by her own people and by Thamyris, she was looked for through the streets as one lost; and one of the fellow-servants of the doorkeeper told that she went out by night. And they examined the doorkeeper and he told them that she was gone to the stranger unto the prison; and they went as he told them and found her as it were bound with him, in affection. And they went forth thence and gathered the multitude to them and showed it to the governor.

20 And he commanded Paul to be brought to the judgement seat; but Thecla rolled herself upon the place where Paul taught when he sat in the prison. And the governor commanded her also to be brought to the judgement seat, and she went exulting with joy. And when Paul was brought the second time the people cried out more vehemently: *"He is a sorcerer, away with him!"* But the governor heard Paul gladly concerning the holy works of Christ: and he took counsel, and called Thecla and said: *"Why wilt thou not marry Thamyris, according to the law of the Iconians?"* But she stood looking earnestly upon Paul, and when she answered not, her mother Theocleia cried out, saying: *"Burn the lawless one, burn her that is no bride in the midst of the theatre, that all the women which have been taught by this man may be affrighted. "*

21 And the governor was greatly moved: and he scourged Paul and sent him out of the city, but Thecla he condemned to be burned. And straightway the governor arose and went to the theatre: and all the multitude went forth unto the dreadful spectacle. But Thecla, as the lamb in the wilderness looketh about for the shepherd, so sought for Paul: and she looked upon the multitude and saw the Lord sitting, like unto Paul, and said: *"As if I were not able to endure, Paul is come to look upon me. And she earnestly paid heed to him: but he departed into the heavens. "*

22 Now the boys and the maidens brought wood and hay to burn Thecla: and when she was brought in naked, the governor wept and marvelled at the power that was in her. And they laid the wood, and the executioner bade her mount upon the pyre: and she, making the sign of the cross, went up upon the wood. And they lighted it, and though a great fire blazed forth, the fire took no hold on her; for God had compassion on her, and caused a sound under the earth, and a cloud overshadowed her above, full of rain and hail, and all the vessel of it was poured out so that many were in peril of death, and the fire was quenched, and Thecla was preserved.

23 Now Paul was fasting with Onesiphorus and his wife and their children in an open sepulchre on the way whereby they go from Iconium to Daphne. And when many days were past, as they fasted, the boys said unto Paul: *"We are an hungered. And they had not wherewith to buy bread, for Onesiphorus had left the goods of this world, and followed Paul with all his house"*. But Paul took off his upper garment and said: *"Go, child, buy several loaves and bring them"*. And as the boy was buying, he saw his neighbour Thecla, and was astonished, and said: *"Thecla, whither goest thou?"* And she said: *"I seek Paul, for I was preserved from the fire."* And the boy said: *"Come, I will bring thee unto him, for he mourneth for thee and prayeth and fasteth now these six days."*

24 And when she came to the sepulchre unto Paul, who had bowed his knees and was praying and saying: *"O Father of Christ, let not the fire take hold on Thecla, but spare her, for she is thine":* she standing behind him cried out: *"O Father that madest heaven and earth, the Father of thy beloved child Jesus Christ, I bless thee for that thou hast preserved me from the fire, that I might see Paul.* "And Paul arose and saw her and said: *"O God the knower of hearts, the Father of our Lord Jesus Christ, I bless thee that thou hast speedily accomplished that which I asked of thee, and hast hearkened unto me. "*

25 And there was much love within the sepulchre, for Paul rejoiced, and Onesiphorus, and all of them. And they had five loaves, and herbs, and water *(and salt)*, and they rejoiced for the holy works of Christ. And Thecla said unto Paul: *"I will cut my hair round about and follow thee whithersoever thou goest"*. But he said: *"The time is ill-favoured and thou art comely: beware lest another temptation take thee, worse than the first, and thou endure it not but play the coward."* And Thecla said: *"Only give me the seal in Christ, and temptation shall not touch me."* And Paul said: *"Have patience, Thecla, and thou shalt receive the water. "*
[… sections omitted.].

34 Then did they put in many beasts, while she stood and stretched out her hands and prayed. And when she had ended her prayer, she turned and saw a great tank full of water, and said: *"Now is it time that I should wash myself."* "And she cast herself in, saying: *"In the name of Jesus Christ do I baptize myself on the last day".* And all the women seeing it and all the people wept, saying: *"Cast not thyself into the water: so that even the governor wept that so great beauty should be devoured by seals."* So, then, she cast herself into the water in the name of Jesus Christ; and the seals, seeing the light of a flash of fire, floated dead on the top of the water. And there was about her a cloud of fire, so that neither did the beasts touch.

35 Now the women, when other more fearful beasts were put in, shrieked aloud, and some cast leaves, and others nard, others cassia, and some balsam, so that there was a multitude of odours; and all the beasts that were struck thereby were held as it were in sleep and touched her not; so that Alexander said to the governor: *"I have some bulls exceeding fearful, let us bind the criminal to them."* And the governor frowning, allowed it, saying: *"Do that thou wilt."* And they bound her by the feet between the bulls, and put hot irons under their bellies that they might be the more enraged and kill her. They then leaped forward; but the flame that burned about her, burned through the ropes, and she was as one not bound.

36 But Tryphaena, standing by the arena, fainted at the entry, so that her handmaids said: *"The queen Tryphaena is dead!"* And the governor stopped the games and all the city was frightened, and Alexander falling at the governor's feet said: *"Have mercy on me and on the city, and let the condemned go, lest the city perish with her; for if Caesar hear this, perchance he will destroy us and the city, because his kinswoman the queen Tryphaena hath died at the entry."*

37 And the governor called Thecla from among the beasts, and said to her: *"Who art thou? and what hast thou about thee that not one of the beasts hath touched thee?"* But she said: *"I am the handmaid of the living God; and what I have about me-it is that I have believed on that his Son in whom God is well pleased; for whose sake not one of the beasts hath touched me. For he alone is the goal (or way) of salvation and the substance of life immortal; for unto them that are tossed about he is a refuge, unto the oppressed relief, unto the despairing shelter, and in a word, whosoever believeth not on him, shall not live, but die everlastingly."*

38 And when the governor heard this, he commanded garments to be brought and said: *"Put on these garments."* And she said: *"He that clad me when I was naked among the beasts, the same in the day of judgement will clothe me with salvation. And she took the garments and put them on."* And the governor forthwith issued out an act, saying: *"I release unto you Thecla the godly, the servant of God."* And all the women cried out with a loud voice and as with one mouth gave praise to God, saying: *"One is the God who hath preserved Thecla: so that with their voice all the city shook."*

39 And Tryphaena, when she was told the good tidings, met her with much people and embraced Thecla and said: *"Now do I believe that the dead are raised up: now do I believe that my child liveth: come within, and I will make thee heir of all my substance.* "Thecla therefore went in with her and rested in her house eight days, teaching her the word of God, so that the more part of the maid-servants also believed, and there was great joy in the house.

40 But Thecla yearned after Paul and sought him, sending about in all places; and it was told her that he was at Myra. And she took young men and maids, and girded herself, and sewed her mantle into a cloak after the fashion of a man, and departed into Myra, and found Paul speaking the word of God, and went to him. But he when he saw her and the people that were with her was amazed, thinking in himself: *"Hath some other temptation come upon her?"* But she perceived it, and said to him: *"I have received the washing, 0 Paul; for he that hath worked together with thee in the Gospel hath worked with me also unto my baptizing. "*

41 And Paul took her by the hand and brought her into the house of Hermias, and heard all things from her; so that Paul marvelled much, and they that heard were confirmed, and prayed for Tryphaena. And Thecla arose and said to Paul: *"I go unto Iconium."* And Paul said: *"Go, and teach the word of God.* "Now Tryphaena had sent her much apparel and gold, so that she left of it with Paul for the ministry of the poor.

42 But she herself departed unto Iconium. And she entered into the house of Onesiphorus, and fell down upon the floor where Paul had sat and taught the oracles of God, and wept, saying: *"O God of me and of this house, where the light shone upon me, Jesus Christ the Son of God, my helper in prison, my helper before the governors, my helper in* *the fire, my helper among the beasts, thou art God, and unto thee be the glory for ever. Amen".*

43 And she found Thamyris dead, but her mother living. And she saw her mother and said unto her: *"Theocleia my mother, canst thou believe that the Lord liveth in the heavens? for whether thou desirest money, the Lord will give it thee through me: or thy child, lo, I am here before thee."* And when she had so testified, she departed unto Seleucia, and after she had enlightened many with the word of God, she slept a good sleep.

[A good many manuscripts add that Theoeleia was not converted, but the Coptic does not support them: it ends the episode as above. A long appendix is given by other Greek copies, telling how in Thecla's old age (she was ninety) she was living on Mount Calamon or Calameon, and some evil-disposed young men went up to ill-treat her: and she prayed, and the rock opened and she entered it, and it closed after her. Some add that she went underground to Rome: this, to account for the presence of her body there.]

The Acts of Paul
(150 – 200 A.D.)

The Acts of Paul is one of the major works and earliest pseudepigraphal (*noncanonical*) series from the New Testament also known as apocryphal Acts, an approximate date given to the Acts of Paul is 160 CE. The Acts were first mentioned by Tertullian. Tertullian found it heretical because it encouraged women to preach and baptize. The Acts were considered orthodox by Hippolytus, but were eventually regarded as heretical when the Manichaeans started using the texts. The author of the Acts of Paul is unknown and wrote out of respect for Paul, in Asia Minor. The author does not show any dependency on the canonical Acts, but uses oral traditions of Paul's missionary work.

Acts of Paul consists of the third letter to the Corinthians, an account of his martyrdom, and other narratives depicting his preaching and activity. There is a range of literature either about or purporting to be by Paul, including letters, narratives, prayers, and apocalypses. The pseudonymous Third Letter to the Corinthians claims to have been written from prison to correct the misinterpretations that his first and second letter had created. In his first letter to the Corinthians, he stated that "*flesh and blood cannot inherit the kingdom of God*" and this statement is not unrelated to the debates that ensued between the Gnostic and proto-orthodox Christians thereafter.

A Christian concerned to emphasize that people would be physically resurrected rather than merely spiritually forged 3 Corinthians to counter what the Gnostics were saying, presumably because their argument was gaining much ground. The Acts of Paul also appear to be familiar with the traditional account about the martyrdom of Peter, in which, having been arrested and condemned to death, Peter asked to be crucified head-down because he wasn't worthy of having the same death as Jesus.[40]

---

[40] http://en.wikipedia.org/wiki/Acts_of_Paul

Summary notation: *Due to it's importance and historical significance to the early Church, the **Acts of Paul** is presented in some detail but not entirely .Due to the length of the manuscript, only key excerpts or talking points are presented for discussion. Please note sections omitted or missing in the early manuscript.*

Excerpts from the Acts of Paul

[Copt., p.38 of the MS.]

Chapter 3

When he was departed from Antioch and taught in Myra (*Myrrha*). When Paul was teaching the word of God in Myra, there was there a man, Hermoerates by name, who had the dropsy, and he put himself forward in the sight of all, and said to Paul: *"Nothing is impossible with God, but especially with him whom thou preachest; for when he came he healed many, even that God whose servant thou art. Lo, I and my wife and my children, we cast ourselves at thy feet: have pity on me that I also may believe as thou hast believed on the living God."*

Paul said unto him: *"I will restore thee (thine health) not for reward, but through the name of Jesus Christ thou shalt become whole in the presence of all these".* (*And he touched his body*) drawing his hand downwards: and his belly opened and much water ran from him and . . . he fell down like a dead man, so that some said: *"It is better for him to die than to continue in pain".* But when Paul had quieted the people, he took his hand and raised him up and asked him, saying: *"Hermocrates, ask for what thou desirest."* And he said: *"I would eat. And he took a loaf and gave him to eat."* And in that hour he was whole, and received the grace of the seal in the Lord, he and his wife.

But Hermippus his son was angry with Paul, and sought for a set time wherein to rise up with them of his own age and destroy him. For he wished that his father should not be healed but should die, that he might soon be master of his goods. But Dion, his younger son, heard Paul gladly.

Now all they that were with Hermippus took counsel to fight against Paul so that Hermippus . . . and sought to kill him. Dion fell down and died: but Hermippus watered Dion with his tears.

But Hermocrates mourned sore, for he loved Dion more than his other son. (*Yet*) he sat at Paul's feet, and forgat that Dion was dead. But when Dion was dead, his mother Nympha rent her clothes and went unto Paul and set herself before the face of Hermocrates her husband and of Paul. And when Paul saw her, he was frightened and said: "*Wherefore art thou thus, Nympha?*" But she said to him: "*Dion is dead; and the whole multitude wept when they beheld her.*" And Paul looked upon the people that mourned and sent young men, saying to them: "*Go and bring me him hither*". And they went: but Hermippus caught hold of the body (*of Dion*) in the street and cried out.

[A leaf lost.]

...the word in him (*them?*). But an angel of the Lord had said unto him in the night: Paul, thou hast to-day a great conflict against thy body, but God, the Father of his Son Jesus Christ, will protect thee. When Paul had arisen, he went unto his brethren, and remained (*sorrowful?*) saying: "*What meaneth this vision?* "And while Paul thought upon this, he saw Hermippus coming, having a sword drawn in his hand, and with him many other young men with staves. And Paul said unto them: "*I am not a robber, neither a murderer. The God of all things, the Father of Christ, will turn your hands backward, and your sword into its sheath, and your strength into weakness: for I am a servant of God, though I be alone and a stranger, and small and of no reputation (?) among the Gentiles. But do thou, 0 God, look down upon their counsel and suffer me not to be brought to nought by them*".

And when Hermippus ran upon Paul with his sword drawn, straightway he ceased to see, so that he cried out aloud, saying: "*My dear comrades, forget not your friend Hermippus. For I have sinned, 0 Paul, I have pursued after innocent blood. Learn, ye foolish and ye of understanding, that this world is nought, gold is nought, all money is nought: I that glutted myself with all manner of goods am now a beggar and entreat of you all: Hearken to me all ye my companions, and every one that dwelleth in Myra. I have mocked at a man who hath saved my father: I have mocked at a man who hath raised up my brother Dion . . . I have mocked at a man who . . . without doing me any evil. But entreat ye of him: behold, he hath saved my father and raised up my brother; he is able therefore to save me also".* But Paul stood there weeping alike before God, for that he heard him quickly, and before man, for that the proud was brought low. And he turned himself and went up . . . But the young men took the feet and bore Hermippus and brought him to the place where Paul was teaching and laid him down before the door and went unto their house. And when they were gone a great multitude came to the house of Hermocrates; and another great multitude entered in, to see whether Hermippus were shut up there. And Hermippus besought every one that went in, that they would entreat Paul, with him. But they that went in saw Hermocrates and Nympha, how they rejoiced greatly at the raising up of Dion, and distributed victuals and money unto the widows for his recovery. And they beheld Hermippus their son in the state of this second affliction, and how he took hold on the feet of every one, and on the feet of his parents also, and prayed them, as one of the strangers, that he might be healed. And his parents were troubled, and lamented to every one that came in, so that some said: Wherefore do these weep? for Dion is arisen. But Hermocrates possessed goods . . . and brought the value of the goods and took it and distributed it. And Hermocrates, troubled in mind and desiring that they might be satisfied, said: *"Brethren, let us leave the food . . . . and occupy ourselves . . . Hermocrates."* And immediately Nympha cried out in great affliction unto Paul . . they said: *"Nympha, Hermocrates calleth upon God that your son Hermippus may see and cease to grieve, for he hath resisted Christ and his minister.* "But they and Paul prayed to God. And when Hermippus recovered his sight, he turned himself to his mother Nympha, and said to her: *"Paul came unto me and laid his hand upon me while I wept, and in that hour I saw all things clearly".* And she took his hand and led him unto the widows and Paul. But while Paul wept bitterly, Hermippus gave thanks, saying unto them: *"Every one that believeth, shall . . . "*

[A leaf gone]

. . . concord and peace . . . Amen.

And when Paul had confirmed the brethren that were in Myra, he departed unto Sidon.

Chapter 4

When he was departed from Myra . Now when Paul was departed from Myra and would go unto Sidon there was great sadness of the brethren that were in Pisidia and Pamphylia, because they yearned after his word and his holy appearance in Christ; so that some from Perga followed Paul, namely Thrasymachus and Cleon with their wives Aline (?) and Chrysa, Cleon's wife. And on the way they nourished Paul: and they were eating their bread under a tree (?). And as he was about to say Amen, there came

[five lines broken: the words 'the brethren' and 'idol' occur]

table of devils . . . he dieth therefor, but every one that believeth on Jesus Christ who hath saved us from all defilement and all uncleanness and all evil thoughts, he shall be manifest. And they drew near unto the table

[three lines broken. 'Idol' occurs]

. . . stood . . . a mighty idol. And an old man . . . . stood up among them, saying unto them: "*Ye men, (wait a little and see) what befalleth the priests which would draw near unto our gods: for verily when our fellow-citizen Charinus hearkened and would . . . . against the gods, there died he and his (father). And thereupon died Xanthus also, Chrysa (?), and (Hermocrates?) died, sick of the dropsy, and his wife Nympha.*"

[Two leaves at least gone. (Paul is speaking)]

"*...after the manner of strange men. Wherefore presume ye to do that which is not seemly (?)? Or have ye not heard of that which came to pass, which God brought upon Sodom and Gomorrha, because they robbed . . . . after the manner of strangers and of women? God did not . . . . them but cast them down into hell. Now therefore we are not men of this fashion that ye say, nor such as ye think, but we are preachers of the living God and his Beloved. But that ye may not marvel, understand . . . the miracles (?) which bear witness for us*". But they hearkened not unto him, but took the men and put them into the temple of Apollo, to keep them until the morrow, whereon they assembled the whole city. And many and costly were the victuals which they gave them.

But Paul, who was fasting now the third day, testified all the night long, being troubled, and smote his face and said: *"O God, look down upon their threatenings and suffer us not to slide, and let not our adversaries cast us down, but save us and bring down quickly thy righteousness upon us. And as Paul cast himself down, with the brethren, Thrasymachus and Cleon, then the temple fell . . . . so that they that belonged to the temple and the magistrates that were set over it . . . . others of them in the . . . . for (the one part) fell down . . . . fell down . . . . round about, in the midst of the two parts. And they went in and beheld what had happened, and marvelled that . . . . in their . . . . and that the . . . . rejoiced over the falling of the temple (?).* "And they cried out, saying: *"Verily these are the works of the men of a mighty God!"* And they departed and proclaimed in the city: *"Apollo the god of the Sidonians is fallen, and the half of his temple."* And all the dwellers in the city ran to the temple and saw Paul and them that were with him, how they wept at this temptation, that they were made a spectacle for all men. But the multitude cried out: *"Bring them into the theatre. And the magistrates came to fetch them; and they groaned bitterly with one soul. "*

[About two leaves gone. (Paul speaking)]

"...through me. Consider . . . . (nine lines much broken, 'the way of life (conversation) of Christ', 'not in the faith', occur) . . . . Egyptians . . . . and they . . . But the multitude . . . . and followed after Paul, crying: Praised be the God . . . . who hath sent Paul . . . that we should not . . . . of death. "But Theudes . . . . and prayed at Paul's feet and embraced his feet, that he should give him the seal in the Lord. But he commanded them to go to Tyre . . . . in health (or farewell), and they put Paul (in a ship?) and went with him. The purpose of confining Paul and his companions in the temple appears to have been connected with the sins of the cities of the plain of which Paul speaks.

[The Acts of Titus, quoted before, have a sentence referring to this and the next episode: ']

And Paul healed Aphphia the wife of Chrysippus who was possessed with a devil: and fasting for seven days he overthrew the idol of Apollo.'

[The Acts place this immediately after the conversion and preaching at Damascus, and put the Panehares episode later. They are not to be trusted, therefore, as a guide to the order of our book.]

Chapter 5

When he was departed out of Sidon and would go unto Tyre. Now when Paul was entered unto Tyre there came a multitude of Jews . . . . in to him. These . . . . and they heard the mighty works . . . They marvelled . . . . Amphion *(= Aphphia of the Acts of Titus)* . . . . saying . . . . in . . . . Chrysippus . . . . devil with him . . . . many . . . . When Paul came . . . . he said: He . . . . God and will not be an evil spirit (?) . . . . in (?) Amphion . . . . through the evil spirit . . . . without any one's having . . . . she said to him: *"Save me that I die not."* And while the multitude . . . . then arose the other (?) evil spirit . . . . And forthwith the devils fled away. And when the multitude saw this, by the power of God, they praised him who had *(given such power)* unto Paul. And there was there one by name... rimus, who had a son born to him which was dumb.

[On the next page is a proper name, Lix (or perhaps Kilix, a Cilician), and later the words, 'I preach the good tidings of the Saviour . . . . Son of God'. [On the next page. Lix perhaps occurs again, and 'Moses'. The next begins: for that which we say cometh to pass forthwith.]

Behold we will bring him hither ...unto thee that he may . . . . thee, to hear the truth of thy . . . .

[Next page.]

On God whose desire is come to pass in him, this is the wise man . . . . . . the Father and he hath sent Jesus Christ.

[Next page]

turned toward the East. Moses . . . . . . in Syria in Cyrene   Again I say unto you . . . I, that do the works . . . that a man is not justifed by the Law, but that he is justified by the works of righteousness, and he . . .

[Next page]

has the words 'liberty', 'and the yoke', 'all flesh'; and, 'and every one confess that Jesus Christ is the glory of the Father'.

[Next page]

lower part: is not water in him, but . . . being water, I am not hungry but I am thirsty; I am not but not to . . . . to suffer them, to be (devoured) by wild beasts, not to be able . . . . from the earth, but not to suffer them to be burnt by the fire, are these things of the present age testified, he which was a persecutor . . .

[Next page]

lower part, (Cle)anthes. the law of God which is called . . . . who walketh here before them, hath he not followed us throughout all the cities . . . And when . . . . he turned himself toward the East after this (after two lines) such words, neither preacheth he as thou preachest them, 0 Paul, that thou mayest not . . . .

[Next page begins: Thou art in the presence (sight, face) of Jerusalem, but I trust in the Lord that thou wilt . . . The name 'Saul' is almost certain some lines later. Next page]

begins: whom they crucified. And at the end: raised up our flesh.

[Next page, 7th line]

For since the day when . . . . persecuted the apostles which were (*with me? se. Peter*) out of Jerusalem, I hid myself that I might have comfort, and we nourish them which stand, through the word according to the promise (?) of his grace. I have fallen into many troubles and have subjected myself to the law, as for your sakes. But thought by night and by day in my trouble on Jesus Christ, waiting for him as a lamb . . . . when they crucified him he did not . . . did not resist . . . . was not troubled.

[The above may be a speech of Peter. We have seen some indication that Paul is now at Jerusalem, and the conjecture is that a dialogue between him and Peter occurred in this place. The next page undoubtedly mentions Peter. Line 1 has 'Paul', line 3, 'twelve (?) shepherds'. Line 5, through Paul.]

...But . . . . was troubled because of the questioning *(examination)* that *(was come)* upon Peter and he cried out, saying: *"Verily, God is one, and there is no God beside him: one also is Jesus Christ his Son, whom we . . . this, whom thou preachest, did we crucify, whom expect in great glory, but ye say that he is God and Judge of the living and the dead, the King of the ages, for the in the form of man. "*

Chapter 6

Paul is condemned to the mines in an unknown place. Longinus and Firmilla have a daughter, Frontina, who is to be thrown down from a rock, and Paul with her. It is my distinct opinion that Fontina is already dead: her body is to be thus contumeliously treated because she has become a Christian.

[upper part of the page has Longinus twice in lines 1, 2; 'Paul' in 1.7.]

...Then: For since . . . . the mine, there hath not . . . nothing good hath befallen mine house. And he advised that the men which were to throw Frontina down, should throw down Paul also with her, alive. Now Paul knew these things, but he worked fasting, in great cheerfulness, for two days with the prisoners. They commanded that on the third day the men . . . . should bring forth Frontina: and the whole city followed after her. And Firmilla and Longinus lamented and the soldiers . . . But the prisoners carried the bed (bier). And when Paul saw the great mourning with the daughter and eight . . .

[Next page, line 8]

Paul alive with the daughter. But when Paul had taken the daughter in his arms, he groaned unto the Lord Jesus Christ because of the sorrow of Firmilla, and cast himself on his knees in the mire . . . . praying for Frontina with her in one (a) prayer. In that hour Frontina rose up. And the whole multitude was afraid, and fled. Paul took the hand of the daughter and led her through the city unto the house of Longinus, and the whole multitude said with one voice: God is one, who hath made heaven and earth, who hath granted the life of the daughter in the presence of Paul . . . a loaf. and he gave thanks to him.

[Some lines later. to Philippi (?).]

Chapter 7

When he was departed from . . . and would go . Now when Paul was come to Philippi . . . he entered into the house of . . . . and there was great joy (among the brethren) and to every one.

[On the following page begins the episode of the correspondence with the Corinthians, which was circulated separately in Syriac, Latin, and Armenian, and found a place in the Syriac collection of Pauline epistles (and is commented on with the rest by Ephraem the Syrian), and in the Armenian Bible. We have it in (a) many Armenian MSS., (b) in Ephraem s commentary-only extant in Armenian, (c) in three Latin MSS., at Milan, Laon, and Paris: as well as in the Coptic MS., which is here less fragmentary than in the preceding pages. We begin with a short narrative, introducing the letter of the Corinthians to Paul; then follows another short piece of narrative, extant in Armenian only; then Paul's reply, commonly called the 'Third Epistle to the Corinthians'. There are various phrases and whole sentences, especially in the Armenian and the Milan MS. of the Latin, which are absent from the Coptic and the Laon MS. and are regarded, rightly, as interpolations. These will be distinguished by small capitals. The page of the Coptic MS. on which the correspondence begins is fragmentary at the beginning.

1.1. the lawless one
1.2. the reward. They . . . . in
1.3. a prayer . . . . every
1.4. one, and every one (?)
1.6. Paul . . . . again (or together).]

1.7. prayed that a messenger be sent to Philippi. For the Corinthians were in great trouble concerning Paul, that he would depart out of the world, before it was time. For there were certain men come to Corinth, Simon and Cleobius, saying: There is no resurrection of the flesh, but that of the spirit only: and that the body of man is not the creation of God; and also concerning the world, that God did not create it, and that God knoweth not the world, and that Jesus Christ was not crucified, but it was an appearance (i.e. but only in appearance), and that lie was not born of Mary, nor of the seed of David. And in a word, there were many things which they had taught in Corinth, deceiving many other men, (and deceiving also) themselves. When therefore the Corinthians heard that Paul was at Philippi, they sent a letter unto Paul to Macedonia by Threptus and Eutychus the deacons. And the letter was after this manner.

I. 1 Stephanus and the elders (presbyters) that are with him, even Daphnus and Eubulus and Theophilus and Zenon, unto Paul Their brother eternal greeting in the Lord.

2 There have come unto Corinth two men, Simon and Cleobius, which are overthrowing the faith of many with evil (corrupt) words,

3 which do thou prove And examine:

4 for we have never heard such words from thee nor from the other apostles:

5 but all that we have received from thee or from them, that do we hold fast.

6 Since therefore the Lord hath had mercy on us, that while thou art still in the flesh we may hear these things again from thee,

7 if it be possible, either come unto us or write unto s.

8 For we believe, according as it hath been revealed unto Theonoe, that the Lord hath delivered thee out of the hand of the lawless one (enemy, Laon).

9 Now the things which these men say and teach are these:

10 They say that we must not use the prophets,

11 and that God is not Almighty,

12 and that there shall be no resurrection of the flesh,

13 and that man was not made by God,

14 and that Christ came not down *(is not come, Copt.)* in the flesh, neither was born of Mary,

15 and that the world is not of God, but of the angels.

16 Wherefore, brother, We pray thee use all diligence to come unto us, that the Church of the Corinthians may remain without offence, and the madness of these men may be made plain. Farewell Always in the Lord.

II. 1 The deacons Threptus and Eutyches brought the letter unto Philippi,

2 so that Paul received it, being in bonds because of Stratonice the wife of Apollophanes, And he forgat his bonds, and was sore afflicted,

3 and cried out, saying: It were better for me to die and to be with the Lord, than to continue in the flesh and to hear such things An the calamaties of false doctrine, so that trouble cometh upon trouble.

4 And over and above this so great affliction I am in bonds and behold these evils whereby the devices of Satan are accomplished. (4 Harnack: may not the priests (*intrigues*) of Satan anticipate me while (*or after*) I suffer (*have suffered*) fetters for the sake (?) of men.)

5 Paul therefore, in great affliction, wrote a letter, answering thus:

III.1 Paul, a prisoner of Jesus Christ, unto the brethren which are in Corinth, greeting.

2 Being in the midst of many tribulations, I marvel not if the teachings of the evil one run abroad apace.

3 For my Lord Jesus Christ will hasten his coming, and will set at nought (*no longer endure the insolence of*) them that falsify his words.

4 For I delivered unto you in the beginning the things which I received of the Holy apostles which were before me, who were at all times with Jesus Christ:

5 namely, that our Lord Jesus Christ was born of Mary Which is of the seed of David According to the flesh, the Holy Ghost being sent forth from heaven from the Father unto her By the angel Gabriel,

6 that he (*Jesus*) might come down into this world and redeem all flesh by his flesh, and raise us up from the dead in the flesh, like as he hath shown to us in himself for an ensample.

7 And because man was formed by his Father,

8 therefore was he sought when he was lost, that he might be quickened by adoption.

9 For to this end did God Almighty who made heaven and earth first send the prophets unto the Jews, that they might be drawn away from their sins.

10 For he designed to save the house of Israel: therefore he conferred a portion of the spirit of Christ upon the prophets and sent them unto the Jews had no compassion unto the first Jews),

and they proclaimed the true worship of God for a long space of time.

11 But the prince of iniquity, desiring to be God, laid hands on them and slew them (banished them from God, Laon MS.), and bound all flesh by evil lusts (And the end of the world by judgment drew near).

12 But God Almighty, who is righteous, would not cast away his own creation, But had no compassion on them from heaven,

13 and sent his spirit into Mary In Galilee,

[**14** *Milan MS. and Arm.: Who believed with all her heartand received the Holy ghost in her womb, that Jesus might come into the world*]

15 that by that flesh whereby that wicked one had brought in death (*had triumphed*), by the same he should be shown to be overcome.

16 For by his own body Jesus Christ saved all flesh [*and restored it unto life*],

17 that he might show forth the temple of righteousness in his body.

18 In whom (or whereby) we are saved (Milan, Paris: in whom if we believe we are set free).

19 They therefore (*Paris MS with them*) are not children of righteousness but children of wrath who reject the wisdom (providence?) of God, saying that the heaven and the earth and all that are in them are not the work of God.

20 They therefore are children of wrath, for cursed are they, following the teaching of the serpent,

21 whom do ye drive out from you and flee from their doctrine.

[Arm., Milan, Paris:]

22 For ye are not children of, but of the well-beloved church.

23 Therefore is ther time of resurrection proclaimed unto all.]

24 And as for that which they say, that there is no resurrection of the flesh, they indeed sha

25 because they believe not in him that is risen from the dead, notd believing nor understanding,

26 for they know not, O Corinthians, the seeds of wheat or of other seeds (grain), how they are cast bare into the earth and are corrupted and rise again by the will of God with bodies, and clothed.

27 And not only that [*body*] which is cast in riseth again, but manifold more blessing itself [i.*e. fertile and prospering*].

28 And if we must not take an example from seeds only but from more noble bodies,

29 ye know how Jonas the son of Amathi, when he would not preach to them of Nineve, But fled, was swallowed by the sea-monster;

30 and after three days and three nights God heard the prayer of Jonas out of the lowest hell, and no part of him was consumed, not even an hair nor an eyelash.

31 How much more, O ye of little faith, shall he raise up you that have believed in Christ Jesus, like as he himself arose.

32 Likewise also a dead man was cast upon the bones of the prophet Helisaetis by the children of Israel, and he arose, both body and soul and bones and spirit (Laon: arose in his body); how much more shall ye which have been cast upon the body and bones and spirit of the Lord [*Milan, Paris: how much more, O ye of little faith, shall ye which have been cast on him*] arise again in that day having your flesh whole, ven as He arose?

[**33** Arm., Milan, Paris:]

likewise also concerning the prophet Helias: He raised up the widow's son from death. How much more shall the Lord Jesus raise you up from death at the sound of the trumpet, in the twinkling of n eye? For He hath showed us an ensample of His own body.]

34 If, then, ye receive any other doctrine, God shall be witness against you. And let no man trouble me,

35 for I bear these bonds that I may win Christ, and I therefore bear his marks in my body that I may attain unto the resurrection of the dead.

36 And whoso receiveth (*abideth in*) the rule which he hath received by the blessed prophets and the holy gospel, shall receive a recompense from the Lord, And when He riseth ffrom the dead shall obtain eternal life.

37 But whoso trans- gresseth these things, with him is the fire, and with them that walk in like manner.

[Milan, Paris:]

with them that go before in the same way, Who are men without God),

38 which are a generation of vipers,

39 whom do ye reject in the power of the Lord, 40 and peace, grace and love shall be with you.

[... sections omitted.].

Chapter 9

[Fragments: scenes of farewell. (Paul speaking) . . . thanksgiving (?)]

The grace of the Lord will walk with me until I have fulfilled all the dispensations which shall come upon me with patience. But they were sorrowful, and fasted. And Cleobius was in the Spirit and said unto them: Brethren, (*the Lord*) will suffer Paul to fulfil every dispensation and thereafter will suffer him to go up (*to Jerusalem*). But thereafter shall be . . . . in much instruction and knowledge and sowing of the word, so that men shall envy him, and so he shall depart out of this world. But when Paul and the brethren heard this, they lifted up their voices, saying:

[Next page, first extant line]

beheld'. Second, 'shall say'. Third, But the Spirit came upon Myrte so that she said unto them: Brethren . . . and look upon this sign, that ye . . . For Paul the servant of the Lord shall save many in Rome, so that of them shall be no number, and he will manifest himself more than all the faithful. Thereafter shall . . . . of the Lord Jesus Christ come . . . . a great grace is . . . .at Rome. And this is the manner wherein the Spirit spake unto Myrte. And every one took the bread, and they were in joy, according to the custom of the fast, through . . . . and the psalms of David and . . . . he rejoiced.

[On the next page]

the only significant words are 'to Rome'; 'the brethren'; 'grieved'; 'took the bread'; 'praised the Lord'; 'were very sorrowful'.

[The next has ends of lines:]

'the Lord'; 'risen'; 'Jesus'; 'Paul said to him'. The last is 'he (or they) greeted'.

[Two more pages have nothing of moment. The next is concerned with the Martyrdom.]

Chapter 10

The Martyrdom

[This, preserved separately to be read on the day of Commemoration, exists in two Greek copies, an incomplete Latin version, and versions in Syriac, Coptic, Ethiopic, Slavonic, besides fragments in our Coptic MS.]

I. Now there were awaiting Paul at Rome Luke from Galatia (Gaul, Gk.) and Titus from Dalmatia: whom when Paul saw he was glad: and hired a grange outside Rome, wherein with the brethren he taught the word of truth, and he became noised abroad and many souls were added unto the Lord, so that there was a rumour throughout all Rome, and much people came unto him from the household of Caesar, believing, and there was great joy.

And a certain Patroclus, a cup-bearer of Caesar, came at even unto the grange, and not being able because of the press to enter in to Paul, he sat in a high window and listened to him teaching the word of God. But whereas the evil devil envied the love of the brethren, Patroclus fell down from the window and died, and forthwith it was told unto Nero.

But Paul perceiving it by the spirit said: *"Men and brethren, the evil one hath gained occasion to tempt you: go out of the house and ye shall find a lad fallen from the height and now ready to give up the ghost; take him up and bring him hither to me".* And they went and brought him; and when the people saw it they were troubled. But Paul said: *"Now, brethren, let your faith appear; come all of you and let us weep unto our Lord Jesus Christ, that this lad may live and we continue in quietness. And when all had lamented, the lad received his spirit again, and they set him on a beast and sent him back alive, together with the rest that were of Caesar's household. "*

II. But Nero, when he heard of the death of Patroclus, was sore grieved, and when he came in from the bath he commanded another to be set over the wine. But his servants told him, saying: *"Caesar, Patroclus liveth and standeth at the table. And Caesar, hearing that Patroclus lived, was affrighted and would not go in".* But when he went in, he saw Patroclus, and was beside himself, and said: *"Patroclus, livest thou?"* And he said: *"I live, Caesar."* And he said: *"Who is he that made thee to live?* "And the lad, full of the mind of faith, said: *"Christ Jesus, the king of the ages."* And Caesar was troubled and said: *"Shall he, then, be king of the ages and overthrow all kingdoms?"* Patroclus saith unto him: *"Yea, he overthroweth all kingdoms and he alone shall be for ever, and there shall be no kingdom that shall escape him."* And he smote him on the face and said: *"Patroclus, art thou also a soldier of that king?"* And he said: *"Yea, Lord Caesar, for he raised me when I was dead."* And Barsabas Justus of the broad feet, and Urion the Cappadocian, and Festus the Galatian, Caesar's chief men, said: *"We also are soldiers of the king of the ages."* And he shut them up in prison, having grievously tormented them, whom he loved much, and commanded the soldiers of the great king to be sought out, and set forth a decree to this effect, that all that were found to be Christians and soldiers of Christ should be slain.

III. And among many others Paul also was brought, bound: unto whom all his fellow-prisoners gave heed; so that Caesar perceived that he was over the camp. And he said to him: *"Thou that art the great king's man, but my prisoner, how thoughtest thou well to come by stealth into the government of the Romans and levy soldiers out of my province?"* But Paul, filled with the Holy Ghost, said before them all: *"0 Caesar, not only out of thy province do we levy soldiers, but out of the whole world. For so hath it been ordained unto us, that no man should be refused who wisheth to serve my king. And if it like thee also to serve him (Lat. thou wilt not repent thereof: but think not that the wealth, &c., which seems better), it is not wealth nor the splendour that is now in this life that shall save thee; but if thou submit and entreat him, thou shalt be saved; for* *in one day (or one day) he shall fight against the world with fire."* And when Caesar heard that, he commanded all the prisoners to be burned with fire, but Paul to be beheaded after the law of the Romans.

But Paul kept not silence concerning the word, but communicated with Longus the prefect and Cestus the centurion.

Nero therefore went on (*was*) (*perhaps add 'raging'*) in Rome, slaying many Christians without a hearing, by the working of the evil one; so that the Romans stood before the palace and cried *" It sufficeth, Caesar! for the men are our own! thou destroyest the strength of the Romans! Then at that he was persuaded and ceased, and commanded that no man should touch any Christian, until he should learn throughly concerning them".*

IV. Then was Paul brought unto him after the decree; and he abode by his word that he should be beheaded. And Paul said: *"Caesar, it is not for a little space that I live unto my king; and if thou behead me, this will I do: I will arise and show myself unto thee that I am not dead but live unto my Lord Jesus Christ, who cometh to judge the world."* But Longus and Cestus said unto Paul: *"Whence have ye this king, that ye believe in him and will not change your mind, even unto death?"* And Paul communicated unto them the word and said: *"Ye men that are in this ignorance and error, change your mind and be saved from the fire that cometh upon all the world: for we serve not, as ye suppose, a king that cometh from the earth, but from heaven, even the living God, who because of the iniquities that are done in this world, cometh as a judge; and blessed is that man who shall believe in him and shall live for ever when he cometh to burn the world and purge it thoroughly".* Then they beseeching him said: *"We entreat thee, help us, and we will let thee go".* But he answered and said: *"I am not a deserter of Christ, but a lawful soldier of the living God: if I had known that I should die, O Longus and Cestus, I would have done it, but seeing that I live unto God and love myself, I go unto the Lord, to come with him in the glory of his Father".* They say unto him: *"How then shall we live when thou art beheaded?"*

V. And while they yet spake thus, Nero sent one Parthenius and Pheres to see if Paul were already beheaded; and they found him yet alive. And he called them to him and said: *"Believe on the living God, which raiseth me and all them that believe on him from the dead".* And they said: *"We go now unto Nero; but when thou diest and risest again, then will we believe on thy God".* And as Longus and Cestus entreated him yet more concerning salvation, he saith to them: *"Come quickly unto my grave in the morning and ye shall find two men praying, Titus and Luke. They shall give you the seal in the Lord."*

Then Paul stood with his face to the east and lifted up his hands unto heaven and prayed a long time, and in his prayer he conversed in the Hebrew tongue with the fathers, and then stretched forth his neck without speaking. And when the executioner *(speculator)* struck off his head, milk spurted upon the cloak of the soldier. And the soldier and all that were there present when they saw it marvelled and glorified God which had given such glory unto Paul: and they went and told Caesar what was done.

VI. And when he heard it, while he marvelled long and was in perplexity, Paul came about the niuth hour, when many philosophers and the centurion were standing with Caesar, and stood before them all and said: *"Caesar, behold, I, Paul, the soldier of God, am not dead, but live in my God. But unto thee shall many evils befall and great punishment, thou wretched man, because thou hast shed unjustly the blood of the righteous, not many days hence."* And having so said Paul departed from him. But Nero hearing it and being greatly troubled commanded the prisoners to be loosed, and Patroclus also and Barsabas and them that were with him.

VII. And as Paul charged them, Longus and Cestus the centurion went early in the morning and approached with fear unto the grave of Paul. And when they were come thither they saw two men praying, and Paul betwixt them, so that they beholding the wondrous marvel were amazed, but Titus and Luke being stricken with the fear of man when they saw Longus and Cestus coming toward them, turned to flight. But they pursued after them, saying: *"We pursue you not for death but for life, that ye may give it unto us, as Paul promised us, whom we saw just now standing betwixt you and praying."* And when they heard that, Titus and Luke rejoiced and gave them the seal in the Lord, glorifying the God and Father of our Lord Jesus Christ

[Copt. and glorified the Lord Jesus Christ and all the saints]

Unto whom be glory world without end. Amen.

The Gospel of Philip (*Gnostic*)
(180 – 250 A.D.)

Because of the contents, the eccentric arrangement, and the literary types exhibited, it is likely that *The Gospel of Philip* is a collection of excerpts mainly from a Christian Gnostic sacramental catechesis. It explains the significance of sacramental rites of initiation, the meaning of sacred names, especially names of Jesus, and provides paraenesis for the life of the initiated. It interprets Biblical passages, particularly from the book of Genesis, makes use of typology, both historical and sacramental, and, as catechists do, argues on the basis of analogy and parable.

The work called *The Gospel According to Philip* is a Valentinian anthology containing some one hundred short excerpts taken from various other works. None of the sources of these excerpts have been identified, and apparently they do not survive. To judge from their style and contents, they were sermons, treatises, or philosophical epistles (typical Valentinian genres), as well as collected aphorisms or short dialogues with comments. Only some of the sources can definitely be identified as Valentinian. Because of their brevity and the lack of context it is difficult to assign any of them to particular schools of Valentinian theology. On the other hand, nothing indicates that all come from one and the same branch of the Valentinian church. It is possible that some of the excerpts are by Valentinus himself. Others, however, refer to etymologies in Syriac, the Semitic language (a dialect of Aramaic) used in Edessa and western Mesopotamia; these must be the work of a Valentinian theologian of the East, writing in a bilingual milieu such as Edessa. Probably the language of composition of all the excerpts was Greek.

Summary notation: Due to it's importance and historical significance to the early Church, the **Gospel of Philip** *presented in some detail but not entirely .Due to the length of the manuscript, only key excerpts or talking points are presented for discussion. Please note sections omitted or missing in the early manuscript. It strongly suggests that Jesus Christ had sexual relations with Mary Magdalene and she was His companion.* It was condemned as heretical.

Excerpts from the Gospel of Philip

Before Christ came, there was no bread in the world, just as Paradise, the place were Adam was, had many trees to nourish the animals but no wheat to sustain man. Man used to feed like the animals, but when Christ came, the perfect man, he brought bread from heaven in order that man might be nourished with the food of man. The rulers thought that it was by their own power and will that they were doing what they did, but the Holy Spirit in secret was accomplishing everything through them as it wished. Truth, which existed since the beginning, is sown everywhere. And many see it being sown, but few are they who see it being reaped.

Some said, "Mary conceived by the Holy Spirit." They are in error. They do not know what they are saying. When did a woman ever conceive by a woman? Mary is the virgin whom no power defiled. She is a great anathema to the Hebrews, who are the apostles and the apostolic men. This virgin whom no power defiled [...] the powers defile themselves. And the Lord would not have said "My Father who is in Heaven" (Mt 16:17), unless he had had another father, but he would have said simply "My father".

[... sections omitted.].

"Jesus" is a hidden name, "Christ" is a revealed name. For this reason "Jesus" is not particular to any language; rather he is always called by the name "Jesus". While as for "Christ", in Syriac it is "Messiah", in Greek it is "Christ". Certainly all the others have it according to their own language. "The Nazarene" is he who reveals what is hidden. Christ has everything in himself, whether man, or angel, or mystery, and the Father. Those who say that the Lord died first and (then) rose up are in error, for he rose up first and (then) died. If one does not first attain the resurrection, he will not die. As God lives, he would [...].

[... sections omitted.].

Some are afraid lest they rise naked. Because of this they wish to rise in the flesh, and they do not know that it is those who wear the flesh who are naked. It is those who [...] to unclothe themselves who are not naked. "Flesh and blood shall not inherit the kingdom of God" (1 Co 15:50). What is this which will not inherit? This which is on us. But what is this, too, which will inherit? It is that which belongs to Jesus and his blood. Because of this he said "He who shall not eat my flesh and drink my blood has not life in him" (Jn 6:53). What is it? His flesh is the word, and his blood is the Holy Spirit. He who has received these has food and he has drink and clothing. I find fault with the others who say that it will not rise. Then both of them are at fault. You say that the flesh will not rise. But tell me what will rise, that we may honor you. You say the Spirit in the flesh, and it is also this light in the flesh. (But) this too is a matter which is in the flesh, for whatever you shall say, you say nothing outside the flesh. It is necessary to rise in this flesh, since everything exists in it. In this world, those who put on garments are better than the garments. In the Kingdom of Heaven, the garments are better than those that put them on. It is through water and fire that the whole place is purified - the visible by the visible, the hidden by the hidden. There are some things hidden through those visible. There is water in water, there is fire in chrism.

Jesus took them all by stealth, for he did not appear as he was, but in the manner in which they would be able to see him. He appeared to them all. He appeared to the great as great. He appeared to the small as small. He appeared to the angels as an angel, and to men as a man. Because of this, his word hid itself from everyone. Some indeed saw him, thinking that they were seeing themselves, but when he appeared to his disciples in glory on the mount, he was not small. He became great, but he made the disciples great, that they might be able to see him in his greatness.

[... sections omitted.].

There were three who always walked with the Lord: Mary, his mother, and her sister, and Magdalene, the one who was called his companion. His sister and his mother and his companion were each a Mary.

[... sections omitted.].

He who has been created is beautiful, but you would <not> find his sons noble creations. If he were not created, but begotten, you would find that his seed was noble. But now he was created (and) he begot. What nobility is this? First, adultery came into being, afterward murder. And he was begotten in adultery, for he was the child of the Serpent. So he became a murderer, just like his father, and he killed his brother. Indeed, every act of sexual intercourse which has occurred between those unlike one another is adultery.

[... sections omitted.].

An ass which turns a millstone did a hundred miles walking. When it was loosed, it found that it was still at the same place. There are men who make many journeys, but make no progress towards any destination. When evening came upon them, they saw neither city nor village, neither human artifact nor natural phenomenon, power nor angel. In vain have the wretches labored.

[... sections omitted.].

As for the Wisdom who is called "*the barren*," she is the mother of the angels. And the companion of the [...] Mary Magdalene. [...] **loved her more than all the disciples, and used to kiss her often on her mouth.** The rest of the disciples [...]. They said to him "*Why do you love her more than all of us?*" **The Savior answered and said to them,** "*Why do I not love you like her? When a blind man and one who sees are both together in darkness, they are no different from one another. When the light comes, then he who sees will see the light, and he who is blind will remain in darkness.*"

[... sections omitted.].

If one goes down into the water and comes up without having received anything, and says "*I am a Christian,*" he has borrowed the name at interest. But if he receives the Holy Spirit, he has the name as a gift. He who has received a gift does not have to give it back, but of him who has borrowed it at interest, payment is demanded. This is the way it happens to one when he experiences a mystery. Great is the mystery of marriage! For without it, the world would not exist. Now the existence of the world [...], and the existence of

[...] marriage. Think of the [...] relationship, for it possesses [...] power. Its image consists of a defilement.

The forms of evil spirit include male ones and female ones. The males are they which unite with the souls which inhabit a female form, but the females are they which are mingled with those in a male form, though one who was disobedient. And none shall be able to escape them, since they detain him if he does not receive a male power or a female power, the bridegroom and the bride. One receives them from the mirrored bridal chamber. When the wanton women see a male sitting alone, they leap down on him and play with him and defile him. So also the lecherous men, when they see a beautiful woman sitting alone, they persuade her and compel her, wishing to defile her. But if they see the man and his wife sitting beside one another, the female cannot come into the man, nor can the male come into the woman. So if the image and the angel are united with one another, neither can any venture to go into the man or the woman.

[... sections omitted.].

He who has knowledge of the truth is a free man, but the free man does not sin, for "He who sins is the slave of sin" (Jn 8:34). Truth is the mother, knowledge the father. Those who think that sinning does not apply to them are called "free" by the world. Knowledge of the truth merely makes such people arrogant, which is what the words, "it makes them free" mean. It even gives them a sense of superiority over the whole world. But "Love builds up" (1 Co 8:1). In fact, he who is really free, through knowledge, is a slave, because of love for those who have not yet been able to attain to the freedom of knowledge. Knowledge makes them capable of becoming free. Love never calls something its own, [...] it [...] possess [...]. It never says,"This is yours" or "This is mine," but "All these are yours". Spiritual love is wine and fragrance. All those who anoint themselves with it take pleasure in it. While those who are anointed are present, those nearby also profit (from the fragrance). If those anointed with ointment withdraw from them and leave, then those not anointed, who merely stand nearby, still remain in their bad odor. The Samaritan gave nothing but wine and oil to the wounded man. It is nothing other than the ointment.

V. APPENDIX

Additional Pseudepigraphical Manuscripts

As indicated, approximately 200+ manuscripts have been found which did not carry over to the New Testament canon in the first few centuries after Christ's ministry. Due to book size and date considerations, the author has chosen to focus on approximately 30 of the most important foundational, earliest works including those of the Apostolic and early Church fathers and Apologists as well as historical accounts from non-Christian sources shortly after the resurrection of Jesus the Christ.

The remaining 164+ or so apocryphal works are either extremely fragmentary, or highly suspect as forgeries; However, they are mentioned by name only and approximate date for future reference and study. Many of these claim to have been written by some well-known Apostle, disciple or early Church father but comprehensive scholarship has revealed many flaws in the authorship claims. These are called *"Pseudepigrapha"*. The word "pseudepigrapha"[41] (from the Greek: ψευδής, *pseude*, "false" and ἐπιγραφή, *epigraphē*, "name" or "inscription" or "ascription"; thus when taken together it means "false superscription or title"; see the related *epigraphy*) is the plural of "pseudepigraphon" (sometimes Latinized as "pseudepigraphum"). Pseudepigraphy covers the false ascription of names of authors to works, even to authentic works that make no such claim within their text. Thus a widely accepted but an incorrect attribution of authorship may make a completely authentic text pseudepigraphical. Assessing the actual writer of a text locates questions of pseudepigraphical attribution within the discipline of literary criticismAuthorship and pseudepigraphy:

Many of the apocryphal works were written to either deny or confirm an heretical theology valled Gnosticis. The word "Gnosticism", (from *gnostikos*, "learned", from Ancient Greek: γνῶσις *gnōsis*, knowledge; Arabic: ةي صونغ لٱ *al-ġnūṣīh*) is the

---

[41] http://en.wikipedia.org/wiki/Pseudepigrapha

belief that the material world created by the demiurge should be shunned[and the spiritual world should be embraced (God's world). Gnostic ideas influenced many ancient religions[1] which teach that *gnosis (variously interpreted as knowledge, enlightenment, salvation, emancipation or 'oneness with God')* may be reached by practicing philanthropy to the point of personal poverty, sexual abstinence (as far as possible for *hearers*, total for *initiates*) and diligently searching for wisdom by helping others.

Levels of Authenticity:

Scholars have identified seven levels of authenticity which they have organized in a hierarchy ranging from literal authorship, meaning written in the author's own hand, to outright forgery:

1. **Literal Authorship.** A Church leader writes a letter in his own hand.
2. **Dictation.** A Church leader dictates a letter almost word for word to an amanuensis.
3. **Delegated Authorship.** A Church leader describes the basic content of an intended letter to a disciple or to an amanuensis.
4. **Posthumous Authorship.** A Church leader dies, and his disciples finish a letter that he had intended to write, sending it posthumously in his name.
5. **Apprentice Authorship.** A Church leader dies, and disciples who had been authorized to speak for him while he was alive continue to do so by writing letters in his name years or decades after his death.
6. **Honorable Pseudepigraphy.** A Church leader dies, and admirers seek to honor him by writing letters in his name as a tribute to his influence and in a sincere belief that they are responsible bearers of his tradition.
7. **Forgery.** A Church leader obtains sufficient prominence that, either before or after his death, people seek to exploit his legacy by forging letters in his name, presenting him as a supporter of their own ideas

Appendix

Christian writing (*G* = *Gnostic writings*)	Date A.D.
1. Pre-Markan Passion Narrative(hypothetical)	30-60
2. Oxyrhynchus 1224 Gospel	50-140
3. Lost Sayings Gospel Q	50–140
4. Apocalypse of Adam	50-150
5. Eugnostos the Blessed	50-150
6. Egerton Gospel	70-120
7. Fayyum Fragment	70-200
8. Secret Mark	70-160
9. Testaments of the Twelve Patriarchs	70-200
10. Gospel of the Twelve	70-200
11. Mara Bar Serapion	73-200
12. Christian Sibyllines	80-250
13. Gospel of the Ebionites	100-160
14. Gospel of the Nazoreans	100-160
15. Odes of Solomon	100-200
16. Gospel of Eve	100-200
17. Thunder, Perfect Mind	100-230
18. Book of Elchasai	101-220
19. Papias	110-140
20. Oxyrhynchus 840 Gospel	110-160
21. Gospel of Matthias	110-160
22. Traditions of Matthias	110-160
23. Pliny the Younger	111-112
24. Suetonius	115
25. Quadratus of Athens	120-130
26. Naassene Fragment **(G)**	120-140
27. Valentinus **(G)**	120-160
28. Apocryphon of John **(G)**	120-180
29. Gospel of the Savior (G)	120-180
30. 2nd Apocalypse of James **(G)**	120-180
31. Trimorphic Protennoia	120-180
32. Gospel of Perfection	120-180
33. Genna Marias	120-200
34. Marcion **(G)**	130-140
35. Aristo of Pella	130-150
36. Epiphanes On Righteousness **(G)**	130-160
37. Ophite Diagrams **(G)**	130-160
38. Gospel of Judas **(G)**	130-170
39. Epistle of Mathetes to Diognetus	130-200
40. The Epistula Apostolorum	140-150
41. Ptolemy **(G)**	140-160
42. Isidore **(G)**	140-160
43. Fronto	140-170

Appendix

Christian writing (*G* = *Gnostic writings*)	Date A.D.
44. Heracleon **(G)**	150-180
45. Excerpts of Theodotus (G)	150-180
46. Ascension of Isaiah	150-200
47. Interpretation of Knowledge	150-200
48. Testimony of Truth	150-200
49. Tne Acts of Peter and the twelve (G)	150–225
50. Thomas the contender (Gnostic)	150–225
51. Paraphrase of Shem	150-250
52. Fifth and Sixth Books of Esra	150-250
53. Authoritative Teaching **(G)**	150-300
54. Coptic Apocalypse of Paul **(G)**	150-300
55. Prayer of the Apostle Paul	150-300
56. Discourse on the Eighth and Ninth**(G)**	150-300
57. Melchizedek **(G)**	150-300
58. Preaching of Paul	150-350
59. Epistle to the Laodiceans	150-350
60. Questions of Mary	150-350
61. Allogenes, the Stranger	150-350
62. Hypsiphrone	150-350
63. Valentinian Exposition	150-350
64. Concept of Our Great Power	150-360
65. Acts of Pilate	150-400
66. Anti-Marcionite Prologues	150-400
67. Dialogue Between John and Jesus	150-400
68. Tatian's Address to the Greeks	160-170
69. Claudius Apollinaris	160-180
70. Apelles **(G)**	160-180
71. Julius Cassianus **(G)**	160-180
72. Octavius of Minucius Felix	160-250
73. Acts of Carpus	161-180
74. Melito of Sardis	165-175
75. Hegesippus	165-175
76. Dionysius of Corinth	165-175
77. Lucian of Samosata	165-175
78. Marcus Aurelius	167
79. Diatessaron	170-175
80. Dura-Europos Gospel Harmony	170-200
81. Muratorian Canon	170-200
82. Treatise on the Resurrection **(G)**	170-200
83. Letter of Peter to Philip **(G)**	170-220
84. Thought of Norea	170-230
85. Rhodon	175-185
86. Theophilus of Caesarea	175-185

Appendix

Christian writing (*G = Gnostic writings*)	Date A.D.
87. Galen	175-190
88. Celsus	178
89. Letter from Vienna and Lyons	178
90. Passion of the Scillitan Martyrs	180
91. Acts of Apollonius	180-185
92. Bardesanes	180-220
93. Kerygmata Petrou	180-220
94. Hippolytus of Rome	180-230
95. Sentences of Sextus	180-230
96. 1st Apocalypse of James **(G)**	180-250
97. Clement of Alexandria	182-202
98. Maximus of Jerusalem	185-195
99. Polycrates of Ephesus	185-195
100. Talmud	188-217
101. Victor I	189-199
102. Pantaenus	190-210
103. Second Discourse of Great Seth	190-230
104. Anonymous Anti-Montanist	193
105. Inscription of Abercius	193-216
106. Serapion of Antioch	200-210
107. Apollonius	200-210
108. Caius	200-220
109. Philostratus	*200-220*
110. Ammonius of Alexandria	200-230
111. Zostrianos	200-230
112. Three Steles of Seth	200-230
113. Exegesis on the Soul	200-230
114. Didascalia	200-250
115. Books of Jeu **(G)**	200-250
116. Pistis Sophia **(G)**	200-300
117. Tripartite Tractate	200-300
118. Hypostasis of the Archons	200-300
119. Prayer of Thanksgiving	200-300
120. Coptic Apocalypse of Peter (G)	200-300
121. Apostolic Church Order	200-330
122. Holy Book of the Great Invisible Spirit	200-350
123. Monarchian Prologues	200-450
124. Acts of Perpetua and Felicitas	203
125. Origen	203-250
126. Lucian of Antioch	210-245
127. Callistus	217-222
128. Acts of Thomas	230-250
129. Dionysius of Alexandria	230-265

Appendix

Christian writing (*G* = *Gnostic writings*)	Date A.D.
130. Firmilian of Caesarea	230-268
131. Commodian	240-260
132. Cyprian	246-258
133. Gospel of Mani	250-274
134. Teachings of Silvanus	250-300
135. Excerpt from the Perfect Discourse	250-300
136. Coptic Apocalypse of Elijah	250-350
137. Apocalypse of Paul	250-400
138. Pope Cornelius	251-253
139. Novatian	251-258
140. Pope Stephen	254-257
141. Dionysius of Rome	259-268
142. Theognostus	260-280
143. Gregory Thaumaturgus	265-282
144. Pope Felix	269-274
145. Victorinus of Pettau	270-310
146. Methodius	270-312
147. Marsanes	270-330
148. On the Origin of the World	270-330
149. De Recta in Deum Fide	270-350
150. Hesychius	280-300
151. Pierius	280-310
152. Pamphilus of Caesarea	280-310
153. Arnobius of Sicca	297-310
154. Peter of Alexandria	300-311
155. Pseudo-Clementine Homilies	300-320
156. Eusebius of Caesarea	300-340
157. Manichean Acts of Leucius Charinus	300-350
158. Letters of Paul and Seneca	300-390
159. Apocalypse of Thomas	300-400
160. Freer Logion	300-400
161. Gospel of Gamaliel	300-600
162. Lactantius	303-316
163. Reticius of Autun	310-334
164. Pseudo-Clementine Recognitions	320-380

References for Further Study

- http://www.interfaith.org/christianity/apocrypha/

- http://www.earlychristianwritings.com/

- http://www.newadvent.org/cathen/01601a.htm

- http://www.sacred-texts.com/chr/apo/

- Michael Coogan, The New Oxford annotated Apocrypha, (Oxford Press, New York, 2010)

- Little, Williams. Onions, C.T., editors. The Oxford Universal Dictionary. (Oxford University Press,New York), 1955

- Clontz, T.E. and J., "The Comprehensive New Testament", (Cornerstone Publications), 2008

- Bruce, F.F. "The Canon of Scripture". IVP Academic, 2010, Location 1478-86 (Kindle Edition)

- Metzger, Bruce M. An Introduction to the Apocrypha. (Oxford University Press New York), 1977

- Joseph Lumpkin, The Lost Books of the Bible: the Rejected Texts, (Fifth Estate Publishers, Blountsville,Al), 2009

- Wilis Barnstone, the Other Bible, (HarperCollins Publishers,New York), 2005

Appendix

Index

Appendix

Appendix

Appendix

CPSIA information can be obtained
at www.ICGtesting.com
Printed in the USA
LVOW04s0055221016

509645LV00011B/152/P